THE *Practica mvsicae* OF FRANCHINUS GAFURIUS

THE *Practica*

The University of Wisconsin Press

musicae OF

FRANCHINUS GAFURIUS

Translated and
edited
with musical transcriptions
by
IRWIN YOUNG

Madison, Milwaukee
and London
1969

Published by
The University
of Wisconsin Press
Box 1379
Madison, Wisconsin 53701
The University
of Wisconsin Press, Ltd.
27–29 Whitfield Street
London, W.1
Copyright © 1969
by the Regents of
The University of Wisconsin
All rights reserved
Printed in
the United States of America by
Buckbee-Mears Co.
St. Paul, Minnesota
Standard Book Number
299–05180–3
Library of Congress
Catalog Card Number 69–16113

JENNY & JESSE

Filiae filioque optimis
D. D. D.

$\mathcal{A}$cknowledgments

I owe a very special debt of gratitude to Dr. Ortha L. Wilner, emeritus professor and former chairman of the Department of Classics at the University of Wisconsin—Milwaukee, without whose prompting and counseling this work probably would never have reached fruition. No thanks could possibly begin to compensate for the inspiration, understanding, and wisdom she lent to this undertaking. Her assistance with problems of Latin syntax particularly helped open new avenues of ingress into the wonderful world of Renaissance music.

Grateful appreciation is tendered to Mrs. Kate Trauman Steinitz of the Elmer Belt Library of Vinciana and to the Huntington Library in Pasadena, whose facilities and rare incunabula, including many first editions of works by Gafurius and others, were made available to me. I wish, too, to express my indebtedness to Miss Cordelia A. Procope, who assisted in the typing of the manuscript.

Illustrations I through III are reproduced from Franchino Gafori, *Practica musicae*, facsim. ed. (Farnborough, Eng.: Gregg International Publishers, Ltd., 1967), by permission of the publishers.

Irwin Young

La Crescenta, California
October 1968

Contents

Illustrations

Introduction

No single incunabulum on music achieved as great an influence upon the musical thought of sixteenth-century Western Europe as did the *Practica musicae* of Franchinus Gafurius. Printed first at Milan in 1496, the *Practica* ran through four additional editions—three in neighboring Brescia in 1497, 1502, and 1508, and a fifth edition in Venice in 1512—and circulated the length and breadth of Europe. Leading theorists of diverse national origins—including the German Ornithoparcus and his English translator, the lutenist John Dowland, Galliculus and Listenius of Leipzig, the Swiss humanist Glarean, Aron and Zarlino of Italy, Jacques LeFevre (Faber Stapulensis) of France, and even the Hungarian Monetarius—cited, paraphrased, or plagiarized text and music from the pages of Gafurius' *Practica*.

Gafurius' writings, and the music of his time, were almost completely forgotten in the course of the seventeenth and early eighteenth centuries; but when, in the early eighteenth century, travel in Italy inspired an interest in Italian ruins, music, and art, the English historian Sir John Hawkins was led to refer to Gafurius as "the Father of Modern Music." In spite of Sir John's glowing attribution, Gafurius and Renaissance music remained outside the mainstream of musical development throughout the nineteenth century. Twentieth-century resurgence of interest in this style makes the study of the *Practica* important again, however, so that there is need now for an English translation of its Latin text and for a modern transcription of its musical examples.

Any valid appreciation of Renaissance music must hinge upon an understanding of both the theory and practice of that era and of the patterns of tradition commingling with patterns of change. In the person of Franchinus Gafurius the two talents of teaching and practice were fortuitously merged, and in his *Practica* the reciprocal thrust of *musicus* and *phonascus*, theorist and practitioner, may be conveniently studied, affording an unusual opportunity for understanding a great age in the history of music.

Franchinus Gafurius was born in 1451 in the town of Lodi, a little southeast of the capital of the duchy of Lombardy, Milan. His contemporary biographer Pantaleo Melegulus reports that Gafurius' early education was directed toward the priesthood but that gradually he channeled his life and energies in the direction of music and humanism.[1] His musical education began in his hometown (1473–74) under the tutelage of the Flemish Carmelite musician, Johannes Gutentag, or Bonadies as the name was Latinized. Bonadies, a composer as well as a theorist, had been exposed to the humanist influences of Vittorino da Feltre's school at Mantua before his arrival in Lodi. He provided the youthful Gafurius with a firm foundation in Flemish musical doctrine and also an early appreciation of Boethius, and Gafurius refers gratefully to his teacher in several of his books.

In the subsequent ten-year period Gafurius undertook a course of independent study in Mantua (1474–76), Verona (1476–77), Genoa (1477–78), Naples (1478–80), Monticelli (1480–83), and Bergamo (1483–84). Systematically and painstakingly he researched, copied, annotated, and learned the musical manuscripts of Boethius, Guido, Franco, De Muris, Marchettus, and others. His quest for knowledge impelled him to search out what was available in Greek music theory, and he investigated with much thoroughness literary, scientific, and philosophical works of the great classical authors for references to music of antiquity.

The attainment of this broad scholarship elevated him above contemporaries who were less educated and less endowed with the accoutrements of humanism and the faculty for abstract speculation. By 1480, having already completed several minor tracts, he applied his learning to the completion of his first major work, *Theoricum opus musicae disciplinae* (Naples, 1480). The *Theoricum* was accorded the honor of being the first book printed before 1500 to treat in broad dimension the study of music theory.[2] The work fit the requirements of the fledgling art of typography in Italy, whose humanist printers displayed a preference for works of pedagogical content and humanistic quality.

Gafurius' impressive credentials as a scholar and musician led to his invitation to Milan in 1484 to occupy the important post of director of music at the great Ambrosian Cathedral during the reign of Ludovico Sforza, surnamed Il Moro. Until the time of his death in 1522, a period of almost forty years, Gafurius manifested a boundless dedication to his craft. He

---

1. Melegulus' biography appears as an appendix to *De harmonia*.

2. Thus, Gafurius' 1480 *Theoricum* antedates by two years Bartolomeo Ramis' *Practica musicae*, which was published in the rival city of Bologna in 1482. Under its variant title, *Theorica musicae*, the 1492 edition discloses considerable change from the 1480 version. A facsimile of the 1492 edition superintended by Gaetano Cesari (Rome, 1934) provides a useful introduction to and valuable collative remarks on the two editions. References hereinafter are to the Cesari edition.

directed his singers, composed a substantial amount of music in all the forms then prevalent, served as Professor of Music at the University of Pavia,[3] and most important, continued to explain the theory and practice of music in his books.

Gafurius was well prepared by his era and location to write a definitive textbook on music. His living in northern Italy during the period of the fruition of the Renaissance meant that many opportunities presented themselves for study and intellectual employment. It meant being born into an environment of enthusiasm for research and zeal for learning, excitement over ancient ideas newly discovered or newly understood, speculative disputation, competition among scholars, fraternity for intellectuals, a market for books, poems, and compositions, pleasure in music, literature, and art. The secularism, the rise of capitalistic economy, and the humanism that characterize this first modern epoch all shaped the thought of Franchinus Gafurius along with other Renaissance men, and no one of these so much as humanism.

Unquestionably the Mantuan period (1474–76) was crucial to his development as a humanist. Mantua, cradle of Italian humanism and home of the famous school of Vittorino da Feltre, provided that milieu of respect for classical tradition to which he became unalterably attached. The *De ritu canendi* of Johannes Gallicus, or Carthusiensis, one of Vittorino's musical disciples, made the impressionable Gafurius a lifelong champion of Boethius. In Mantua Gafurius learned those classical ideas which were to color his thinking and work as a theorist: that the value of a practical musician lay in proportion to his grounding and integrity as a speculative musician, that reason is supreme over the errant faculties of sense, that music has an ethical purpose to educate the higher faculties and to mollify men's minds. In Mantua he embraced the thesis that music is first and foremost a philosophical science and a proper vehicle for abstract speculation.

Practica reflects his devotion to these ideas of antiquity. The last book which he produced, the vitriolic *Apologia,* he wrote to refute the Bolognese

3. See Paul Oscar Kristeller, *Studies in Renaissance Thought and Letters* (Rome, 1956), pp. 457–62, where it is reported that "the only certain example of a chair of music at any Italian university is that held by Gafurius at Pavia between 1494 and 1499." Kristeller regards Gafurius as an outstanding representative of musical humanism and an example of a blend of Burgundian musical tradition and Italian literary influences.

theorists who dared to impugn the authority of Pythagoras and Boethius. His purpose was, he declared, "to bring back into the light the truth abounding in Greek and Latin sources." His allegiance to classical tradition persists throughout his books.

Each of Gafurius' books, the *Practica* included, relies for support on statements made by or attributed to ancient authorities. His scholarly desire to compile and explain, his enthusiasm and respect for Greek and Roman figures and ideas, and his urge to help bring classical ideas into living experience again are all the attitudes of a humanist. In fact, it is one of Gafurius' achievements that he gathered ideas of Ptolemy, Aristides, and Boethius, and through Boethius Nicomachus and Pythagoras, not to mention those which Peter of Abano reported as Aristotle's, Virgil's, Cicero's, Pliny's, and Euclid's. His contemporary readers and those who have followed are impressed that he patronized the rebirth of learning himself in a small way when learned Greek exiles came to Italy by commissioning translations from the Greek of Briennius, Bacchius, Ptolemy, and Aristides. He owned a copy of Marsilio Ficino's Latin translation of the works of Plato.

Gafurius was not only conversant with the writings of antiquity. Like many of his contemporaries he emulated the ancients. Naturally he cultivated a pure Latin style as his medium of expression, and the dedicatory remarks addressed to Ludovico Sforza at the beginning of the *Practica* may be compared to Pliny's dedication of his *Natural History* to the Emperor Titus. As Gafurius himself points out, however, the technical nature of his subject made such belletristic Latin inexpedient, so that the rest of the *Practica*, except for a few passages here and there, employs a straightforward Latin expression relying generally upon uninvolved sentence constructions. Classical allusions are evident throughout the work.

Like a true humanist, Gafurius had many friends among the *literati*. Lancinus Curtius, a Milanese poet and humanist, contributed his poetic talent to the *Theorica* and *De harmonia* while Lucinus Conagus penned his elegiac distichs for the *Practica*. When Gafurius needed to prod Ludovico for a benefice, he found a sympathetic ally in his well-placed friend Jacobus Antiquarius, secretary to Il Moro.

The author of the *Practica* was the most prolific and published writer on music of his time. He endorsed the classical proposition that the theoretical and practical aspects of music had to be sorted out and explained separately. Accordingly, over a period of two decades from about 1480 to

1500, Gafurius "wrote with the utmost care three volumes on music: *Theorica, Practica,* and *Harmonia instrumentorum.*"[4] These works comprise a complete and unified course of instruction in music theory and practice as it had evolved both from ancient and medieval tradition and from the demands of performance by the late fifteenth century in the most civilized location in Europe, northern Italy.

In line with standard, traditional procedure, *Theorica* treated music as a science, summarizing classical music doctrine as it had been preserved or pieced together in the western world. In general *Theorica* followed Boethius, the synthesizing sixth-century scholar on whose teachings Europeans were nourished for a thousand years. *De harmonia* amplified this scientific approach to music with an exhaustive presentation and analysis of intervallic sizes, stressing Greek contributions in particular. Together *Theorica* and *De harmonia* offer the rationale of music which Gafurius had been educated to believe was the primary goal of study in his field.

But if he was convinced of the superiority of musical theory over practice as an intellectual and moral discipline, Gafurius nevertheless argued that this study is sterile unless it is put to use in composition and performance. He had not spent his own life as a choir director and composer without realizing that the fruition of theory lies only in its use. Thus the inception of the *Practica* antedates publication of his *Theoricum* in 1480. In Book V, Chapter 6, of *Theoricum* Gafurius was already referring to the second work he contemplated. At Bergamo in 1483–84 a manuscript version of the *Practica* had in fact been executed; a copy of this manuscript, bearing the date 1487, is preserved in the Biblioteca Civica de Bergamo.[5] More extensive and specific references to the yet-unpublished *Practica* appear in the second, revised and expanded edition of the

4. This legend adorns three borders of the woodcut frontispiece of Gafurius' *Angelicum ac divinum opus musicae* (Milan, 1508).

5. Melegulus says that the *Practica* was completed in Bergamo, or possibly in Monticelli, just before Gafurius' departure for Milan in 1484. This MS is unfortunately no longer extant. The Biblioteca Civile di Bergamo holds the earliest surviving MS in a codex which bears the date 1487. This early script, prepared by the Carmelite brother, Allesandro Assolari, in Bergamo, does not provide a complete text of the *Practica*. The MS consists of 103 leaves, of which only the first nineteen are devoted to the *Practica*. Here Book I appears in substantially the form which was to be printed by Le Signerre some nine years later. Books II, III, and IV are not included.

Leaves 20 to 103 of the Bergamo Codex appear to be notes and excerpts on music theory from Guido, de Muris, and Marchettus. They do not appear to have been collected by Gafurius but by Brother Assolari. It is as though the Carmelite had con-

Theoricum printed under the variant title *Theorica musicae* in Milan in 1492.

Besides the trilogy which was issued in so many editions, Gafurius produced two years before his death the little volume of polemic called *Apologia adversum Joannem Spatarium.*[6] *Apologia*, which was printed at Turin in 1520, culminated forty years of controversy between the rival schools of music of Bologna and Milan. A scholar's penchant for making marginal notes had embroiled him in this bitter dispute: the quarrel erupted when he returned to Giovanni Spataro a copy which he had borrowed of Bartolomeo Ramis' *Practica*, in which he had not refrained from writing disparaging marginal notes.

Besides these printed works by Gafurius there exist in Codex 1158 of the Palatine Library in Parma two autographed but undated manuscripts bearing the titles *Extractus parvus musicae* and *Tractatus brevis cantus plani*. These youthful efforts, both dedicated to native Lodians, may probably be assigned to the years 1473–75. Two other early tracts, bearing the titles *Musicae institutionis collocutiones* and *Flos musicae*, are mentioned in *Theorica* IV; and *Practica* III, 8, also refers to *Flos musicae*. These two tracts, now missing, were written around 1476, while he was in Verona.

In the Biblioteca del Liceo Musicale di Bologna there is preserved another tract in Gafurius' hand called *Proportioni practicabili*, which in its arrangement of topics and contents seems to follow very closely Tinctoris' *Proportionale*. This manuscript was composed at Monticelli around 1481–83 and indicates the influence which Tinctoris had on Gafurius while they were both staying in Naples.

Practica seems important to present in English first because it has the most meaning for our time. This work treats music not as a philosophical or scientific discipline leading a few persons to a higher moral and intel-

---

cluded that only Book I of Gafurius' work contained material appropriate to his work "written for the honor and glory of God."

A comparison of the Bergamo MS copy of Book I with the *editio princeps* of 1496 demonstrates how Gafurius matured as a scholar during the intervening period of nine years. The Bergamo Codex omits the classical allusions that flourish in the printed *Practica*. The musical illustrations were improved. In addition, the 1487 MS reveals that he had not yet had access to Anselm's *De musica*, to the Latin translations of several Greek works on music theory, nor to the Aristotelian *Musical Problems* and their exegesis by Peter of Abano.

6. For Latin text and English translation, see "The *Apologia* of Franchinus Gafurius," a research paper submitted by Irwin Young to the University of Southern California, June 1952.

lectual plane, the way music was considered in antiquity, but as an art, the way it is considered in modern times. *Practica* explains how to read, compose, and play Renaissance compositions. Music, like the other arts, had come to be appreciated as the conscious application of creative imagination and taste to the production of something to be enjoyed by the many. With the modern era a secular, materialistic attitude toward art replaced a religious and philosophical attitude, and the fact that Gafurius related his *Practica* to this new frame of mind shows him participating in this modern spirit. More than any other work of its period, the *Practica* helped bridge the gap between music as a philosophical science and as a secular art.

In addition to being a definitive theorist, the author of the *Practica* was an accomplished and fertile composer. His extant compositions include fourteen masses (some *missae breves*), thirty-eight motets in one, two and three *partes*, eleven Magnificats, assorted hymns, Stabat Maters, litanies, and a half dozen secular pieces as well. The latter are preserved in Parma Codex 1158 (46v–52r), among them a textless canzona based upon the famous tune "De tous biens pleine" which also provides the thematic material for Gafurius' mass of the same name.

Except for two hymns, "Christe redemptor" and "Hostis Herodes," which are preserved in MS. 871 of the Abbey of Monte Cassino, all of the liturgical music that remains to us is conserved in three great Milanese Codices 2267, 2268, and 2269 of the Ambrosian Cathedral. Gafurius himself supervised the preparation of these elephantine anthologies of fifteenth-century sacred music. His own compositions and those of the Flemish masters whose music was also sung in the Cathedral of Milan were copied out for his choir, some of it indeed by his own hand.[7]

At least eight masses by Gafurius are missing. In his *Apologia* Gafurius reports that at the behest of Pope Leo X, three of the masses, *L'homme armé, Illustrissime Princeps,* and *Le Souvenir,* were forwarded to the Vatican some time before 1520, but they have not been mentioned among the treasures of the Papal Seat since 1533. A fourth, Milanese Codex 2266, was tragically destroyed by a fire while on display at the International Exposition in Milan in 1906. Only a few fragments remain. Three masses, including one entitled *La Bassadanza,* five motets, three Magnificats as

7. Knud Jeppesen, "Die Drei Gafurius-Kodices der Fabbrica del Duomo, Milano," *Acta Musicologica,* III (1931).

well as a Pater Noster, a Te Deum, two canzoni sacre, and a Lauda on the nativity with Italian text—all from the pen of Gafurius—were consumed in the fire.

Gafurius' surviving music constitutes a valuable repertory of Renaissance music. The style of composition bears elements of Franco-Netherlandish tradition commingled with autochthonous traits. His compositional style is also in evidence in the numerous musical examples which were incorporated into the *Practica*. The generous supply of monodic and polyphonic examples tremendously enhances the value of the *Practica* as a textbook on theory.

These examples should not be regarded as merely conventional or pedantic essays designed to clarify troublesome matters of mensuration or mode, although they accomplish that purpose, to be sure. It is worthwhile also to view them as miniature specimens of the larger works of an experienced and seasoned craftsman, and as such they offer entrée to the contrapuntal and harmonic thinking of his time. They are a file of late *quattrocento* techniques.

The musical examples reflect Gafurius' adherence to the classical concept of proportion as the foundation for aesthetic beauty and perfection. Proportion enabled musicians to assemble that variety of horizontal relationships which distinguishes Renaissance mensural music in its multiform divisions of the *tactus* and in its linear elasticity. It also provided a theoretical basis for the composite interval, that vertical aggregate of two or more intervals which is the logical progenitor and equivalent of the modern triad.

Renaissance composers were moving into new ground, and their music necessarily deviated and grew increasingly remote from established classical theory. Pythagorean authority was in conflict with the contemporary and vibrant world of music about it. In its definition of intervals in terms of detailed mathematical proportions, Pythagorean tradition came under closer scrutiny by the theorists. Gafurius, practical musician that he was, was forced to concede that in composition the logic of theory often had to give way to the amenities of sound. He appreciated the *suavitas* of a composite fifth consisting of a major and minor third tuned in the ratios of 5:4 and 6:5 respectively, and he endorsed these "sweet"-sounding modifications of their Pythagorean counterparts 81:64 and 32:27 as eminently suitable in practice. But at the same time he felt the need to justify these changes on rational grounds, and he resented innovations not supported by scientific explanation. By the addition and the subtraction of the minute interval of a comma in an 81:80 ratio, Gafurius was able to justify the conversion of Pythagoras' thirds into the more artless formulae of just intonation.

With the exception of the octave, the *Practica* lay open to examination every interval in Pythagoras' hitherto sacrosanct arsenal. Even the perfect fifth was assaulted, and in a discussion of a practice which foreshadowed equal temperament, Gafurius mentions the way the organists tampered with this basic interval by minutely tempering its 3:2 dimension.

At the turn of the century proportion as a factor in temporal relationships had reached and passed the zenith of its development, but Gafurius, seemingly unmindful of this, explains temporal proportion in the most definitive and exhaustive way. In Book IV of the *Practica* he carries horizontal proportion to its theoretical extremes. Eighty-one mathematical ratios, ranging from the basic sesquialter to such esoteric formulations as 4:19 and 22:5, are introduced and illustrated.

The musical examples conceived and executed by means of such a technical apparatus gave rise to a great multiplicity and variety of rhythmic patterns both in their horizontal and their vertical juxtapositions. Certainly the majority of these musical proportions found limited outlet in the practical composition of the time, and even in Gafurius' own compositions, only a few samples of the five proportional genera are in evidence.

Of all the proportional devices to which Gafurius addressed himself in the *Practica,* none bears his imprint more than his deft exploitation of the sesquialter and its equivalent, coloration. Sesquialter manipulations abound in his compositions and may well constitute the most distinctive aspect of his rhythmic craftsmanship. As illustrated by text and example in the *Practica,* the injection of a sesquialter proportion, or coloration, into a melodic line in minor prolation afforded an excellent means for attaining variety, relief, and contrast. The horizontal juxtaposition of binary and ternary divisions of the *tactus* effected a basic contrast in the rhythmic design. In conjunction with another part or parts the additional factor of vertical conflict results. Interest in the rhythmic fabric is further heightened by Gafurius' predilection for this dual sesquialter technique among parts written in contrasting mensurations. In the Gloria of his *Missa Montana,* for example, his use of sesquialter evokes an idyllic scene appropriate for Christmas.

Gafurius also made effective use of duple sesquialter (5:2), a species of the multiple superparticular genus, in his own compositions. Near the end of his motet, "O beata Sebastiane," which he composed in honor of Milan's patron saint, this proportion is invoked to produce a short, melismatic touch of tone painting in the top voice. For the "Et in terra" of his *Missa Montana* a subduple sesquialter (2:5) conveniently augments the value of each of the tenor's notes, while *superius* and baritone sing what he refers to in *Practica* III, 2, as "the most famous progression" in tenths.

The medieval device of indicating proportion by canonic inscription which is described in IV, 5, occasionally occurs in Renaissance composition. In Gafurius' *Missa de tous biens pleine,* "Crescit in duplo haec prima conclusio" directs the tenor in the "Et in spiritus" to augment the notes of the first phrase of Hayne's popular chanson in a ratio of 1:2.

Both text and musical examples in IV, 13, explain the mathematical cerebrations required when proportions were applied cumulatively. That this kind of operation was sometimes actually used is also demonstrated in some of Gafurius' compositions. The soloistic duo in the "Benedictus" of his *Missa sine nomine,* for example, introduces a series of superparticular species requiring the singers to make swift, accurate mathematical computations during the course of the movement. In this case a sesquitertia (4:3) is supplanted by a sesquiquarta (5:4), compelling the singer to perform the succeeding notes in the superpartient 5:3. Happily the latter proportion encounters a sesquiquinta (6:5), and by conjunction these two unite into the relatively simple first multiple species 6:3, or as reduced, 2:1. Unless exposed to the kind of instruction contained in IV, 13, of the *Practica,* the members of his choir in the Ambrosian Cathedral might have experienced some difficulty in coping with this problem in performance, not to mention sight-reading.

More than a score of the polyphonic examples in the *Practica* are engaging demonstrations of the synchronization of parts scored in contrasting metrical signatures. Gafurius was less academic than his famous Flemish predecessor, Ockeghem, in his treatment of both proportion and mensuration. Ockeghem in his *Missa prolationum* used four contrasting mensurations at once in a tour de force. Gafurius similarly deployed four different mensurations in the "Hosanna" of his *Missa sine nomine* ($\oplus\frac{3}{2}$, $\mathbb{C}\frac{3}{2}$, $\mathbb{C}\frac{3}{2}$, $\mathbb{C}\frac{3}{1}$), but here the technical display defers to the musical sense. As actually realized in modern transcription, the complicated process finds the parts moving more or less uniformly and substantially as though the entire passage had been written in a single mensuration.

Gafurius served Ludovico Sforza as music master in the Cathedral of Milan at the very time that Leonardo da Vinci served the same patron. No one is likely to claim for Gafurius the range of invention and the creative genius that lift Leonardo above his age. Yet Gafurius' impact in the field of music theory was enormous. He wrote his *Practica musicae* at exactly the right time and place — in the very decade and the very region where they could benefit from the technological revolution of moveable type. The availability of his works as well as their authority and clarity insured their wide use in Europe for a century or more. His *Practica* is important because it summarizes music theory and practice in a culminating age and because it attends the innovations that would affect the direction of modern music. Gafurius is the first of a succession of Italian theorists who would guide and direct the course of Western music until the advent of the Baroque era.

$\mathcal{T}$exts and Editorial Policy

The present edition of the *Practica* is based upon the original edition (Hain No. 7407) published in Milan in 1496, specifically a fine copy belonging to the Henry E. Huntington Library. All subsequent editions of Gafurius' *Practica* derived from this one; the publishers did not revise it, and it is notable for its completeness and purity.

Of the more than eight hundred incunabula produced in Milan, the *princeps* edition of the *Practica* has been singled out as a superior example of craftsmanship in the new art of typography.[8] Elegant copper engraving, attractive and symmetrical lettering, the artistic format of the title page, borders, and handsomely foliated and framed initials, bespeak the accomplished hands and artistry of its printer, Guillermus Le Signerre of Rouen.

Le Signerre's engraved borders for the lead chapters of the *Practica*'s four books attest to his understanding of the work and the care he took with its printing. In broad terms Books I and III of the *Practica* are concerned with vertical proportion as the basis for the production of intervals, while II and IV explain temporal relationships based on horizontal proportion. In apparent deference to this dualism Le Signerre executed one border pattern for the odd-numbered books and a second for the even-numbered books. The border for I and III shows various combinations of instrumentalists and vocal ensembles. In the upper right-hand corner is seated Apollo, god of poetry and music, holding a lute in one hand and an aulos in the other. In the lower right-hand corner Professor Gafurius sits at a lectern before a group of attentive students. For II and IV Le Signerre's engraving shows three figures of classical mythology—Amphion, Orpheus, and Arion — with the supporting legends "Amphion built the walls of Thebes with his lyre," "Orpheus in the woods," and "Arion among the dolphins."[9]

8. F. J. Norton, *Italian Printers, 1501–1520* (London, 1958), p. 45. See also William Dana Orcutt, *The Book in Italy During the Fifteenth and Sixteenth Centuries* (New York, 1928), p. 131, where the 1496 *Practica* is reported to have been the first book printed in Milan to contain copper engravings.

9. These are conventional humanist references. Gafurius seems to have learned the story of Amphion from Horace's *De arte poetica* (vss. 394–95). The Orpheus and Arion legends he drew from Virgil's *Eclogue* VIII.56. (See Virgil, *Eclogues Georgics Aeneid*, tr. H. Rushton Fairclough [London, 1925], I, 58.)

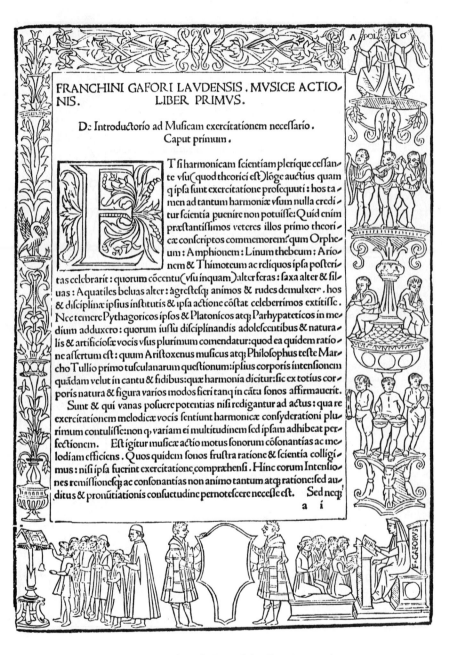

FRANCHINI GAFORI LAVDENSIS . MVSICE ACTIO-
NIS.   LIBER PRIMVS.

De Introductorio ad Muſicam exercitationem neceſſario.
Caput primum.

ET ſi harmonicam ſcientiam pleríque ceſſan-
te vſu(quod theorici eſt)lóge auctius quam
q̃ ipſa ſunt exercitatione proſecuuti: hos ta-
men ad tantum harmoniæ vſum nulla credi-
tur ſcientia puenire non potuiſſe:Quid enim
præſtantiſſimos veteres illos primo theoricæ conſcriptos commemorem?quum Orphe-
um : Amphionem : Linum thebeum : Ario-
nem & Thimoteum ac reliquos ipſa poſteri-
tas celebrarit : quorum cócentu(vſu inquam)alter feras : ſaxa alter & ſil-
uas : Aquatiles beluas alter : agreſteſq̃ animos & rudes demulxere . hos
& diſciplinæ ipſius inſtitutis & ipſa actione cóſtat celeberrimos extitiſſe .
Nec temere Pythagoricos ipſos & Platonicos atq̃ Parhypateticos in medium adduxero: quorum iuſſu diſciplinandis adoleſcentibus & natura-
lis & artificioſæ vocis vſus plurimum comendatur:quod ea quidem ratione aſſertum eſt: quum Ariſtoxenus muſicus atq̃ Philoſophus teſte Mar-
cho Tullio primo tuſculanarum queſtionum:ipſius corporis intenſionem
quádam velut in cantu & fidibus:quæ harmonia dicitur:ſic ex totius corporis natura & figura varios modos fieri tanq̃ in cátu ſonos affirmauerit.
    Sunt & qui vanas poſuere potentias niſi redigantur ad actus : qua re
exercitationem melodicæ vocis ſentiunt harmonicæ conſyderationi plurimum contuliſſe:non q̃ variam ei multitudinem ſed ipſam adhibeat per-
fectionem.   Eſt igitur muſicæ actio motus ſonorum cóſonantias ac me-
lodiam efficiens . Quos quidem ſonos fruſtra ratione & ſcientia colligi-
mus : niſi ipſa fuerint exercitatione,compræhenſi . Hinc eorum Intenſio-
nes remiſſioneſq̃ ac conſonantias non animo tantum atq̃ ratione:ſed au-
ditus & pronútiationis conſuetudine pernoteſcere neceſſe eſt.   Sed neq̃

                                                    a   i

Opening page of Book One of the *Practica musicae,*
1496 edition.

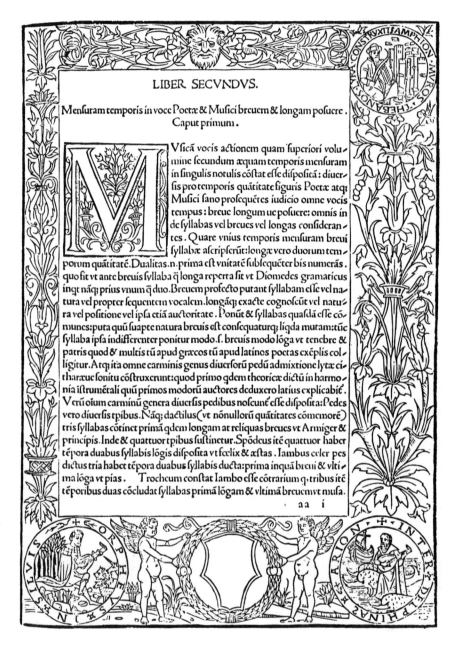

LIBER SECVNDVS.

Mensuram temporis in voce Poetæ & Musici breuem & longam posuere. Caput primum.

Vsicã vocis actionem quam superiori volu-
mine secundum æquam temporis mensuram
in singulis notulis costat esse disposita: diuersis pro temporis quãtitate figuris Poetæ atqꝫ
Musici sano prosequêtes iudicio omne vocis
tempus: breue longum ue posuere: omnis in
de syllabas vel breues vel longas consideran-
tes. Quare vnius temporis mensuram breui
syllabæ ascripserũt:longæ vero duorum tem-
porum quãtitate.Dualitas.n.prima est vnitatê subsequêter bis numerãs.
quo fit vt ante breuis syllaba q̃ longa reperta sit vt Diomedes gramaticus
inqt nãqꝫ prius vnum q̃ duo.Breuem profecto putant syllabam esse vel natura vel propter sequentem vocalem.longãqꝫ exacte cognoscũt vel natura vel positione vel ipsa etiã auctoritate. Ponũt & syllabas quasdã esse cõ-
munes:puta quũ suapte natura breuis est consequaturqꝫ liqda mutam:tũc
syllaba ipsa indifferenter ponitur modo.s. breuis modo lõga vt tenebre &
patris quod & multis tũ apud græcos tũ apud latinos poetas exêplis col-
ligitur.Atqꝫ ita omne carminis genus diuersorũ pedũ admixtione lytæ ci-
tharæue sonitu cõstruxerunt:quod primo qdem theoricæ dictũ in harmonia istrumétali quũ primos modorũ auctores deduxero latius explicabiť.
Verũ oium carminũ genera diuersis pedibus noscunť esse disposita:Pedes
vero diuersis tpibus. Nãqꝫ dactilus(vt nõnullorũ quãtitates cõmemorê)
tris syllabas cõtinet primã qdem longam at reliquas breues vt Armiger &
principis. Inde & quattuor tpibus sustinetur.Spõdeus itê quattuor habet
tépora duabus syllabis lõgis disposita vt fœlix & æstas . Iambus celer pes
dictus tria habet tépora duabus syllabis ducta:prima inquã breui & vlti-
ma lõga vt pias.   Trochæum constat Iambo esse cõtrarium qꝫ tribus itê
téporibus duas cõcludat syllabas primã lõgam & vltimã breuemvt musa.

aa i

Opening page of Book Two of the *Practica musicae*,
1496 edition.

As a felicitous setting for the entire *Practica* Le Signerre provided a frontispiece which includes a great many humanistic references to the classics. Apollo again presides, at the head of muses and naked graces, planets and elements, the lower octave of the *systema teleion,* and corresponding modes. Python, serpent symbol of the Delphic oracle, bisects the design. Across the top a banner proclaims: "The power of the Apollonian mind sets the muses in motion on all sides." So the frontispiece displays in a unifying way the three Boethian categories of music: *mundana, humana,* and *instrumentalis.*

In addition to its artistic merit, it is indeed fortunate that a work of the size and scope of the *Practica* should have been released to the public with a minimum of error. The profusion of musical examples scattered throughout the work must have been prepared under Gafurius' watchful eye. The music was not set in typeface but was printed from wood engravings, and this original set of woodcuts was used for the first four editions of the treatise. Only supervision by an experienced musician can account for their accuracy.

Le Signerre's production looms the more significantly in view of the fact that each of the subsequent editions reproduces verbatim text and music of the original edition, even maintaining the dedication to Ludovico after the Duke had been deposed prior to the publication of the third, fourth, and fifth editions. The 1496 *Practica* thus served as an exemplar for each of the succeeding editions, thereby insuring accurate preservation and dissemination of its contents by other hands.

Layout and decoration varied from one printing of the *Practica* to the next. There are differences in colophons, and titles are modified. These nominal variations, however, and those in spelling, capitalization, abbreviations, punctuation, and paragraphing, demonstrate the lack of standardization at the time in orthography and linguistics, not emendation of text or ideas. Publisher's idiosyncrasies appear in the arbitrary use of Roman and Arabic numerals, the meager or lavish use of initials of assorted dimensions, the spatial arrangement of text and accompanying examples, and in the omission or inclusion of marginal rubrics. Le Signerre's designs for the borders of the opening chapter of each of the four books in the original edition are lacking in the more mundane edition of 1497. In analogous places rubrics are substituted.

This second edition the very next year after the first was prompted by the warm reception accorded Le Signerre's *Practica* and by Gafurius' increasing stature as an authority on music theory. It was done in Brescia, which is near Milan, the work of another *ultramontani,* one Angelicus Britannicus. Even a cursory examination discloses that this 1497 edition is slavishly beholden to its predecessor. Britannicus had access to the original woodcuts. Moreover, he neglected to correct the misprints in the first edition and then contributed a few of his own—an inverted rubric, for example, accompanying a musical example in II, 7. The title was modified to *Music[a]e utriusque cantus practica,* there is no frontispiece, and there are some disparities in spelling, abbreviations, and capitalization. The 1497 edition uses a font which accommodates more text per line. In general, Britannicus' second edition is an artistically inferior but workmanlike reproduction of the original edition.

Britannicus published two more editions of the *Practica,* in Brescia in 1502 and 1508, each bearing the title *Practica musicae utriusque cantus.* Both of these editions also conform closely to the original. They make one slight improvement by lining up musical examples with relevant text more exactly. Each of his editions presented small, delicately framed initials for all the chapters except the opening one for each of the four books. No doubt the publisher had planned to add something more elaborate here which he did not manage to execute.

The next edition of the *Practica* was made in Venice in 1512 by Augustinus de Zannis of Portesio. De Zannis' edition illustrates the advanced state of Venetian typography, with its more modern font, its diagrams and examples, its many large initials with draped figures, animal and human, and above all, its three-dimensional frontispiece, which shows a choir of men and boys gathered in front of a lectern upon which a giant-sized musical score rests. The fifth is a production of artistic excellence. It also marks the first effort by an editor to expunge some of the errors of the previous editions and was advertised "multisque erroribus expurgata." Thus in I, 2, a line of text which had been inadvertently repeated in the original edition is excised in the 1512. A few misprints in I, 3 and 5, and in II, 10, did elude de Zannis' proofreading, and there is a place in IV, 1, where a breve was placed in the cantus of the first musical example where a circle, the sign for tempus, was intended. The more modern and artistic 1512 edition for the first time provided Arabic numbers on the recto pages with which to designate the consecutive folios, and for the first time the Table of Contents carried page numbers.

Several authorities, including the Lodi publication in honor of the five hundredth anniversary of Gafurius' birth, list two further editions of the *Practica,* one in Venice in 1517 and a posthumous edition in 1522. No copies of such editions have been located, however, and evidence of their ever existing is inconclusive.[10]

Besides these five editions in Latin, two vernacular versions made available certain parts of the *Practica* in Italian. The master musician was embarrassed to lend his name to a book published in the vernacular. For him Latin was the only language proper for a scholarly work. But his concern as a teacher vied with his pride as a humanist, so that he did permit a student of his, Francesco Caza, to publish excerpts from the *Practica* in the Italian language, and Gafurius even wrote a Latin preface for it. This was the *Tractato vulgare de canto figurato*, Milan, 1492.[11] Caza's *Tractato* was actually published, then, four years before the Latin manuscript of *Practica* found its way to the printing press. In the same year a second edition of *Theorica* was printed.

Caza's economical volume "imitating," as he frankly states, "the ideas and organization of my teacher Franchinus Gafurius in the second part of his book on practice," included only Book II, Chapters 3 through 15, of the *Practica*, in abridged form, without musical examples. Staves were blocked in, but the reader was expected to draw in the musical notes for himself. Gafurius' first two chapters, which are of a more general, historical nature, were omitted. But the basic mensural theory of *Practica* was made available for a lay audience without compromising his status as a humanist scholar.

Sixteen years later Gafurius allowed the publication of a vernacular edition of certain books from the *Practica* under his own name. The text is in Italian with the retention of much Latin vocabulary and mantled under the respectability of a Latin title: *Angelicum ac divinum opus musicae*, Milan, 1508. He prepared this edition, he explained, to meet the needs of a growing number of people who were illiterate in Latin, especially the "many nuns who hold the intention to praise the Lord and all the Heavenly Court." In the introduction to *Angelicum* Gafurius explains his goal with the usual clarity for which Glarean complimented him:

> . . . now to be sure, since the publication in the Latin language, as was fitting and proper, of the *Theorica* and *Practica* and also the *Instrumentorum Harmonia*, I have composed by request a work on the same subject in the

10. Alessandro Caretta, Luigi Cremascoli, and Luigi Salamina, *Franchino Gaffurio* (Lodi, 1951), p. 134.

11. Johannes Wolf prepared a modern edition of this work: Francesco Caza, *Tractato vulgare de canto figurato*, facsim. ed. with German trans. and notes (Berlin, 1922).

vernacular, to the end that those who have not learned letters [that is, Latin literature] may be able to derive some profit from the work I have done. . . .

Reports on the contents of the *Angelicum* have in the past been inaccurate. The eighteen chapters of *Angelicum,* Book II, present an Italianate version of *Practica*'s Book I, covering the Guidonian system, mutation, and the modes. *Angelicum* III summarizes in eleven chapters the material from *Practica* II. *Angelicum* IV repeats the counterpoint theory of *Practica* III, while *Angelicum* V treats the problem of mensural proportion as discussed in *Practica* IV but without the benefit of the musical examples. Book I of *Angelicum* uses material from the *De harmonia* MS which Gafurius had completed in 1500.

It remains to discuss the policies of translation and transcription. In general the goal has been to bring the text and the musical examples of the *Practica* into modern language and notation as clearly and as faithfully as possible.

Aside from its preface and an occasional literary flourish, the *Practica* hews to an expository Latin construction, as befits a technical treatise. But the span of time which separates the Latin original from its English replica, and the attendant etymological metamorphosis in musical terminology, content, and style, raise some problems for the translator. The process of translation, accordingly, must be a flexible one. It must permit the use of Latin terms where common English terms lack the broader implications inherent in the former, or of a phrase sometimes to stand for a single word. If a Latin word has several meanings, the translator is obliged to select the right one in English to suit each individual use of the word. *Chorda* has been translated "note," "string," or "pitch," as appropriate to the text. *Vox* sometimes had to be translated "voice" but at other times "syllable," "vocable," or "sound." Words that carry modern connotations not relevant to Renaissance thinking have had to be avoided.

Retention of certain Latin technical terms and derivatives is sometimes indicated. The hexachord and mutation provide an example. Each of the hexachords built on G, F, and C has the same structure (T T S T T). Yet for Renaissance theorists they were not identical. Each was considered to possess a particular quality of its own. The hexachord commencing on G was deemed to possess a "hard" *(durus)* quality because its third pitch, B-natural, was *quadratus:* that is to say, the letter name B had a square shape. The hexachord on F was considered to be "soft" *(mollis)* because it

contained a B-flat which was *rotundus,* or round. The C hexachord was
the proprietor of "natural" quality by virtue of the fact that it had neither
the square nor the round B in its structure. Using the Latin neuters *durum,*
molle, and *naturale* to distinguish the respective hexachords on G, F, and
C also prevents the likelihood of confusion between the B-natural of the
G hexachord and the "natural" hexachord on C. "B-*molle*" is, at the very
least, as felicitous a description of the hexachord on F as "B-soft."

The technical terms of the *systema teleion* also seem, to this translator,
worthy of retention and superior to letter pitch names in many instances.
Proslambanomenos may be translated as "A" but at a sacrifice of its status
as the foundation of the Greater Perfect System, leaving no room for those
adjustments in tuning attained by tightening or loosening the string.

English cognates for Latin terms are sometimes useful and preferable to
more familiar synonyms in conserving the sense of the original. "Composite interval" for *intervallum compositum* more truly reflects the Renaissance idea of an aggregate of two or more intervals in vertical proportion
than the modern entity connoted by the word "triad" or "chord." Similarly, the translation "a fourth" would sacrifice the broader meaning of the
Greek derivative "diatessaron." In some contexts, to be sure, a diatessaron
is only a simple fourth. Elsewhere, however, it might consist of three or
four sounds, in two or three species, in one or more intonations depending
upon the genus. The old-fashioned cognate "propriety" is used as a translation for *proprietas* to alert the reader to the concept that a particular
attribute or quality was conferred on each hexachord.

Unless cognates were specifically required to state a concept, however,
every effort has been made to put Gafurius' Latin into modern terminology.

Transcription of the *Practica*'s music into modern notation entails mechani-
cal and editorial decisions. Initially, the transcriber must elect a particular
scale of reduction for the basic unit of Renaissance time, and here Gafurius
provided concrete advice. The modern equivalents for Renaissance metrical signatures emerge in natural course. Secondly, the transcriber must
make judgments regarding *musica ficta,* bar lines, clefs, and a method of
effecting practical resolution of the proportions.

Gafurius supplies us with a physiological basis for the speed of the *tactus,*
the rhythmic beat or unit of time. He draws the analogy between the tempo
of a semibreve and its component parts, two minims, and the time required for a normal pulse to dilate and contract. Thus it seems highly appropriate that the basic semibreve be transcribed as a modern quarter note

in a reduction of 4:1. Unless otherwise indicated, the metrical signatures for each of the so-called four prolations ◯, ◖, ⊙, ◖ are transcribed as 3/4, 2/4, 9/8, and 6/8, respectively. In the latter two mensurations, of course, the ternary semibreve translates as a dotted quarter note.

Modern bar lines have been supplied to facilitate analysis and performance of the music in the *Practica*. Without necessarily implying accent, the bar line offers a convenient means for visualizing the metrical groupings of a particular mensuration. In those instances where Gafurius pits one mensuration against another, it becomes a useful aid. When tempus perfectum, for example, is set against tempus imperfectum—triple meter or 3/4 time in one voice against duple meter (2/4) in another voice—rhythmic conflict is engendered. After every sixth beat, or tactus, the bar line bisects both staves at once to show points of synchronization for the different mensurations.

Treble and bass clefs have been employed for all the two-part examples. For the three- and four-part examples, however, alto and tenor clefs have occasionally been used to avoid an excessive number of ledger lines. A treble clef with a subscript numeral 8 indicates, of course, the transposition of the cantus an octave lower. Its use is necessitated by the lower range characteristic of the cantus voice in Renaissance music and defined by C clefs in the original notation.

In a few instances, in order that all the parts might synchronize at final cadence points, it was deemed politic to shift the bar line in one or another part by one beat. Thus, in transcription, the end of the penultimate measure where contrasting mensurations are involved or the conclusion of a proportional passage will have a bar line bisecting both staves, so that the final beat is synchronized as to each of the parts.

Transcription of these polyphonic examples in the *Practica* inevitably involves the problem of *musica ficta* or *musica acquisita*. The problem is one of determining when and where notes *extra manum Guidonis* or "beyond the Guidonian Hand"—that is to say, notes foreign to the diatonic genus—are ordered by the musical context. Whether a sharp, flat, or natural sign is implied where none is explicitly indicated persists as an enigma which thus far has withstood all musicological attempts at solution. No theorist, Gafurius included, gives clear-cut instruction in the application of accidentals: in a sense, these accretionary tones were a means of stretching the musical ideas of a time past to suit evolving ideas of the future, and few theorists seem to have been willing to risk compromising the venerable system of Guido by the overt intrusion of chromatics into the diatonic edifice. Yet it is impossible to ignore the fact that these notes were being used.

Gafurius recognized the fact that his music and the music he knew took liberties with rules, and he himself added notes "beyond the Hand." Take his far-from-helpful remark, for instance, that it is not the note itself but rather the sound ordered by the musical syllable that matters, or his pains to explain the cabalistic process wherein appropriate vocables are intoned without any accidentals being indicated and with identical notes being written to indicate different species of tetrachords (*Practica* I, 5). His own *Missa quarti toni* (Milan Codex 2268, 101v–109r) also offers a case in point. He had stated in *Practica* I, 9, that "frequently the [Hypophrygian] fourth mode [*B–b*] proceeds by means of acquired species and so is terminated on the acute *a la mi re*." This means that when he wrote the diapente species A-B-C-D-E in the Kyrie of this mass, he intended the performer to intone the fictive series A-Bb-C-D-E. The tenor range *E* to *e* and its final A are ostensibly the mode Glarean was to call Hypoaeolian, but by the application of musica ficta it becomes Hypophrygian once-transposed. Some advice with respect to chromatic use is thus available in the *Practica*.

The rules of the theorists, such as the popular verse *Una nota supra la semper est canendum fa,* or the generalities asserted in the phrases *causa pulchritudinis, causa necessitatis,* or *causa subsemitonii,* are useful, but they cannot always be applied with certainty. An accidental inserted "for the sake of beauty" or "because it is needed" or to convert a modal whole tone into a semitone may throw off the intent of the melodic line or run counter to an harmonic implication in *quattrocento* music.

The music here evidences a more equitable apportionment of linear and vertical forces. Insertion of a single editorial chromatic can sometimes initiate a chain reaction of musica ficta carrying alien tonal implications. Whether or not any, some, or all of them, even cadential subsemitones, are valid, whether they represent the composer's intent or the performer's license or lack thereof, remains unfortunately largely conjectural. In view of the convoluted aspect of the musica ficta problem, a policy of editorial reserve seems indicated. Signs for musica ficta have been placed directly above the notes whose pitches are judged to be subject to modification.

More than a score of the polyphonic examples in the *Practica* carry the anachronistic partial signature, but the guidance that one might expect in adding accidentals is not forthcoming in these examples. In five of Gafurius' own secular compositions partial signatures appear where the parts occupy dual pitch levels at the distance of a fifth, bearing out the hypothesis that this was their purpose. Generally, Gafurius' practice suggests that partial or conflicting signatures were expedient notational devices used in order to accommodate purely melodic considerations of mode and range, probably carrying over from the medieval technique of successive composition.

For the more exotic mensural proportions in Book IV, where reduction or augmentation makes it impossible to transcribe note values precisely, approximations had to be used. Gafurius himself acknowledges this kind of technical difficulty by comparing these indistinct quantitative values to the fusing colors of a rainbow and to the continuous mutation of sound generated by a struck string. A mensural passage, for instance, utilizing the superparticular proportion 7:6 calls for seven notes or their equivalent to be equated with six like notes or an equivalent quantity. This equation is to be accomplished by abstracting one seventh of the value of each of the seven notes, not an easy assignment for even the most experienced musician. For readier grasp of these imprecise values, the affected notes have been transcribed in minuscule form, and the pertinent proportional numbers have been written in above.

In a proportion such as 6:5, modern notational means are available to effect the required reduction. A transcribed quarter or eighth note can be diminished by a sixth of its value by recourse to triplets or sextuplets. But the congested appearance of large numbers of diminished notes often makes such a literal solution undesirable. For the 8:7 passage on p. 205 minuscule notes plus the proportional formula were used in order to avoid a great many thirty-second and sixty-fourth notes. The 16:14 passage in the same example, however, involves larger note values to begin with and can therefore be effectively reduced without clutter. Again, in the example on p. 218, minuscule notes are employed for the 8:5 measures, while the 16:10 proportional passage, with its larger mensural values, has been transcribed into full-sized notes.

Students of music will undoubtedly wish to compare these transcriptions with the original examples. A parallel text may be found in the facsimile edition of the *Practica* published by Gregg International Publishers, Ltd., Farnborough, England.

$\mathcal{L}$ist of Abbreviated Titles

Couss.

    Edmond de Coussemaker, ed. *Scriptorum de musica medii aevi.* 4 vols. Paris, 1864–76.

Gerbert

    Martin Gerbert, ed. *Scriptores ecclesiastici de musica.* 3 vols. Milan, 1784.

Meibom

    Marcus Meibom, ed. *Antiquae musicae auctores septem.* 2 vols. Amsterdam, 1652.

PL

    J. P. Migne, ed. *Patrologiae cursus completus: Series Latina.*

    Except for the works listed above, all works are cited in full upon their first appearance in each Book.

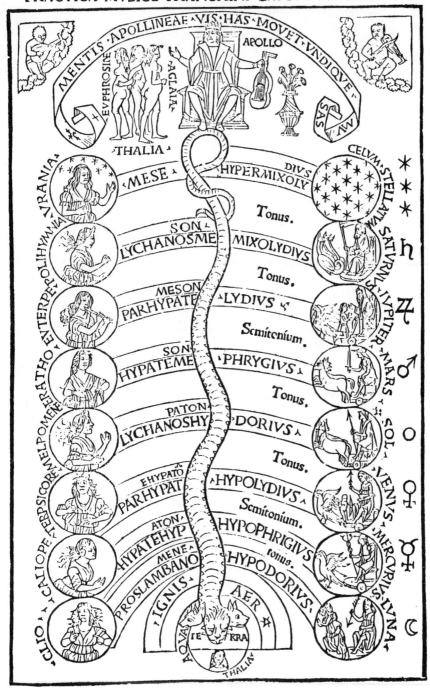

Frontispiece of the *Practica musicae,*
1496 edition.

$\mathcal{T}$o his Lordship, most Illustrious and Excellent Prince, Ludovico Maria Sforza Anglus, Invincible Duke of Milan, Franchinus Gafurius, Professor of Music, sends Greetings.

It is readily apparent, illustrious Prince,[1] how much influence the profession of the art of music had and with what veneration it was held among the ancients. We know this both from the example of the greatest philosophers, who, when they were very old, devoted themselves to this discipline as if in it they put the finishing touch to their studies, and from the practice of the strictest governments, which with the utmost diligence saw to it that whatever was harmful to public morals should be eliminated. Not only did these states not banish the art of music; they cultivated it with the utmost zeal as the mother and nurse of morals. In a word, the position of music is firmly established by the unanimous and steadfast conviction of all people and all nations who have held this art in greater honor than any other.

What other discipline has ever been accepted with so much approval? What other discipline has ever been accepted with so much unanimity by people of every age or sex, so that no one, in any condition of life, has yet been found who was not eager to soothe his cares with music, even crude

1. Ludovico Maria Sforza (1451–1508) inherited the surname Anglus from the Visconti who ruled in Milan immediately before the Sforzas. The surname was the product of a legend concocted in 1360 by enterprising genealogists. Upon the investiture of Giangaleazzo Visconti with the title of Count of Angera, they proceeded to trace the family tree of the Visconti back to one Anglus, founder of Angleria (now called Angera) and a grandson of Aeneas. Thus the Visconti and their successors, the Sforzas, acquired a pedigree, distinguished if fictitious, that related them to the heroes of classical antiquity. (See D. M. Bueno de Mesquita, *Giangaleazzo Visconti* [Cambridge, Eng., 1941], p. 176.)

During the comparatively brief period of his ascendancy, from 1479 when he usurped the duchy of Milan, the humanist trained and educated Ludovico maneuvered aggressively and ambitiously in the particularistic political structure of Renaissance Italy. It was an era of strongly independent city-states mired in Machiavellian intrigue, warring factions, and tenuous alliances, which facilitated the invasion and despoliation of Italian soil by alien forces; and Ludovico's career was aborted by Charles VIII and terminated by Louis XII. The Prince of Milan died in a French prison in 1508.

music? It is proved not only by the testimony of the greatest minds but also by faith made manifest, so to speak, that nothing stirs people so quickly to diverse emotions as music does—so much so that in antiquity there was no hesitation about calling professors of music not just musicians, but seers and philosophers. To this testimony is added the authority of poets, who imagined that Linus and Orpheus were descended from the gods because they reduced the harsh, rustic life of certain men to a gentler culture. They imagined that these musicians moved stones and forests.

But in case you put little confidence in the words of poets, as men who exaggerate everything by the figurative language usual to them, philosophers too may be cited, who have not hesitated to assert that things with senses and even things without sense, insofar as they have some sort of life, are soothed by strains of music. For this reason some people have thought that the famous author, Virgil, in his *Eclogues,* was not using poetic hyperbole when he said that tough oaks really did move their heads to the strains of Silenus.[2] In fact, if we believe Plato, who said that the soul of the universe consists of music,[3] I surely do not see how it can be doubted that other things which are endowed with life of any kind whatever—which, it is clear, was given to them by heaven—are not also affected and made happy by that which is harmonious to their own nature.

Notwithstanding the political turbulence and social upheaval, Milan prospered under Ludovico's aegis and attained a degree of cultural eminence unrivalled except by the Florence of Lorenzo the Magnificent. Nicknamed "Il Moro" after his heraldic emblem, the mulberry tree, symbol of wisdom because it is the first tree to bear fruit and the last to shed its leaves, Ludovico provided a favorable milieu for scholarship and art. He staffed his reorganized University of Pavia with leading humanists; and outstanding figures, including Leonardo da Vinci, Bramante, and Josquin des Prez, gravitated towards the Lombardian citadel and the patronage of Il Moro to help record that historic efflorescence of art and genius known as the golden age of the Renaissance.

2. Virgil, *Eclogue* VI. 27–28, in *Eclogues Georgics Aeneid,* tr. H. Rushton Fairclough (London, 1925), Vol. I.

3. Plato's *Timaeus,* in *The Dialogues of Plato,* tr. B. Jowett (New York, 1937) II, 17, where the creation of the world is recounted in terms of Pythagorean dimensions of the diatonic system. Gafurius' knowledge of Plato derives largely from Marsilio Ficino (1433–99), founder of the Platonic Academy in Florence and a musician and music theorist in his own right. Gafurius' copy of Ficino's translation of the works of Plato is now the property of Harvard University. Beneath its colophon the copy bears a handwritten note by Gafurius indicating May 6, 1489, as the date of his purchase. The book contains copious marginal annotations by Gafurius, many on passages of a purely musical character. See Otto Kinkeldey, "Franchino Gafori and Marsilio Ficino," *Harvard Library Bulletin,* I (1947), 379–82.

After all, it is universally agreed that there is a natural tendency to like what is like oneself.

These reasons, illustrious Prince, influenced me, and nature too; and the impulse of nature is not easy to resist. Since my childhood I have applied myself continuously to this discipline, a discipline especially designed to enhance character, as the wisest men agree. And it has not been inconsistent with my [religious] profession. For the belief that this is a service preeminently suitable to clerics has long been accepted. Therefore, lest my studies should profit me alone, I also published a book,[4] following the technique of the most ancient scholars, on the rationale of this art, which the Greeks call Theory. I did this both to establish a rational basis for my studies and to disseminate the fruits of my labors more widely. That book I dedicated to your name, illustrious Prince—with hesitation and timidity, to be sure, lest I annoy you with my ill-timed trifles when you were occupied with weighty cares and the burdens of important concerns. But when I saw how favorably and how kindly you took an interest in my little work, slight and sketchy though it was, I was spurred on, and your liberality was an added incentive. Indeed, my zeal was kindled more than ever, so that I have produced the second part of this study also, without any anxiety that I might annoy you.

Now music is not, like the other learned disciplines, merely a speculative pursuit: it reaches out into practice, and as was said previously, is connected with morality. I would not have fulfilled my duty if I had remained in the field of research only, serving a few without toiling diligently for the public good too.

Thus this field of music theory is valuable not only because of the knowledge it gives of music itself, but also because its roots extend very far; it aids other disciplines. This has been verified by the testimony of very influential men who have acknowledged that they learned literature from music above all else. Fabius Quintilian declares, on the authority of Timagenes, that this art "is the most ancient of all studies in liberal education."[5]

4. The reference here is to the *Theorica*.

5. Quintilian, *Institutio oratoria*, I.x, tr. H. E. Butler (Loeb Classical Library, 1921) I, 165. This influential and most celebrated work of the Spanish-born Roman rhetorician and author, thanks to Poggio's discovery of a perfect copy in the monastery of St. Gall, provided primary fare for students of the Renaissance and later generations. Quintilian's source was the Alexandrian Greek Timagenes (fl. 61–31 B.C.), who was captured and transported to Rome in 55 B.C. as a slave, gained his freedom from the Emperor Augustus, and opened a famous school of rhetoric in Rome.

Now when I talk about music, I do not mean that theatrical and effeminate music which destroys rather than forms public morals, but rather that moderate, manly music celebrated by the ancient heroes, that music which was presented at the tables of kings and festive banquets when the guests, vying with one another as the cithara circulated among them, sang famous deeds of famous men, which was certainly a great inducement to kindle their eagerness for brave deeds. Truly this music rose even higher: she penetrates the heavens, and according to the testimony of the most celebrated bards, tells of the labors of the sun and the wandering moon and the titan stars,[6] and as if not content to have filled the spaces of earth with merit, she invades the skies and takes her place among the mysteries of things divine.

Therefore, most farseeing Prince, under your auspices and leadership this work has been born as my most recent offspring, to use an expression of Pliny the Elder,[7] and I have dedicated it when printed to your name with all due respect. To whom shall I refer my work more appropriately than to him to whom not only all Italy but also the most distant nations are accustomed to refer the legality of their plans and decisions, as to an arbiter of honor?

I have not been afraid that this little work of ours would come as an annoyance to you while you are busy with very important affairs because I know that you are accustomed to manage the most important things without feeling disdain for the smallest matters, and that you manage all affairs with such a happy talent that they are carried out in an even tenor. And yet you do not consider insignificant those things which are concerned with the perfection of scholarship. Famous schools for all kinds of disciplines, to be sure, bear witness to this, but especially the schools of Greek and Latin eloquence which you have established with utmost care throughout the cities you govern. Who else of your position and fortune inspires to virtue, protects and favors with greater authority, the talents of his subjects? For my part, I do not ask that my writings be compared with those of the great authors or that I be numbered among distinguished writers. If there should prove to be any value in what I write, I gladly acknowledge that this value derives from their teaching. It will be quite suf-

6. *Aeneid* I.742.

7. The phrase "natos apud me proxima fetura," which Gafurius quotes here in an inverted form, appears in the opening paragraph of the Preface to Pliny's *Natural History*, tr. H. Rackham (Loeb Classical Library, 1938), I, 3.

ficient for me if I strive to accomplish this much, and to this extent I would like my industry to win approval: that I be said to have helped the progress of students by a brevity which is both well ordered and comprehensive, so that things which had to be sought here and there throughout the volumes of various authors can be found collected in one volume in a suitable arrangement of subject matter. For we have taken great pains that all subjects, starting from their very beginnings, are carried through in logical succession to their conclusion; so that, however difficult the art may be, no reader will wander aimlessly or struggle because of the ineptness of the writer even more than because of the obscurity of the subject matter. This is the only job I have undertaken. It is on this basis that I think I ought to seek approval of my hard work.

Accept, therefore, most cultured Prince, my little work with the same generosity that you are wont to show in other matters. Let it win support at least by the prefixing of your name, for in this way it will be well received. Then the dedication of the book will win the commendation which it cannot gain for itself on its own merits. In conclusion, just as in general we attribute to you all the good gifts of fortune and talent that we have received, so whatever we have accomplished by study and hard work we want to be dedicated and consecrated to your name for all time.

A Poem by Lucinus Conagus

I would offer you your meed of praise; it is an honor to do so.
But who will extol you as you deserve, Ludovico?
Blessed and golden the era you give us, oh Prince.
The glory of none of our leaders has been so great.
Your deeds surpass that which man can tell of or believe,
To say nothing about your other accomplishments.
When, in what age, have the arts so flourished,
Or Pallas Athena been so favorable to the genius of man?
Men like Isaeus, Euclid, Pythagoras, we see today,
Apollo-born men who aim for the heavens above.
Nor do you lack men like Chrysippus and men learned as Solon,
And your times give you painters like Parrhasius.
Music too has blossomed forth, drawn from her Stygian abode,
And she herself has brought us new, unfamiliar rhythms.
Behold! Franchinus Gafurius proffers his resources; he brings his gifts.
None flourishes more brilliantly than he in the muses' art.

Reader, seek these gifts yourself. You'll see nothing but what is praise-
    worthy.
    From this source you will learn to be trained, and then to speak.
Whatever you do as a singer you can learn from this book;
    And you will be able to bring forth each sound correctly.
So if you are pleased with the author of this gift,
    Do offer pious prayers for him to the Lord God.[8]

8. This eulogy by the local poet and humanist, Lucinus Conagus, is addressed to both
Ludovico and Gafurius and employs the customary elegiac distichs replete with classical allusions. With this procession of Greek genius—Isaeus, the Attic orator and
teacher of Demosthenes; Euclid; Pythagoras; the Stoic philosopher Chryssipus; Solon;
and the celebrated Greek painter Parrhasius—Conagus complimented the author of
the *Practica* in a manner conventional to the period, which must nevertheless have
pleased him very much. Another of Conagus' poems appears in the *Rudimenta gram-
matices* of Nicolaus Perottus (Milan, 1483). (See Mario Emilio Cosenza, *Biographical
and Bibliographical Dictionary of the World of Classical Scholarship in Italy, 1300–
1800* [Boston, 1962], V, 1364–65.)

BOOK ONE

OF *The Practice*
of Music

[THE
SYSTEM OF
GUIDO AND THE
CHURCH MODES]

Chapter one The System Necessary to the Practice of Music

Even though the majority of scholars have pursued the science of harmony, while neglecting its practical application, far more extensively than those who have studied the practical application of the science — after all, the science of harmony is the domain of the theoretician — nevertheless, it is incredible that musicians could have attained the practical skill in harmony which they did attain without any study of theory. Why on earth should I mention the distinguished men of antiquity who were the first recruits to the ranks of theorists when succeeding generations have kept alive the names of Orpheus, Amphion, Linus of Thebes, Timotheus, and the rest,[9] who by their harmony (in practice, I mean) charmed — one of them beasts, another stones and forests, another sea-creatures, another uncivilized and rustic spirits? These men, it is generally agreed, were most eminent and renowned both in the precepts of their discipline and in their actual practice. It is pertinent also to bring into the discussion the Pythagoreans, Platonists, and Peripatetics, according to whose directions the practice of singing and playing is highly recommended for the education of youth. Such a recommendation is justified by this reasoning: according to Marcus Tullius [Cicero] in the first of the *Tusculan Disputations*, Aristoxenus, a musician and philosopher, held that a certain tension of the body exists in the same way that a certain tension exists in vocal and instrumental music, a tension called harmony; so various vibrations are caused from the nature and configuration of the whole body like sounds in music.[10]

9. In attempting to explain the historical origins of music, theorists customarily resorted to accounts of the feats of the legendary musician-poets Orpheus, Amphion, and Linus, of the Greek poet and cithara-player Arion of Lesbos (fl. 700 B.C.), or of the celebrated Athenian Timotheus of Miletus (c. 446–357 B.C.), who by his "music of the future" offended Plato and Aristotle.

10. Cicero, *Tusculan Disputations*, I.x, tr. J. E. King (Loeb Classical Library, 1945), p. 25. Aristoxenus, the "most celebrated musical scholar of antiquity," was an Aristotelian and author of an incomplete *Harmonics* and a fragmentary *Elements of Rhythm*. Aristoxenus represents the school of thought opposed to Pythagoras in that he recommended an empirical auditory approach to the determination of intervallic sizes rather than exclusive reliance upon mathematically-based relationships. The

There are also those who hold things valueless if they are not put to use. These people feel that the practice of vocal music has contributed most to the development of harmony, not because of the multitude of possibilities inherent in practice, but because it exhibits perfection itself.

The mechanics of music are found in the movement of sounds producing consonances and melody. It is true that these sounds are assembled in vain by theory and science unless they are expressed in practice. Hence one must become thoroughly conversant with the highness, lowness, and the combinations of these sounds not only through one's mind and reason but also through the habit of listening to and articulating them.

Nor do I deny, moreover, that musical procedure is a good deal different from that of grammar. The choice of whether a short or a long syllable is to be employed in grammar is made altogether according to the authority of those who have preceded us, but the musician must proceed by a rational measurement of sounds. One should not allow one or another syllable to be articulated before the full measure of sound and time for the preceding one has been completed. This matter is more conveniently treated in Chapter 1, Book II of this work. Let it suffice to say that the divine Augustine is known to have approved of this, using the most efficacious arguments in Book II of his *De musica*.[11]

In any event, sounding voices fall into four categories. The first category consists of those who are versed in prose, who express their ideas in words rather than in melody, as for example, orators and lecturers, and also those who intone antiphons and psalms for divine services. Their lines our Ambrosians and Gregorian clerics call plain chant (though improperly) because they intone the individual notes simply, on one level in the even measure of a temporal breve. Now it is recognized that plain chant does not obey the nature of harmony but rather those defined limits and endings of the modes (which they also call tones) and the tonal conjunctions and passages which are well known to follow along the lines of the natural arrangement of the diatonic genus. The beginnings of songs and of an entire melody are extremely well regulated in plain chant. Hence I call plain chant a sonorous reading, like a reading that sustains sounds or a reading

---

three books of the *Harmonic Elements* are available in Greek and Latin translation in Meibom, I, 1–74. A Greek and English version is provided by Henry S. Macran in *The Harmonics of Aristoxenus* (Oxford, 1902).

11. The six books of the *De musica* by the classically trained St. Augustine are almost exclusively concerned with the materials of poetry—verse, meter, and number. See *PL*, XXXII, 1081–1194.

in lieu of the sounds themselves. The ancients, however, as Aristotle maintains in the Twenty-eighth Problem of the "Harmonics," used to call the
first observations of sounds of this type, which they proposed for the musical instruction of youth, laws.[12]

The second category belongs to those who utter in metrical style not
only the idea but also the short and long syllables which pertain to poetry.
A freer discussion of this will occur in Chapter 1 of Book II.

The third category consists of those who produce melody and sweet
song by means of the reciprocal sonority of one sound and another in
fixed intervallic dimensions. This is well explained in Book III of the present work. This type properly includes musicians and singers.

The fourth category is devoted in general to the art of the actor and
mimic and to those who are inspired to vocal imitation by means of bodily
gestures, as in pantomimic dances and dances accompanying choral singing. Theophrastus explained this as music that is expressed in the movement of the voice and body.[13] Since this unseemly conduct is unfit for our
ceremonies, we turn our attention to that which concerns the praise of
God.

Now we know that Guido Aretinus wrote down a helpful system of
music well equipped with seven letters and six syllables which denominate
all the pitches in keeping with the tones of the natural perfect diatonic
system.[14] Indeed, it is exceedingly worthwhile for the human voice to
imitate the harmonious strings that are sounded by the action of the lyre,
cithara, or monochord. Of these sounds, the Greeks called some graves,

12. Aristotle, *Problems,* XIX ("Problems Connected with Harmony"), tr. W. S. Hett
(Loeb Classical Library, 1936), I, 395. This is one of fifty assorted musical problems
which form Book XIX of an encyclopedic tome consisting of thirty-eight sections
(*particulae*) on a wide variety of scientific topics. Long attributed to Aristotle, the
Problems are now conceded to be a compilation by later hands of material drawn
from the great philosopher. (See the preface to *De rebus musicis problemata* in Karl
von Jan, *Musici scriptores Graeci* [Leipzig, 1895].)

13. An encyclopedist and Aristotle's pupil, Theophrastus of Eresus (c. 372–287 B.C.)
may have formulated some of the *Problems* (see von Jan, *Musici scriptores Graeci*).
Theophrastus, successor to Aristotle as head of the Peripatetic School, is remembered
today chiefly for two botanical works and a series of thirty short character sketches.
He is reported to have belittled the attribution of certain therapeutic and medical
powers to music.

14. Guido of Arezzo (c. 995–1050) taught the technique of solmization, notational
procedure, and his basic system of interlocking hexachords. An authoritative edition
by Jos. Smits Van Waesberghe of Guido's *Micrologus,* based upon some seventy-seven
extant manuscripts, was published by the American Institute of Musicology in 1955 as

some acutes, and the rest medians. Our ecclesiastics, however, modify
Guidonian tradition, which they call the hand, and classify these sounds
into "grave," "acute," and "superacute," so that twenty-two pitches are
inscribed alternately on lines and on intervals, or spaces; two conjunct
hexachords having been figured in, undoubtedly, in imitation of, and for
the sake of, the synnemenon tetrachord.

They call the first eight pitches graves, as though closest to silence and
taciturnity, and the eight pitches arranged above the lower eight acutes,
and the rest superacutes. There exists, however, a high pitch in each of
those eight low pitches, and a low pitch among the highs. This is the way
that a consonance, which Boethius was accustomed to define as "the mixture of a high and low sound falling sweetly and uniformly upon the ear,"
springs up out of each different combination of these pitches.[15]

Therefore, seven pitches, arranged in order by letter, are organized in
lines and spaces in this way: in the lowest position of the system, marked
on a certain line, they wrote the Greek letter *Gamma* and also the syllable
ut. In the adjacent space came the letter *A* together with the syllable *re.*
For the second line next above, they wrote the letter *B*-square made out

---

part of its *Corpus scriptorum de musica.* Guido's tracts have been preserved in *PL,*
CVLI, and in Couss., II.

The *introductorium* of Guido, a twenty-two–pitch system segmentalized into seven
overlapping hexachords, served as basic musical apparatus in the Middle Ages, but
its cumbersome mutational procedure had a restrictive effect on the burgeoning music of the Renaissance with its more expansive range and registration and the increasing incidence of musica ficta. Guido's authority stood unchallenged until the 1482
release of Ramis' *Practica.*

15. Boethius, *De institutione musica,* I.viii, ed. Gottfried Friedlein (Leipzig, 1867).
Gafurius' growth as a music theorist was substantially conditioned and oriented by
Boethius and the conception of music as a science closely allied with its sister sciences
of the quadrivium; and he relied heavily upon both the *De arithmetica* and *De musica*
in writing his own books, particularly the *Theorica.* Indeed, it was not inappropriate
that the Sforza poet Lancinus Curtius, in his long poem which concludes the second
edition of the *Theorica,* should have emphasized Gafurius' indebtedness to Boethius
with the verses

> Unus post veterum longa volumina
> Cantantem sequitur voce Boetium.
> [After the long tomes of the ancients,
> One man echoes the singing Boethius.]

Boethius' definition of consonance quoted here is the one most frequently encountered in the books on music theory written during the millenium following his
execution.

of two gammas, one laid across the other, and the syllable *mi*. In the next space above they located the letter *C* and the syllable *fa*. I understand an interval or space to be an open area between two adjacent lines, one above and one below. In the same way they annotated the pitches of the seven hexachords with letters and syllables.

There is a great deal more that could be said here in reference to this subject, but since the Guidonian system has been lucidly expounded in Book V of the *Theorica*, I am led for brevity's sake to pass over it in silence here. Let Guido's diatonic system of letters and syllables described by lines and spaces be set forth in the accompanying diagram [p. 16].

Chapter two   The Syllabic Names of the Notes and Their Intervals

The authority of Virgil, in Book VI of the *Aeneid*, recognized only seven basic notes: "There, too, the long-robed Thracian priest matches their measures with the seven distinct notes."[16] These notes were written down by Gregory with seven letters. Later Guido perfected his tonal system also in seven overlapping hexachords.

The hexachord is a group of six tones arranged in diatonic sequence whose syllabic names are *ut, re, mi, fa, sol, la.*[17] There are (and I go along with the Greeks) the graves [or low tones] *ut, re;* the acutes [or high tones] *sol, la;* and the medians [or middle tones] *mi, fa.* It is the custom of church musicians, however, to call *ut* and *re* graves, *mi* and *fa* acutes, and *sol* and *la* superacutes.

Of course Guido himself arranged these syllables in such a way that he defined the different intervals of the perfect diatonic system by means of just two of these syllables. Thus between *ut* and *re* there is enclosed an interval of a whole tone in 9:8 ratio; similarly between *re* and *mi*. But between *mi* and *fa* the distance is that of a minor semitone. Between *fa* and

16. *Aeneid* I.645–46.

17. This diatonic sequence of six vocables with a semitone interval in the middle forms the basic unit of medieval music, a hexachord (*deductio*) of the Guidonian system.

The Diatonic System of Guido
Arranged According to Pythagorean Measurement

Greek name	No.	Note	I	II	III	IV	V	VI	VII	Synemmenon	Int.
	1536	e″							la		T
	1728	d″						la	sol		T
	1944	c″						sol	fa		S
	2048	b′							mi		Ap
	2187	b♭′						fa			S
Nete hyperbolaion	2304	a′					la	mi	re		T
Paranete hyperbolaion	2592	g′					sol	re	ut		T
Trite hyperbolaion	2916	f′					fa	ut			S
Nete diezeugmenon	3072	e′				la	mi				T
Paranete diezeugmenon	3456	d′			la	sol	re			Nete synemmenon	T
Trite diezeugmenon	3888	c′			sol	fa	ut			Paranete synemmenon	S
Paramese	4096	b				mi					Ap
	4374	b♭			fa					Trite synemmenon	S
Mese	4608	a		la	mi	re				Mese	T
Lichanos meson	5184	g		sol	re	ut					T
Parhypate meson	5832	f		fa	ut						S
Hypate meson	6144	e	la	mi							T
Lichanos hypaton	6912	d	sol	re							T
Parhypate hypaton	7776	c	fa	ut							S
Hypate hypaton	8192	B	mi								T
Proslambanomenos	9216	A	re								T
[Gamma]	10368	G	ut								

[T = tone, 9:8]
[S = minor semitone, 256:243]
[Ap = apotome (major semitone), 2187:2048]

sol and between *sol* and *la* there is the space of a whole tone. Accordingly, *re* is a whole tone higher than *ut,* and likewise *ut* is a whole tone lower than *re. Re* is exceeded by *mi* by a pitch, a whole tone higher, and is below it by a whole tone. *Fa* is lower than *sol* by a whole tone, and *sol* reaches above *fa* by a whole tone. *Sol* is lower than *la* by the interval of a whole tone, and *la* surpasses *sol* by an *epogdoa* [9:8] distance higher. But *fa* is known to be higher than *mi* by only the space of a minor semitone. Hence *mi* is necessarily lower than *fa* by the same distance.

From this it is apparent that in each hexachord four whole tones, deployed on different pitches, enclose a natural minor semitone in the middle. It can be seen that this semitone occurs here out of necessity. When one wishes to consider the three diatessaron species in a variety of tetrachords, one will never be able to find them in diatonic arrangement in any hexachord except as these four whole tones enclose a middle semitone. Everyone can readily come to see this by himself as he follows along in this explanation. Accordingly, the individual semitones arranged diatonically and naturally in the perfect system are clearly recognized to fall between the two syllables *mi* and *fa.*

Guido paid great attention to the arrangement of the seven interlocking hexachords. He either joined the beginning of each hexachord to the first tetrachord of the preceding hexachord, or he set it up a whole step away from the preceding hexachord. Thus the first tetrachords of two hexachords make up a heptachord.

But where the first tetrachord of the second hexachord ends, the third hexachord, called the B-*molle* hexachord, which can also be called conjunct, begins and is contiguous to it. This is done in order that the harshness of the tritone may be made sweeter in modulation and also so that the composition of several of the modes may proceed by means of different species of consonances of the "commixed" and also "acquired" variety.[18] The fourth hexachord is separated from the first tetrachord of the second hexachord by the interval of a whole tone above. The fifth hexachord is joined onto the first tetrachord of the fourth hexachord. The

18. Here Gafurius introduces almost casually the vexatious problem of musica ficta. Also called *musica acquisita,* these notes or pitches foreign to the diatonic genus and "acquired" from the chromatic and enharmonic genera were applied in response to some alleged melodic or harmonic exigency. The failure of Renaissance composers to write these accidentals into the music shifts the burden to the transcriber, who must determine whether or not an accidental is feasible and fitting in a given musical context where one may or may not be competent.

sixth hexachord is connected to the first tetrachord of this fifth hexachord and can be called synemmenon, or conjunct. The seventh hexachord is set apart from the first tetrachord of the fifth hexachord by the interval of a whole tone higher.

The whole tone is a proper interval circumscribed by two sounds in a 9:8 ratio. It supports in a single division two adjacent parts: one of these is minor, the other major. The latter they denominate an *apotome* or major semitone; the former, a minor semitone. When a minor semitone is abstracted from a whole tone, an apotome remains; and because of its great difficulty a discordant tonal progression issues. This is not the case with the minor semitone, for a harmonious and sweet temperament is manifested among the tones and consonances themselves. This I shall clearly prove in the *De harmonia instrumentali*,[19] since in the diatonic system particularly, the minor semitone is recognized to be introduced naturally either below, above, or in between two whole tones. Hence the semitone itself may be defined as an interval which when added to two sesquioctaves [9:8 whole tones] produces a sesquitertia proportion [4:3 ratio, or interval of a fourth]. When it is joined with two whole tones, it yields with its outer, sounding terms the consonance of a diatessaron.

An interval, or space, can be understood to be the distance between a high and a low sound. Moreover, the mental concept of sound is symbolized in given notes. One must express the fixed, raised and lowered pitches of these notes arranged on a variety of lines and spaces vocally. Consequently, these notes are called vocal symbols. Further, sounds which cannot be written down are committed to memory by usage and practice so that they will not be lost, for their delivery flows imperceptibly into the past.[20]

There follows then a threefold categorizing of notes: simple, composite, and intermediate. A simple note is one which is not joined to another and is written in a square shape like this: ■ . It is also sometimes written with

19. Gafurius refers here to the final volume of his trilogy, which was completed in manuscript form in 1500 but was not published until 1518. At that time it appeared in Milan under the auspices of the great French bibliophile and treasurer of Francis I, Jean Grolier, with the title *De harmonia musicorum instrumentorum*.

20. This concept of music as a transitory sensory impression had been advanced by several classical and medieval theorists and can be found in the *Etymologiarum* (III.xv) of Isidore of Seville (*PL*, LXXXII, 163). See Oliver Strunk, *Source Readings in Music History* [New York, 1950], pp. 93–100, for an English translation of III.xv–xxiii, of the *Etymologiarum*.

a stem descending on its right side in the manner of a mensurable long, like this: ▮ . A composite note [ligature] is one which is tied to another note. It can therefore be written in many ways. When a ligature ascends, that is, when the second note is higher than the first, the first note requires no stem ascending or descending on either of its sides, like this: ▮ ▮ ▮ . When, however, the ligature descends, that is, when it has a lower second note, then a stem is assigned to the first note, descending on its left side, whether the note is oblique or square, in this way: ▮ ▮ ▮ ▮ .

Indeed, the weight of antiquity decreed that a suitable name for the beginnings of ligatures ought to be "propriety." Thus propriety, as established by musical authorities, is a nomenclature appropriate for the first notes of ligatures. Moreover, since according to the Philosopher[21] perfection is attributed to the end of all things, they assigned the name "perfection" to the final notes of ligatures. This is denoted in three ways. Either the final note of the ligature, written in the form of a square, is below the penultimate note, like this: ▮▮, or it is directly above the penultimate note, as here: ▮ ▮ ▮, or it is not directly above the penultimate note, that is, a step to the right, with a square shape and a stem descending from its right side, as follows: ▮ ▮ ▮. Perfection, therefore, is the nomenclature proper for final notes of ligatures. Those who disagree with this point of view are rejecting established authority. Hence, those who write the final note of a ligature in oblique form, like this: ▮ ▮, fall into error. An exception is made for two notes only in oblique form, as follows: ▮ . However, practice shudders at the ascending oblique form, as follows: ▮.

For the middle notes of ligatures, that is, for those which are joined together between the extremes, there is no variation in form. They are written as simple square or oblique shapes, like this: ▮ ▮. Now every ligature, no matter how many notes it comprehends, prolongs the production of a single syllable in singing. Therefore, all the notes of such a musical progression ought to be articulated in equal temporal values even if they are written in different shapes.

The intermediate note is that which assumes the shape of neither simple nor composite notes. In its simplicity it bears a certain resemblance to the oblique shape, but it is not written alone but rather with at least two or more descending notes, generally in the form of a mensurable semibreve,

---

21. Aristotle. Undoubtedly Boethius' Latin commentaries provided Gafurius' primary access to the wisdom of Aristotle.

as follows: ❜♦♦ . These semibreves are equal to the other notes in articulation and temporal value, although some count them twice as fast as the
others. We believe this must be attributed not to reason but rather to the
arbitrary whim of the singer. For the great majority by their own authority have elected to follow the articulation and measurement of plain chant
notes. Hence Persius' dictum is not irrelevant: "Each has his own desires;
no two men offer the same prayers."[22]

There are also those who write these notes of the plain chant all alike,
and at the same time, count them in mensurable dimension as longs,
breves, and semibreves. This is evident in the *Symbolum Cardineum*[23] and
in several sequences and hymns. Quite frequently this technique is followed by Gallic musicians especially for the purpose of expressing a more
ornate articulation of their music by this very diversity.

Chapter three   The Clefs and the Naming of the Notes

Now it is necessary to reveal with what signs the names of the
notes, the low, high, and intermediate pitches, are identified by means of
lines and spaces.

Every letter in the Guidonian system, whether in a lineal or a spatial
location, is called a clef [key], since all the notes are locked up on these
lines or spaces. But obviously, it was unnecessary to identify every line
and space with its own letter and clef because they would be so close together that they would trample all over each other. Accordingly, musicians
thought it sensible to show all the notes of the system in fewer signs, for

22. Persius, Satire V.53, in *Juvenal and Persius*, tr. G. G. Ramsay (Loeb Classical
Library, 1918), p. 375. The satires were first printed in Rome in 1470.
23. *Symbolum* is the Ambrosian synonym for Credo, third item of the Ordinary of
the Mass. This anomaly, a mensurable plain chant, which Gafurius entitles *Symbolum
Cardineum*, is called "Credo Cardinalesco" in Zarlino's *Le istitutioni harmoniche*,
IV.xxxiii (Venice, 1562), p. 341. In his *Handbuch der Notationskunde* (Leipzig, 1913),
I, 153, Johannes Wolf discusses this musical phenomenon as an evolutionary link be-
tween plain chant and mensural music.

as Aristotle held, "it is useless to do with more what can be accomplished with fewer."[24] With two signs called clefs musicians customarily distinguish the grave, acute, and superacute pitches of the system.

The first sign, to explain how the ancients did it, is either on the fourth or fifth line filled in with red alone. When this sign rests on a line in the staff, it signifies the grave *f fa ut,* but written in a space, it signifies the acute *f' fa ut.* The second sign is a single blue-gray line on lines four or five. When this is written on a line, it is read *c' sol fa ut,* but if it is written in a space, it will indicate either the grave *c fa ut* or the superacute *c'' sol fa.* This clef is abundantly present in Ambrosian notation. In addition, the ancients held that a single pitch represented in a space by the celestial color was to be understood as the acute *b fa;* on the line, however, it was understood as the superacute *b' fa.* In like fashion they readily determined that all the remaining pitches and notes from the low to the high register, in order, should be handled by means of lines and spaces.

Since later Gregorians, however, and also composers of mensurable music, strongly assert that all the lines are written in one and the same color, they customarily indicate the lineal grave *f fa ut* clef in their writings with three notes at the head of the line, like this: or this: . They inscribe *c' sol fa ut* as two separate squared notes at the head of the line, as follows: . However, the acute *b fa* is represented by the sign of the letter *b* as follows: . According to this method a clef is written on whatever line the highest note of the first tetrachord of each hexachord occurs. And to be consistent, musicians have by unanimous agreement assigned a clef to that note which yields a semitone next below it. For the semitone is more artificial and more difficult than the whole tone in nature and in art, both in its proportion and its size. Hence it is more in need of a sign to indicate it.

Moreover, sounds represented by notes are generally articulated in three

---

24. "Too many cooks spoil the broth." The aphorism, which Gafurius attributes to Aristotle, is repeated in another context in II, 8, of the *Practica.* Modern editors cite it without giving Aristotle as its author. (See Bohn's *Dictionary of Classical Quotations,* ed. H. T. Riley [London, 1902], p. 133. Riley is silent as to its source.) Gafurius must have learned the expression from some source-translation no longer extant. In the *Topics,* VIII.xi, in *The Works of Aristotle,* tr. W. A. Pickard-Cambridge (Great Books of the Western World; Encyclopaedia Britannica, 1952), I, 220, Aristotle presents the substance of the idea when he says: "It is also a fault in reasoning when a man shows something through a long chain of steps when he might employ fewer steps."

ways. The first way is by solmization, that is, by intoning the syllables and vocal names *ut, re, mi, fa, sol, la,* as follows:

ut   re   mi   fa   sol   la

They say that this method of articulation is indeed almost mandatory for the instruction of youth. The second way is by uttering only the sounds and pitches while omitting entirely letters, syllables, and words, a practice which a singer easily follows in this way:

The third method of singing is by articulating the text, such as antiphons and responses, in the words underscoring the notes of songs. In accordance with this method musicians are conducted, so to speak, through to the end of a given melody, as follows:

Sal-   ve rex   glo-   ri-   ae   Chri-   ste

The notes themselves indicate the intonation of syllables in the following order. For since *re* is a whole tone higher than *ut,* its pitch must be raised by the interval of that whole step, and conversely, *ut* must be lowered by the interval of a whole step from *re,* as follows:

Similarly, the pitch of the note *mi* is elevated a whole step above *re,* and *re* is depressed from *mi* by the interval of the same whole tone. This is reflected in the following notes:

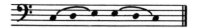

The pitch *fa* is raised above *mi* by the interval of a minor semitone, and from *fa, mi* is lowered by the interval of the same minor semitone, as follows:

The pitch of the syllable *sol* is raised above *fa* by the interval of a whole step, and *fa* is lower than *sol* by the identical interval of a whole step, which these notes show:

Likewise, the syllable *la* is higher than *sol* by the interval of a whole step and *sol* is lower than *la* by the same whole step. This is readily perceived in the following arrangement of notes:

Furthermore, *mi* is higher than *ut* by the interval of a ditone, and *ut* is lower than *mi* by the same distance. This occurs in two ways, both compositely and simply. It happens compositely when the intervals of the two whole tones are defined by two extreme terms with a common, mean term written in between, as follows:

It happens [simply or] incompositely, however, when the interval of two whole tones is enclosed between two extreme terms with no mean written in. This is easy to see in the following musical example:

Boethius and Ptolemy ascribed this incomposite interval as natural to the enharmonic tetrachord.[25]

Now the ditone is a combination of two whole tones. The semiditone, however, is made up of a whole tone and a minor semitone, from the word *semum,* as if it were an imperfect or diminished ditone. Boethius postulated this semiditone as an incomposite trihemitone natural to chromatic tetra-

---

25. Ptolemy's *Harmonicorum libri tres* was one of four Greek works on music which Gafurius had translated into Latin at his own expense, the other three being the *Introductio artis musicae* of Bacchius Senior, the *Harmonica* of Manuel Briennius, and a *De musica* of Aristides Quintilianus. (See Alberto Gallo, "Le traduzioni dal Greco per Franchino Gaffurio," *Acta Musicologica,* XXXV [1963], 172–74; and also the short biography of Gafurius written by his disciple, Pantaleo Melegulus, which appears on the last folio of the 1518 edition of the *De harmonia.*) The Ptolemy opus offers a succinct analysis of the Greek octave species, or *tonoi,* at its stage of evolution in the latter half of the second century A.D. The Greek text and Latin translation are available in John Wallis, ed., *Opera mathematica* (Oxford, 1699), III, 1–152.

chords. According to Pythagorean tradition, in each natural diatonic tetra-chord, an incomposite consonance of a certain quality (discordant, in my opinion, to the ear) is found by the lowering of the middle tones. When this incomposite consonance is taken into consideration in two ways—that is, as a ditone and a trihemitone—those two genera, the chromatic and the enharmonic tetrachords, are interjected into the natural diatonic. But we shall treat these same matters in more detail in our *De harmonia*. Suffice to say, the pitch *fa* is higher than *re* by the interval of a semiditone, and similarly *re* is lower than *fa*. This occurs in two ways, I repeat, compos-itely and incompositely, as each person can perceive for himself in the sub-joined examples:

The pitch *sol* is higher than *mi* again by a semiditone interval, and *mi* is lower than *sol;* and likewise it is considered compositely and incompositely. *Sol* stands apart from the pitch which is deduced between *re* and *fa*. The semitone in the preceding example is higher than the whole step; here the whole step presides over the semitone. This is proved by the following examples:

In each hexachord the pitch *fa* is higher than *ut* by the consonance of a diatesssaron or an *epitritus* [4:3] interval, and the pitch of the syllable *ut* is lower than *fa* by a like distance. This occurs in four ways: (1) either in three separate intervals embracing four notes, that is, it is arranged and proceeds by two whole tones and a semitone; (2) or in two intervals, that is, of a whole tone and a semiditone; (3) or again in two intervals of a di-tone and a semitone; (4) or in a single, incomposite interval of the outer pitches. This is set forth in the following examples:

The pitch *sol* is sustained above *ut* by the interval of a diapente, that is, in three whole tones and a semitone. The diapente interval is strung out in various notes by means of different intervals, as is seen in the following examples:

The pitch *la* is set at an interval of a diapente and a whole tone above *ut*, in four whole tones and a minor semitone. This can be accomplished in various intervals ascending or descending also, as is shown in the accompanying examples:

Chapter four The Proprieties and Mutations of the Vocables

According to Marchettus of Padua propriety in vocal music is the derivation of several vocables from one and the same base.[26] Tinctoris, on the other hand, calls propriety the special quality of arranging vocables in a particular order.[27] Property and propriety are not identical, for property is concrete while propriety is abstract, just as white is to whiteness. Property is a kind of matter and substance joined together with a quality, or if you prefer to say so, with an "accident," and this is concrete. Propriety, however, is a certain feeling or quality or accidence which is called abstract, since it is withdrawn from the substance to which it inheres, just as, moreover, the propriety of whiteness is.

26. The definition of propriety among the vocables, that is, in their hexachordal arrangement, appears in the *Lucidarium musicae planae,* VIII.iv, of the Ars Nova theorist, Marchettus of Padua (See Gerbert, III, 91). A personal copy of *Lucidarium* made by Gafurius in Lodi in 1473 now resides in the Sola-Cabiati Codex in Milan.

27. The important early Renaissance theorist and composer Johannes Tinctoris (c. 1435–1511) was employed from 1475 until 1487 as choir director at the court of Ferdinand of Aragon in Naples. During this time Tinctoris wrote a dozen treatises on music, including *Terminorum musicorum diffinitorium* (Treviso, c. 1495), the earliest printed dictionary of musical terms. According to Melegulus' biographical sketch of Gafurius, Gafurius became acquainted with Tinctoris in Naples in 1478–80, and there, together with the theorists Guarnerius, Hycart, and others, engaged in public debate on musical matters. Gafurius acquitted himself with distinction and became known as a rising theorist in a field theretofore dominated by the Flemish. Tinctoris' definition of propriety appears in his *Expositio manus,* I.v., in Couss., IV, 7.

Indeed, we say that a musical propriety of this sort is the particular pattern of each hexachord, set in its place in the system. The pattern is the natural diatonic progression of six of these syllables, whether ascending in the order *ut, re, mi, fa, sol, la,* or descending, as *la, sol, fa, mi, re, ut.*

They call the following seven hexachords proprieties or qualities. They assign three of these hexachords to B-square, or B-*durum,* two to "nature," and two to B-rotund, or B-*molle.*[28] Now those which are called B-*durum* commence on the letter G. The natural hexachords are known to have their first notes on the letter C, while the B-*molle* hexachords are known to begin on the letter F. This is readily perceived in the structure of the Guidonian system.

And so the lowest pitch, namely the Greek letter *Gamma,* yields the first form of hexachord, a hexachord which the line of B-*durum* quality is known to support. The third letter of the alphabet is recognized to yield the second type of hexachord, deploying the fourth pitch on a space. They designate this as natural propriety or quality. In correct succession the sixth letter of the alphabet, which labels the seventh pitch, produces the third form of hexachord. This they designate as B-*molle* quality. Obviously, in the arrangement of the Guidonian system repeated proprieties of this type are well known.

Moreover, Anselm's reasoning by no means pleases me when he placed natural propriety [hexachord on C] as a mean between B-*quadratum* [hexachord on G] and B-*rotundum* [hexachord on F], or as I prefer to say, between B-*durum* and B-*molle,* as though that sweeter natural propriety were actually arranged according to the chromatic genus, while the harsher propriety of B-natural and the far sweeter propriety of B-flat were arranged in the diatonic and enharmonic genera respectively.[29] Now it is known that

28. The *durum,* or hard, hexachord is distinguished by the square B sign, our natural sign (B♮). The *molle,* or soft, hexachord exhibits the round B sign, our B-flat (B♭), while natural hexachords, commencing on C, contain neither the B♭ nor the B.

29. Anselm named the proprieties on G, C, and F diatonic, chromatic, and enharmonic respectively (*De musica,* III, ed. Giuseppe Massera [*Historiae musicae cultores,* XIV; Florence, 1961], pp. 153–54.) Despite the disagreement voiced here, Gafurius generally admired the early fifteenth-century Italian scholar and humanist, Anselm of Parma (c. 1386–1443). Anselm achieved a reputation as a lecturer at the Universities of Parma and Bologna and as the author of works on astronomy, medicine, and magic as well as the *De musica* of 1434. He is remembered today as a music theorist chiefly because he counseled a four-octave scale in the diatonic genus.

Gafurius' esteem for Anselm derives from a common bond of devotion to Boethius. Like the great Roman transmitter of antiquity, Anselm considered music one of the

every hexachord, whether of the B-*durum,* natural, or B-*molle* quality, is measured according to the diatonic genus. Hence I myself am convinced that that natural quality is preferably ascribed to the fourth pitch [C] rather than to the diatonic tetrachord of the first, lower hypaton [B], that is to say, of the natural genus.

By preference, an interval should contain a B-*molle,* which, forming its first tetrachord by conjunction—on the trite synemmenon pitch [B♭], that is—would soften the tritone's harshness by the position of the *b fa.* Conversely, it will yield the harsher B-*durum* through the disjunct whole tone between mese [A] and paramese [B] by means of *b mi.* But if I select this pitch as the mean term of the chordotone, the first arc drawn in either direction will obtain this mean pitch in a duple relationship by an octave lower than itself but similar to and sounding like itself—to *B mi,* that is.[30] Thus, since *mi* is that third pitch of the hexachord and occupies the third

four scientific disciplines whose mastery constituted an indispensable *gradus ad Parnassum.* Thus his three-part *De musica* on celestial, instrumental, and vocal harmony conforms substantially to the *musica mundana, musica humana,* and *musica instrumentalis* of Boethius. It is not surprising that Gafurius, similarly oriented to Boethius and an avid collector of printed books and manuscripts, should have come into possession of a copy of Anselm's work on music theory. The particular manuscript, bearing Gafurius' autograph and a large number of his marginal annotations, is now the property of the Ambrosian Library in Milan. (See Jacques Handschin, "Anselmi's Treatise on Music Annotated by Gafori," *Musica Disciplina,* II [1948], 123–41.) It is the same copy upon which the Massera edition is based.

Anselm cast his *De musica* in the classical form of the dialogue, with conversations between the author and a close political friend held on three successive sessions. In order to effect the most profitable use of their leisure time, the friends inquire into the realm of music theory while taking the baths at their vacation spa. The bulk of Gafurius' references to Anselm in *Theorica* and *De harmonia* are to the first and second dialogues in Anselm's work, and understandably so, since it is in these two books that Gafurius also treats celestial and instrumental harmony. (It is interesting to note that the manuscript version of Gafurius' *De harmonia musicorum instrumentorum* bore the title *De harmonia instrumentali,* the exact title which Anselm had assigned to his second dialogue.) *Practica's* references apply exclusively to Anselm's more practical dialogue, the third session at the baths, where the subject of vocal, everyday music is discussed.

30. The instrument referred to here appears to be essentially a sophisticated version of the monochord, a multi-stringed (perhaps hypothetical) instrument designed for the purpose of discovering and distinguishing empirically all the intervallic sizes available in the diatonic, chromatic, and enharmonic genera. Gafurius' chordotone is probably the same *chordotonum* described by the Italian humanist, Georgio Valla (d. 1499) in his encyclopedic *De expetendis et fugiendis rebus* published in Venice in 1501.

place in the system, a beginning of its proper quality must commence on the first, lowest pitch, namely, on *G ut.*

It is easy to see to which proprieties or qualities all the vocables are assigned in the three tables which follow:

Everything is sung according to B-*durum:*	Everything is sung according to the natural:	Everything is sung according to B-*molle:*
la on E	*la* on A	*la* on D
sol on D	*sol* on G	*sol* on C
fa on C	*fa* on F	*fa* on B♭
mi on B	*mi* on E	*mi* on A
re on A	*re* on D	*re* on G
ut on G	*ut* on C	*ut* on F

Furthermore, churchmen acknowledge many kinds of pitch mutations. According to Bacchius,[31] mutation is the exchange of substitutes, or the transposition of something similar into a dissimilar place. Hence in his *Morals* Gregory says that to change is to go from one thing into another and not to be stable in respect to one's essential self, for each thing tends to move toward another, by as many steps, so to speak, as its distance requires.[32] Martianus [Capella] calls such mutation transposition, and he explains this as the variation of a pitch into another form of the pitch.[33] Briennius, however, said that mutation was the transference of a substitute system and a vocable.[34]

31. Bacchius Senior (fl. fourth century A.D.) was the author of a musical handbook in question and answer form, *Introductio artis musicae,* whose translation Gafurius hired in his quest for information on Greek music theory. Bacchius' response to the question "What is mutation?" is available in Meibom, I, 14.

32. Pope Gregory's monumental homily, *Moralia,* consisting of thirty-five books of commentary on the Book of Job, appears in *PL,* LXXV, 527–1162; LXXVI, 9–782.

33. This remark on mutation, which accompanies the paragraph heading "De transitu vocis," appears in the "De musica," Book IX of *De nuptiis philologiae Mercurii,* the allegory on the liberal arts in verse and prose by the Carthaginian Martianus Capella (fl. fifth century A.D.). (See Meibom, II, 165-98.) For an account of the place of Capella's "De musica" in medieval learning, see Nan Cooke Carpenter, *Music in the Medieval and Renaissance Universities* (Norman, Okla., 1958).

34. Manuel Briennius (or Bryennius) was a fourteenth-century Byzantine whose *Harmonicorum libri tres* was translated for Gafurius by the Veronese humanist Francesco Burana. The Latin translation of the *Harmonica's* three "books" is preserved in the *Biblioteca Laudense* in Codex XXVIII, and the work appears in parallel Greek

Mutation occurs according to genus, that is, when the lichanos or else the paranete pitch[35] in a diatonic tetrachord is lowered by a semitone, converting into the chromatic species, or by a whole tone transformation into the enharmonic. Such an alteration never occurs in ascending motion, as our Boethius has explained in Book IV [of his *De musica*]. Aristotle himself in the *Musical Problems* also wished this to be understood when he said, "That which partakes of the nature of the acute generally moves to the grave, but that which knows the nature of the grave is not changed into the acute."[36]

There is also another aspect of mutation in pitch and sound: for when these vocables are in motion and are only coming into existence, they are believed to be of the genus of successive entities. The Interpreter explained this in the Twenty-seventh *Problem*.[37] According to him, the generation of pitch and sound itself consists of a certain coming into being and changing. Such a system, according to the writing of Marchettus, results in definite mutation. He says: "Mutation is the change of one vocable into another on the same pitch."[38] For if these syllables which are assigned to

---

and Latin texts in Wallis, *Opera mathematica*, III, 359–508. In substance, the work is a compilation and summarization of Greek music theory based on Nicomachus, Aristides, Bacchius, Euclid, Ptolemy, and Aristoxenus. Briennius' remarks on mutation are to be found in I.ix (Wallis ed., p. 390).

35. That is, lichanos meson (*g*) or lichanos hypaton (*d*) and paranete hyperbolaion (*g'*) or paranete diezeugmenon (*d'*), the Greek technical terms for the third pitch (ascending) in each of the four tetrachords of the *systema teleion*.

36. This and subsequent references reflect Gafurius' familiarity with the apocryphal *Musical Problems* of Aristotle. Gafurius' major source was undoubtedly the exegetical Latin version of Peter of Abano (Petrus Aponensis, c. 1250–1315). Except for a minor change in vocabulary—the use of *sapit naturam* for *habet rationem*—the Latin quotation which Gafurius employs here may be found directly following Peter of Abano's presentation of the thirteenth musical problem in his *Expositio problematum Aristotelis* (Venice, 1482). The Greek exile Theodorus Gaza (c. 1398–1478) also prepared a Latin translation of the pseudo-Aristotelian problems, which was printed in Rome in 1475. Peter of Abano's *Expositio* together with Gaza's *Problemata* contributed much to the rekindling of interest in Greek music theory during the Renaissance. It is quite apparent that in their Latin translations both men had access to manuscripts which are no longer extant. (See Hett, introduction to Aristotle, *Problems*.)

37. Again the Latin phraseology employed here is taken almost verbatim from the exegesis which accompanies the twenty-seventh problem, Book XIX (*decimanona particula*) of Peter of Abano's *Expositio*. The early fourteenth-century professor of medicine and astrology was also surnamed "Reconciliator" and "Elucidator."

38. *Lucidarium*, VIII.iii, in Gerbert, III, 90.

sounds and pitches—to their notes, that is— stand on one and the same line or space, they are called equal in quantity but different in quality or propriety.

Hence, when mutation occurs, the quality of one hexachord is transferred into the quality of another hexachord, the quantity of the sound remaining the same, as Anselm testifies in Book III of his *Musica.*[39] Hence I call mutation the alternative displacement of one vocable into another taken on an identical pitch. I understand sounds to be the syllables of the hexachords. Therefore, no sound is changed into another sound by raising or lowering; rather a syllable is changed into another syllable and a propriety or quality is changed into another quality. Thus when in a musical passage we articulate syllables only, mutation will fit exactly. The alphabetical letters that are used in the system, however, are neither introduced nor changed. Moreover, a syllable which occupies either a line or a space all by itself is not suitable for mutation. Thus, on *G ut, A re, B mi,* and *e″ la* mutation never occurs, because if it should happen to come about by necessity, you would repeat the original order of the interlocked hexachords.

On *c fa ut* two mutations occur alternatively, the first by changing the preceding syllable into the following one, namely *fa* into *ut.* This is called an ascending mutation, from the B-*durum* hexachord into the natural hexachord, as the following musical illustration shows:

(fa)
ut

The second mutation takes place when in singing we alter the succeeding syllable into the preceding one, namely *ut* into *fa.* This, to be sure, is called a descending mutation from the natural hexachord into the B-*durum* hexachord, as is shown here:

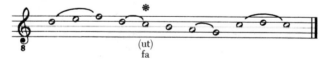

(ut)
fa

It is clear that mutation must result from three causes. First, it is employed so that in a vocal passage the pitches may ascend or descend above or below any hexachord. Second, mutation occurs in order to bring about

39. Massera ed., pp. 159–60.

a more sweetly modulated transition. Generally the varied quality of the
pitches renders a melody no less sweet and delightful than the permuted
quantity of an inflected pitch. Sometimes the B-*molle* quality arranged in
lieu of the B-*durum* is used to produce a sweeter modulation—a technique
which Ambrosians frequently practice. Third, mutation may result from an
effort to facilitate a progression of consonant species, that is, of diatessaron
and diapente, arranged in a mixtures of modes.

On *d sol re* and also on *e la mi* two similar mutations occur. On *f fa ut*
two mutations arise. The first is effected for the purpose of ascending by
changing the quality of the natural hexachord into the B-*molle* or the first
syllable into the second, that is *fa* into *ut*, as the adjoining arrangement of
notes indicates:

In the second mutation one observes a descent from B-*molle* into the
natural hexachord by changing the second syllable into the first, that is *ut*
into *fa*, as can readily be comprehended in the following arrangement of
notes:

Out of *g sol re ut* six mutations issue. The first takes place in the modulated transition of the first syllable into the second, that is, from *sol* into
re, ascending from the natural hexachord into the B-*molle*, as is evident in
this arrangement:

Conversely, the second mutation is made by changing the second syllable
into the first, namely *re* into *sol*, descending from B-*molle* into the natural
hexachord, as is clear here:

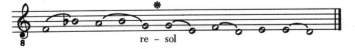

The third mutation is made by converting the first syllable into the third in order to attain an ascent, that is, by converting *sol* into *ut*, from the natural into B-*durum*, which is perceived in this arrangement:

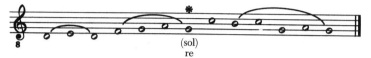

The fourth mutation is made in reverse, that is, seeking a descent with *ut* changed into *sol* from B-*durum* into the natural, as shown here:

The fifth mutation takes place when, in singing, the second syllable is changed into the third, namely *re* into *ut*, in order to ascend from B-*molle* into B-*durum*, as follows:

The sixth mutation arises by changing the third syllable into the second, that is, *ut* into *re*, for the sake of a descent from B-*durum* into B-*molle*, as this example demonstrates:

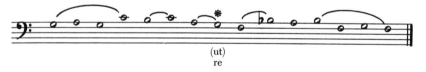

This sixth mutation of the third syllable into the second, *ut* into *re*, is quite common, providing for an ascent in the first step of disjunction. In this case I call the mutation irregular or indirect. It is clearly indicated in the following example:[40]

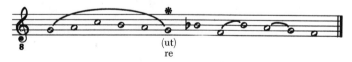

40. That is, normally the sixth mutation should provide for a descent in its initial melodic movement following, in this case, the pivotal point G (*ut* = *re*). Here the first step of disjunction is an ascent from the unisonal pivot on G to Bb.

A mutation is direct and regular when it is opposite to the preceding and following mutation of the unisonal pitch—when, for example, the first mutation takes place in order to ascend, the second to descend, the third to ascend, the fourth to descend, the fifth to ascend, and the sixth to descend. A mutation is called indirect and irregular, however, when it produces a motion of propriety or quality exactly similar to the preceding or following mutation of the unison. This sixth type of ascending mutation is produced in a movement identical to the preceding fifth mutation. The mutation is ascending when the name of the unison pitch has been changed and the initial movement of the voice is upward. It is descending when the first movement of the voice is downward.

On *a la mi re* six mutations occur similar to those which are produced on *g sol re ut.* And the sixth mutation again proceeds irregularly and indirectly, that is, like the preceding fifth, ascending from B-*durum* into B-*molle,* as follows:[41]

(re)
mi

Most authorities agree that on *b fa* and *b mi* no mutation is possible since the syllables do not both have the same pitch and since they are a major semitone apart from one another. This is because *b fa* is a minor semitone higher than *mi* of *a la mi re* and *b mi* is a whole tone higher than *re* of the same *a la mi re;* and since a whole tone is larger than a minor semitone by a major semitone, it is clear that *b mi* is higher than *b fa* by a major semitone. When, therefore, we produce that *b fa-b mi* mutation out of necessity, a mutation both of quality and of quantity will result. I speak (1) of quality, that is, of the propriety of B-*molle* into B-*durum* by changing *fa* into *mi* in order to ascend, or conversely, in order to descend, and (2) of quantity, that is, passing from a lower to a higher sound by means of *fa* into *mi* at the distance of this *apotome,* or conversely, *mi* into *fa,* descending from a higher to a lower pitch. Since this progression is difficult and highly dissonant, the schools of music have advised that it be avoided with every ingenuity. Marchettus and Anselm call this permuta-

41. The Latin here is obviously in error: *molli in duram* should read *dura in mollem.* As the musical example clearly demonstrates, the mutation involves a progression from the hard hexachord on G into the soft hexachord on F, irregular because of the ascent to B♭ in its initial advance after the unisonal pivot on A.

tion. Irregular and indirect mutation was conceived in order to avoid the dissonant passage of such permutation, a passage which must be made by an oppressive arrangement of notes, as is evident in the accompanying example:

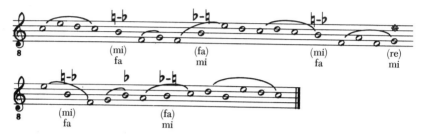

Permutation, therefore, is the simultaneous variation of quality and quantity.

On *c′ sol fa ut* six mutations are produced, the first when in singing we change the first syllable into the second, namely *sol* into *fa,* ascending from the B-*molle* into the B-*durum* hexachord, as follows:

In addition, this first mutation is sometimes accomplished indirectly and irregularly, that is, when it descends in its initial mobile advance in order to escape the dissonant and unsuitable *b fa-b mi* permutation, as is demonstrated in the following musical arrangement:

The second mutation occurs when, in singing, the second syllable is changed into the first, that is, *fa* into *sol* for the sake of a descent from B-*durum* into B-*molle,* as is clear in the following example:

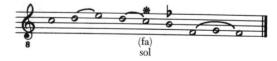

The third mutation occurs when in singing we change the first syllable into the third, namely *sol* into *ut,* by ascending from B-*molle* into the natural hexachord, as is evident in this example:

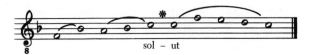

sol – ut

The fourth mutation occurs when in singing we change *ut* into *sol,* descending from the natural hexachord into B-*molle,* as is clear here:

ut – sol

The fifth mutation occurs in singing when we change the second syllable into the third, that is, *fa* into *ut,* ascending from B-*durum* into the natural hexachord, as is plain here:

fa – ut

The sixth and final mutation occurs when, in singing, the third syllable is changed into the second, namely *ut* into *fa,* descending from the natural hexachord into B-*durum,* as can be recognized in the following example:

ut – fa

Many mutations can also occur indirectly and irregularly, as everybody can readily figure out by himself.

On *d' la sol re* six similar mutations are produced, and two each on *e' la mi* and on *f' fa ut.* And among the rest, too, there are similar mutational movements. To discerning musicians they can be understood by comparing individual mutations to the ones to which they are similar.

Further, they say that a plurality of mutations is to be avoided when one comes to the conclusion that the melodic progression has been suitably arranged in a single mutation. It is said too that mutation ought to be managed slowly and over as long a time as possible. Occasionally a disjunct passage of mutations occurs in singing when a progression takes place beyond the range of a hexachord, ascending or descending—for example, through seven, eight, or even more pitches. This is more frequently encountered in mensural composition. Many mutations could be executed through conjunctions if the syllables of the hexachords were arranged in whole-tone intervals and these whole tones were divided into unequal semitones. But since this coincides very closely with the chromatic or mixed genus, the present discussion, concerned only with the Guidonian diatonic system, rejects it.

Chapter five   The Consonance of the Diatessaron and Its Species

The diatessaron is a consonance fashioned out of four sounds embracing two whole tones and a minor semitone. Natural modulation requires this consonance in each tetrachord. It is known to contain three species, since all consonances in natural diatonic arrangement, whether diatessaron, diapente, or diapason, always contain one species or form less than the number of its pitches and just as many species or forms as it has intervals. The word *diatessaron* means "through four," one in genus, to be sure, but diverse in species. Thus it comprehends, as has been said, three different species or forms.

The first species proceeds from low to high by the intervallic distances of a whole tone, semitone, and whole tone defined by the syllables *re mi fa sol*. It commences a A *re*, where the first acquired pitch of the perfect disdiapason system abides, and it is terminated on *d sol re*. Moreover, wherever a similar configuration transpires, one always discerns the first diatessaron species. This species proceeds either in the separate, distinct intervals of the diatonic genus, or in the interval of a whole tone and an incomposite semiditone, or in an incomposite semiditone and whole tone, or as an incomposite fourth, as is evident in the following examples:

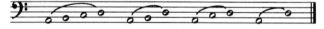

The second diatessaron species proceeds from low to high by means of a semitone and two contiguous whole tones set down in separate and composite intervals, that is, with the syllables *mi fa sol la*. It follows the beginning of the first species, that is, on *B mi*, in accordance with the diatonic dimensions of the first hexachord, and conversely, descends from high to low, namely, by two whole tones and a semitone. Everywhere a similar progression of intervals and syllables occurs, it manifests the second diatessaron species, a species which, as in the former case, is arranged in diverse intervals, as follows:

The third species of diatessaron extends from low to high throughout the diatonic sequence of interlocked hexachords, from *c fa ut* to *f fa ut* with the syllables *ut re mi fa*—that is, by a whole tone, whole tone, and semitone—and conversely, from high to low by a semitone and two whole tones. And so a similar collocation of both syllables and intervals always produces the third form of diatessaron. I have sketched this out in the various intervals which the subjoined example shows, as follows:[42]

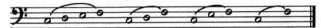

For all that, these three diatessaron species can be considered in a single species by the varied measurement of the middle pitches, as I shall show very clearly in a highly detailed division and numerical representation in my *De harmonia* [I, 16]. Since what we say can be understood here with these syllables alone, however, let us demonstrate in this way:

re   mi   fa   sol   mi   fa   sol   la   ut   re   mi   fa

Chapter six   The Diapente Consonance and Its Species

The diapente is a consonance of five pitches embracing three whole tones and one minor semitone in four diatonic intervals. The term means "through five." The diapente possesses four different species or

42. One of the rare misprints in this early printed work occurs here, a misspelling: *delacrant* for *declarant*.

forms. It is understood that the nomadic location of the semitone here and there determines the order of these species.

The first species of diapente arises from the first diatessaron species plus one whole tone above and retains the natural semitone as its second interval, proceeding with the syllables *re mi fa sol la*. This species begins on *d sol re* and concludes on *a la mi re*. Moreover, a like configuration of intervals and notes will always produce the first diapente species, and it is also formed in different intervals, as is here evident:

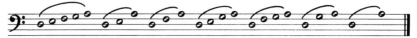

The second diapenté species consists of the second diatessaron species plus a whole tone above and maintains the semitone in its first, lowest interval. It is produced by the syllables *mi fa sol la mi*, beginning on the grave *e la mi* and concluding on the acute *b mi*. Likewise, a similar arrangement of pitches and intervals is always recognized to introduce the second diapente species, which, this arrangement shows, is also formed in different intervals:

The third diapente species is constructed out of a tritone plus a semitone above, that is, having the semitone established as its fourth interval and proceeding syllabically *fa sol la mi fa*. Further, it is begun on the grave *f fa ut* and extends upward to *c' sol fa ut*. Every progression of like pitches and intervals always produces a like diapente species. This can be arranged diatonically also by means of different intervals, as is manifest here:

The fourth diapente species is arranged by means of the third diatessaron plus a whole tone above, proceeding from *g sol re ut* to *d' la sol re* with the syllables *ut re mi fa sol*. It carries the semitone in its third interval. Moreover, wherever a similar succession of pitches and intervals exists, the fourth diapente species will always result. This is commonly also arranged in different intervals as follows:

Similarly, one can demonstrate the pattern of each of the species in a single form of diapente, a fact which we have elected to show in our *De harmonia* [II, 31] by the measurement of these pitches and by numerical annotation. Here, however, we have written the first diapente species separate from the others as an indication of the treatment we propose, as follows:

re   mi   fa   sol   la mi   fa   sol   re   mi fa   sol   re   mi fa   ut   re   mi   fa   sol

Chapter seven   The Diapason Consonance and Its Species

The diapason is a consonance of eight sounds arranged in the diatonic genus and made up of five whole tones and two minor semitones. It results from a diatessaron joined to a diapente with a common, mean term of conjunction present, a term which I shall call common because it marks the terminal point of the diatessaron and the beginning of the diapente, or conversely. The term *diapason* means "through all," as if it supported the musical spectrum or a melodic complex in all its separate sounds.

It is clear that there are only seven distinct sounds in all. The diapason, however, adds an eighth pitch very much like the first sound by duplication. Therefore, they use the name "equisone" (I mean, of course, what Ptolemy called a diapason consonance) for the production of such a conjunction of sound that one and the same sound seems to be delivered up simultaneously.

Bacchius asserts that there are just as many forms of consonances in which the fullness of an entire tonal complex exists as there are diapason species. One form is constituted according to arithmetic mediation, when, that is, the outer pitches of the diatessaron and diapente and their common mean pitch only are struck simultaneously, in such a way that the lower note and the mean define the diatessaron, and the mean and the higher note define the diapente. This phenomenon is present in the collateral modes.

Another form, in the chief or authentic modes, is conceived according to harmonic mediation. This occurs when the extreme pitches and the mean only are struck simultaneously and define the diapente between the low note and the mean, and the diatessaron between the mean and the high note. And so these three pitches struck simultaneously establish a harmonic correspondence. The reason for this correspondence lies in the proportionate agreement on the chordotone of the extremes in relation to each other and the differences between them and the mean in relation to each other, a fact which will be lucidly propounded in the *De harmonia* [III, 2].

Hence the diapason consonance contains seven forms or species. Of these the first is formed from the first diatessaron species, extending from A *re* to *d sol re,* and from the first diapente species, extending from *d sol re* to the acute *a la mi re,* and mediated in an arithmetic correspondence on *d sol re.* It contains five whole tones and two minor semitones. The first of these semitones occupies the second interval or space in diatonic arrangement, and the second semitone is located in the fifth. Furthermore, a similar progression of pitches and intervals always signifies the first diapason species, which can be laid out in various intervals, as is evident here:

The second diapason species is formed out of the second diatessaron species, constructed from the grave B *mi* to the grave *e la mi,* and from the second diapente species, extending from the grave *e la mi* to the acute *b mi.* It is mediated on the grave *e la mi* in an arithmetic relationship. Again, a like pattern of pitches and intervals will everywhere yield the second diapason species, keeping the first semitone in its first interval, the second semitone in its fourth. The arrangement here shows this second diapason species set forth in various intervals:

The third diapason species is formed out of the third diatessaron species, constructed between the graves c *fa ut* and f *fa ut,* and the third diapente species, extending from the grave f *fa ut* to the acute c' *sol fa ut.* It is mediated on the grave f *fa ut* in arithmetic manipulation and keeps the first semitone in its third interval, the second semitone in its seventh interval. Again, a similar arrangement of pitches and intervals establishes the third diapason species, demonstrable in many different intervals, as is evident here:

The fourth diapason species is composed of the first diapente species, extending from *d sol re* to the acute *a la mi re,* and from the first diatessaron, constructed from *a la mi re* to *d' la sol re.* It is mediated harmonically on *a la mi re* and keeps its first semitone in its second interval and its second semitone in its sixth interval. Further, a like collocation of pitches and intervals always produces the fourth diapason species. This can be demonstrated in various intervals, as follows:

The fifth diapason species is formed out of the second diapente species, extending from the grave *e la mi* to the acute *b mi,* and from the second diatessaron, situated between the acutes *b mi* and *e' la mi.* It is mediated, to be sure, on the acute *b mi* in harmonic mediation and contains the first semitone in its first interval and the second in its fifth. All such progressions of pitches and intervals will always form the fifth diapason species, and this can also be constituted in various intervals, as follows:

The sixth diapason species is woven out of the third diapente species, extending from the grave *f fa ut* to the acute *c' sol fa ut,* and from the third diatessaron species, extending from *c' sol fa ut* to the acute *f' fa ut.* It mediates on *c' sol fa ut* according to harmonic mediation, and the first semitone is located in its fourth interval and the second, in its seventh. Furthermore, such a collocation of pitches and intervals will always and everywhere confirm the sixth diapason formula. This can be varied in many different intervals, as follows:

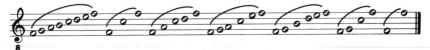

The seventh and final diapason form is conceived from the fourth diapente species, extending from the grave g *sol re ut* to the acute d' *la sol re,*
and from the first diatessaron, extending from the acute d' *la sol re* to the
acute g' *sol re ut.* It is mediated on d' *la sol re,* that is, in harmonic correspondence, and has the first semitone in its third interval and the second in
its sixth. Moreover, a similar disposition of pitches and intervals always
produces the seventh diapason form. Its intervals are delineated in various
forms, as is evident here:

Thus it is clear that these seven diapason forms differ from one another
sometimes in the varied location of their semitones and sometimes in the
diversity of their diatessaron and diapente formulae, and further, that one
diapason species is higher by a whole tone or semitone, that is, in the diatonic distribution of successive pitches; another is lower. In addition, in
any single diapason species with its extreme pitches stationary, the other
species can be discovered by a varied measurement of the intervals. This
is clearly set forth in the *De harmonia* [II, 32, captioned "De septiformi
diapason dispositione"].

The ancients called these diapason formulae constitutions, just as if each
single species, consisting of a conjunction of consonances, might in a certain way produce an entire body of modulation. Furthermore, since they
also denominated these species "modes," distinguished by their own
proper names, Ptolemy added to these scalar patterns an eighth mode on
top in order to complete the whole of the perfect fifteen-chord system.
His eighth mode differs from the first diapason, not in species but in its
separation from the first diapason by the full distance of this first diapason.
He named this the Hypermixolydian ("above the Mixolydian"). We shall
explain all the characteristics of the modes carefully, however, in our *De
harmonia* [IV, 1–10]. It seems good, nevertheless, to review their names
here.

They call the first diapason species, which we reckoned from the grave
A *re* to the acute a *la mi re* and mediated on d *sol re,* the Hypodorian
("beneath the Dorian"), the plagal or lower associate of the Dorian on account of its tetrachord being turned back down from the mean pitch. The
clergy call this mean pitch the *finalis.* The second species was customarily
denominated the Hypophrygian, or "below the Phrygian," and is reckoned

from the grave *B mi* to the acute *b mi* and mediated on its proper final pitch, the grave *e la mi*. The third diapason species was called Hypolydian ("under the Lydian"), since it transposes the upper tetrachord of the Lydian in an inverse direction. We figured this species from the grave *c fa ut* to the acute *c' sol fa ut*, mediated arithmetically on its own final, the grave *f fa ut*.

The fourth diapason species, extending from the grave *d sol re* to the acute *d' la sol re* and mediated harmonically on its *confinalis*, the acute *a la mi re*, was called the Dorian. This was called Dorian, to be sure, by those people who first established this type of tonal structure, or as some maintain, by those who were most delighted by its melodic form. The fifth diapason species, which we have calculated from the grave *e la mi* to the acute *e' la mi* and mediated harmonically on the acute *b mi*, its co-final, they named the Phrygian. Tradition reports that the Phrygians had discovered and made the most use of its melodic form. The sixth diapason species, which we have arranged between the grave *f fa ut* and the acute *f' fa ut* and mediated harmonically on its co-final, *c' sol fa ut*, they named the Lydian, since that people delighted in its modulation the most.

Moreover, the authority of the ancients commends the three modes Dorian, Phrygian, and Lydian as the most celebrated, the most appropriate, as it were, for the more vehement emotions of the soul. Hence they call these modes chiefs and authentics. Their collaterals, which render more gentle emotional effects, they call plagals or associates. They are called collaterals because they are produced by similar components—that is, by diatessaron and diapente species, or out of the inversion of one part —as, for example, out of a higher diatessaron transposed below. But I shall explain the natural harmonies of all of these more extensively, and their authors as well, in the *De harmonia*.

The seventh diapason species, represented between the grave *g sol re ut* and the acute *g' sol re ut* and mediated harmonically on *d' la sol re*, was named the Mixolydian, a "mixed Lydian." Frequently a more beautiful harmony results from the mutual interplay of the Lydian and Mixolydian modes, a fact which our Ambrosians particularly observe in the ecclesiastical modes. They are accustomed to perform these fifth and seventh modes by exchanging the quality of B-*durum* for the B-*molle*, as though they were mixed diapente or diatessaron species.

As has been mentioned, Ptolemy ordained that the Hypermixolydian should be that diapason form which would lie, in its turn, above the seven different species and be reckoned from mese to nete hyperbolaion and mediated arithmetically on paranete diezeugmenon [a-d'-a'].

Further, these eight modes are also called tones, produced, so to speak, out of whole tones and their parts, that is to say, semitones, Some call these modes tropes because of the chromatic conversion of one into another, a conversion which is brought about by the raising or lowering of a whole tone or semitone, or because of the alternate mixture of diapente and diatessaron species.

Ecclesiastical authority categorized these modes in four *maneriae,* denominating the first *maneria Protus,* the second *Deuterus,* the third *Tritus,* and the fourth *Tetrardus,* and bringing together into each one a diapason and a diatessaron in such a way that Protus governed the limits and boundaries of Dorian and Hypodorian. We clearly perceive this in many ecclesiastical chants, in the "Salve Regina," the quadragesimal hymn to the Virgin,[43] for example. Deuterus governed the limits of the Phrygian and Hypophrygian, Tritus the Lydian and Hypolydian, Tetrardus the Mixolydian and its partner, which we can call the Hypomixolydian, in the same way as the others, with its tetrachord transposed below the diapente.

Later generations divided the maneriae in such a way as not to diverge from the order of ancient authority. They placed Protus, which is Dorian, first; Hypodorian second. They put Deuterus, which is also Phrygian, third; Hypophrygian fourth; Tritus, that is, Lydian, fifth; Hypolydian sixth; and Tetrardus, namely Mixolydian, seventh in order. For the eighth mode a name of its own is not allowed unless perhaps, as has been mentioned, in emulation of the other modes, I call it the Hypomixolydian.

And so later ecclesiastics enumerated these modes two by two in such a way that since unity is the first odd number, all the firsts together are proclaimed the odds, authentics, or chiefs; the seconds, from the even number two, are called the evens, collaterals, or associates. This is the way they derive the most renowned order of the modes: the first odd and authentic; the second even, its plagal; the third odd, authentic; the fourth even, its plagal; the fifth odd, authentic; the sixth even, its plagal; the seventh odd, authentic; the eighth and final even, its subject.

---

43. The Ambrosian rite employs this antiphon differently from the Gregorian rite. This compline *BVM* antiphon appears in the Milanese liturgy as a lenten hymn (see *Liber vesperalis juxta ritum sanctae ecclesiae mediolanensis* [Tournai, 1939], p. 808). In the *Liber usualis* (Tournai, 1939), p. 276, the hymn is used during and shortly before Advent. The range of this beautiful melody encompasses the entire *protus maneria; i. e.,* it combines the authentic Dorian and its plagal Hypodorian, *A–d,* or an octave and a fifth.

In short, such a mode, according to Guido, is defined as a rule by which every modulation, ascending and descending, written or capable of being invented, can be distinguished. But these modes and their accidents must be treated individually.

Chapter eight   The Different Characteristics of the Modes and the Formation of the First Mode

The tonal structure of the first mode is formed from the first diapente species, arranged between *d sol re* and *a la mi re,* and from the first diatessaron, from *a la mi re* to the acute *d' la sol re.* This diapason species, where we have located the Dorian, is fourth in order. It ends regularly on *d sol re,* where its diapente begins; and similarly, in the structures of the other modes, the beginnings of their own diapentes are regularly assigned to their individual endings. Indeed, because the human voice is more taxed in the upper than in the lower register (because in descending from high to low it approaches rest), they have therefore concluded that those four terminal pitches of the modes should be selected from among the series of lower sounds. (I mean those lower sounds in which the conjunct tetrachord of each collateral mode would properly abide.)

Ecclesiastics, moreover, following Roman and Ambrosian precepts, set one pitch in the interval of a whole tone below the final of each authentic mode, that is to say, between the first eight pitches of the diapason and this ninth. A whole tone in a sesquioctave relationship [9:8] results between the two. But even though, in the natural diatonic sequence, this suits those three authentic modes—the first, third, and seventh—nevertheless the diatonic sequence of sounds proves to be inapt for the fifth mode because a semitone falls naturally below the pitch of its final, the grave *f fa ut.* Accordingly, some contend that that note must be lowered in between the graves *d sol re* and *e la mi,* that is, by a major semitone below *e la mi,* so that it will then be a whole tone below the final. We believe, however, that when moving diatonically, the natural order of pitches in the scale should by no means be subverted, especially when these eight pitches of the diapason consonance are tuned in duple dimension, that is, in five sesquioctaves and two minor semitones. Hence I think that such a substitution of this pitch as if it were fitting for diapasonic modulation is unnecessary. On the contrary, I think that it is rather superfluous, although approved by ecclesiastic authority.

Generally, therefore, modulations of the first mode properly commence on the graves *c fa ut* (beyond its range,[44] to be sure), *d sol re, f fa ut, g sol re ut,* and on the acute *a la mi re* as natural and proper beginning tones. Further, this first mode begins commixed on the grave *e la mi* and mixed (and similarly beyond its ambitus) on the graves *A re* and *B mi.*

An authentic mode is called commixed if there are species other than its own collateral arranged within it. If, however, the mode is plagal, it will be called commixed when it contains consonant species of an odd or chief mode other than its own.

An authentic mode is called mixed when it appropriates to itself either the entire lower tetrachord of its plagal or at least two of its pitches.

An imperfect mode, whether authentic or plagal, is one which does not complete a diapasonic form. It lacks either part of its diapente or part of its diatessaron or part of both. This is properly called diminished.

An authentic mode is considered to be beyond perfect or superfluous when it supports one or two notes in diatonic sequence above its range. When it is plagal, however, the additional tone [or tones] will be in the lower register.

There are also those who call the melodic structure of individual modes irregular when they terminate on their co-finals. There are four co-final pitches according to the pairings of the eight modes. The co-final for any one of the maneriae is that uppermost pitch on which the diapente species is concluded. Hence the co-final of each mode is distant from its final by the full interval of a diapente. Thus the first and second modes end regularly on *d sol re* but irregularly on *a la mi re;* the third and fourth modes, regularly on the grave *e la mi,* irregularly on the acute *b mi;* the fifth and sixth modes, regularly on the grave *f fa ut,* irregularly on the acute *c' sol fa ut;* the seventh and eighth modes, regularly on the grave *g sol re ut* and irregularly on the acute *d' la sol re,* although for antiphons, graduals, and other Gregorian melodies a co-final is seldom permitted, for they say that

---

44. *Quidem tanquam superflue,* "indeed like a superfluity"; that is, in excess of or beyond the normal octave range *D–d.*

these modes always terminate regularly. The Ambrosians, however, more often end the seventh mode on its co-final but rarely do so with the eighth mode.

Furthermore, each mode in the tonal system can be identified according to where its component parts or species are tuned chromatically. When the tuning occurs outside its natural and primary arrangement, we can call the mode fictive or acquired.

In such modal modulations, the "distinction" must also be considered, which Guido defined in this way: a distinction or phrase is as much as is articulated continuously in any chant up to that point where the voice rests. This is clearly shown by means of neumes. Now a neume is an aggregation of sounds or notes which have to be articulated agreeably in a single breath. The Greek *neuma* is generally translated by the Latin *nutus,* "a nod." In antiphons, nocturnal responsoria, and graduals, composers write this neume with a certain line like the rest used at the end of songs, a line embracing all the spaces of the staff. This neume separates the phrases at the point where they signal the voice to take a breath. One ought not to breathe before the final syllable of any word unless a great many notes have been placed above a single syllable. Then, under pressure of urgent necessity, a performer is allowed to breathe after a syllable that is not the final syllable of the word. Moreover, according to Guido, these phrases ought to begin and end more frequently and properly on those pitches which the particular mode in which the phrases occur may select for its beginnings by rule.

Noteworthy also (not to overwork Guido's authority) is the practice of that highest, most holy Pope Gregory. In the nocturnal responsoria, which are customarily given heavily and laxly, without energy, in the manner of sleepy men, he seems to exhort us to wake up. And in the antiphons he sounds simply and sweetly. But in the introits, as if with the voice of the priest, he clamors to the Divinity and evokes the office. In the alleluias and sequences which the Ambrosians set to music he seems to delight sweetly, with a heavenly jubilation. But in the tracts and graduals he is known to proceed with a simple, relaxed, and submissive voice. In the offerings and communions he has made it clear how much power there is in the effects of the melodic pattern of these chants.

There exists in all these chants every technique of this discipline: ascent, descent, extension, repetition—a sweet delight to those who are knowledgeable, to learners a surcease from labor, an unsurpassed style far removed from the techniques of other composers. Not only did he [Pope

Gregory] introduce these things into the art of music, but he also is known to have codified the content and elevated the authority of the discipline of music. Moreover, the divine Ambrose,[45] as the words of Guido himself attest, has independently undertaken a marvelous job of investigating the charm of music; and innumerable others have contributed various gifts to its treasure house in proportion to what they have learned from the master.

This example demonstrates an ecclesiastical modulation of the first mode:[46]

Al- me pa- ter Am- bro- si no- stras pre- ces au- di

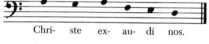

Chri- ste ex- au- di nos.

When, after the announcement of the antiphon, one wishes to proceed with Gregorian psalmody of the first mode—for this is the way it goes, an antiphon of the first mode requiring psalmody of the same mode and similarly for the other modes—one begins the melody of this psalm on the third note above the final of the antiphon by proceeding with the syllables *fa sol la*. Moreover, these psalms are mediated in various ways and ended in many places, that is, according to the annotation of their *Seculorum Amen* or their *Euouae*. Now the term *Euouae* represents nothing other than *Seculorum Amen*, for the letters are all of its vowels collected for the

45. St. Ambrose, Bishop of Milan (c. 340–97), is credited with establishment of the ritual and liturgy of the Milanese church. He composed hymn-texts and introduced the Eastern custom of antiphonal singing into the West. Many of Gafurius' comments on plain chant reveal the fine distinctions which differentiate the Ambrosian dialect from the Gregorian.

46. This musical example provides one instance of the many fine didactic illustrations which pervade the *Practica* and which motivated subsequent theorists—Glarcan, LeFevre, and others—to utilize and quote them in their texts. The Swiss humanist and theorist Heinrich Glarean, who lived one generation later (1488–1563), not only used this example of the first mode but also the monodic examples which Gafurius wrote for each of the other Church modes. See Heinricus Glareanus, *Dodekachordon*, I.xiii. 33 (Basel, 1547; Microcard facsim., Sibley Library, Rochester, New York); and also Heinrich Glarean, *Dodecachordon*, tr. Clement A. Miller, 2 vols. (American Institute of Musicology, 1966). Here the normal, complete ambitus of the Dorian is clothed in a syllabic setting and attractive contour, its structural components (beginning, mediation, and ending) plainly evident.

sake of brevity into one package. Thus Gregorian psalmody of the first
mode unfolds as follows:

To whichever mode the melodies of graduals, alleluias, and responsoria
are assigned, their verses must also be assigned. Thus, just as the beginning
of an *Euouae* is related to the final of an antiphon, so the beginning of the
verses is related to the final of the melodies that just preceded. When a
melody belongs to the authentic mode, its versicle is obedient to the same
mode, and conversely. And yet, the versicle of a plagal chant frequently
touches upon the species of an authentic modulation, and conversely; and
then both parts are considered as belonging to a single maneria. Moreover, the beginning of an *Euouae* of the first mode is a fifth higher than
the final tone of the preceding antiphon. When the need arises the Gregorians are accustomed to select from the verses of the nocturnal responsoria of the first mode certain necessary notes by which the "Gloria patri
et filio et spiritui sancto" is performed in the most attractive way possible,
as shown here:

Chapter nine   The Formation of the Second Mode

The tonal structure of the second mode is formed from the first common species of diapente, a species which coincides with that in the first mode, and from the first diatessaron species, constructed from *A re* to *d sol re.* This [second mode] is that species of diapason which we have ranked first in order between *A re* and the acute *a la mi re,* the one assigned to the Hypodorian. I call that species common which occurs in one fixed position in any authentic mode and its plagal; that is, it is thought of as having identical pitches. Thus it is clear that the diatessaron is not a species common to both an authentic and its collateral mode, as Marchetus asserts, because the diatessaron is situated higher in the authentic mode and lower in the plagal. It is known that in the latter the diatessaron is placed below the diapente and in the former, above the diapente.

Five pitches are proffered as initial tones for the second mode: the graves *A re, c fa ut, d sol re, e la mi,* and *f fa ut.* Further, in rare cases, in its excess or superfluity of ambitus they have entrusted its beginning to *G ut.* It obtains its proper ending regularly on *d sol re.* This example demonstrates its formula:

In ho- no-   rem   a- po- sto- lo-   rum

fa- bri- ca- vit Bas- si- an- us   do- mi- no tem- plum   no- vum.

In addition, many people agree that by ecclesiastical license the plagal modes appropriate for themselves one pitch beyond and above the diapente. Therefore, when an antiphon ends on *d sol re* and its *Seculorum Amen* has its beginning on the grave *f fa ut,* it will be adjudged by the law of the second mode. They begin its psalmody with a pitch a whole tone below the final, proceeding with the notes *ut re fa,* which the present arrangement shows:

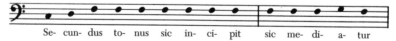

Se- cun- dus to- nus sic in- ci- pit   sic me- di- a- tur

et sic fi- ni- tur.   Euouae.

The versicles of nocturnal responsoria in this second mode also usually proceed in proper modulation with a single pitch lowered by the interval of a whole tone below the final of the preceding chant, that is, with the notes *ut re mi fa.* Likewise the notes to which the "Gloria patri" is harmoniously intoned are customarily picked up from the modulation of these notes:

Glo-   ri- a   pa- tri   et   fi- li-   o   et spi- ri-

tu- i   san-   cto.

Chapter ten   The Tonal Structure of the Third Mode

The tonal pattern of the third mode is formed from the second diapente species, extending from the grave *e la mi* to the acute *b mi,* and from the second diatessaron species, leading from the acute *b mi* to the acute *e' la mi.* This [third mode] is the fifth diapason species, which we have named the Phrygian. For this mode four initial tones are proper: the graves *e la mi, f fa ut, g sol re ut,* and the acute *c' sol fa ut.* Its final tone is the grave *e la mi.* This example conforms to the structure of the third mode:

Bap- ti- zat Au- gu- sti- num   sa- cer- dos Am- bro- si- us

am- bo sta- tim mo- du- lan- tur te de- um lau- da- mus.

Furthermore, the *Euouae* of the third mode is begun on *c' sol fa ut,* according to the Gregorians—that is, on the sixth above the final of the antiphon, where the tetrachord that began the psalmody is ended. But the Ambrosians, proceeding more sweetly, have arranged the beginning of the *Euouae* for this third mode on the fifth tone above the final of the antiphon—that is, on the tone on which its diapente species is terminated— just as they had done in the other authentic modes, on the grounds that this is much sweeter in harmonic mediation. Gregorian psalmody of the type mentioned above, however, is begun on the third above the final of the antiphon, proceeding with the notes *ut re fa.* Its medial and final tones are shown in this melody:

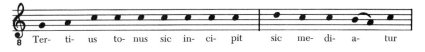

Similarly, too, there exists in the verses of the responses a suitable progression for intoning the "Gloria patri" expressed in the following notes:

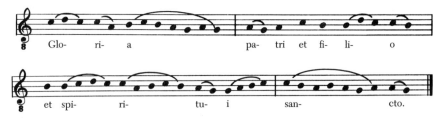

Chapter eleven   The Tonal Structure of the Fourth Mode

The tonal distribution of the fourth mode is derived from the second diapente species, which we have also assigned to the third mode, and from the second species of diatessaron, extending from the grave *B mi* to the grave *e la mi.* It is the diapason species, second in order, extending from the grave *B mi* to the acute *b mi,* which they call the Hypophrygian. Further, the fourth mode appropriates to itself six initial tones, namely the graves *c fa ut, d sol re, e la mi, f fa ut,* and *g sol re ut,* and the acute *a la mi re;* and it is terminated regularly on the grave *e la mi,* as the accompanying example sets forth:

Mar- ce- li-   nus   sa- cer- dos   et   Pe- trus ex-   or- ci-   sta

mar- ti- res Chri-   ste   in- ter- ce- dant pro   no-   bis.

Often this fourth mode, proceeding by means of acquired species, is ended on the acute *a la mi re.*[47] For the second diapente species coincides with the acquired species from this *a la mi re* to the acute *e' la mi,* brought about by the introduction of the B-*molle* quality or by proceeding from mese [*a*] to nete diezeugmenon [*e*] by means of the synnemmenon tetrachord [A-Bb-C-D]. Moreover, the second diatessaron species appropriate for such an acquired fourth mode extends from the grave *e la mi* to that *a la mi re* which then is its proper final, or from hypate meson [*e*] to mese [*a*].

Further, every *Euouae* of the fourth mode is begun on the fourth tone above the final of the preceding antiphon, whose psalmody commences on the same pitch, proceeding with the notes *la sol la,* as is perceived in this arrangement:

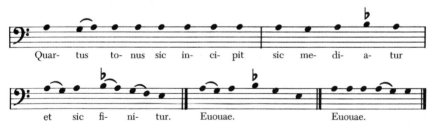

Quar- tus   to- nus sic in- ci- pit   sic me- di- a-   tur

et   sic fi- ni- tur.   Euouae.   Euouae.

But if the versicle of the response, which terminated on the grave *e la*

47. The "Kyrie" of Gafurius' own melodious *Missa quarti toni* (Milan Codex 2268, 101r–109r) provides an excellent example of the use of acquired species that is highly suggestive of minor tonality.

mi, begins on the acute *a la mi re*—namely, on a fourth above the final of the preceding chant—it will belong to the fourth mode; or when the response ends on the acute *a la mi re* and the beginning of the verse is on *d′ la sol re* (brought about by the soft quality of the B-flat), it will also belong to the acquired fourth mode. The natural modulation proceeds in the "Gloria patri" with these notes:

Glo- ri-   a   pa- tri   et   fi- li-   o

et spi- ri-   tu- i   san-   cto.

Chapter twelve The Composition of the Fifth Mode

The tonal outline of the fifth mode is formed from the third diapente species extending from the grave *f fa ut* to the acute *c′ sol fa ut*, and from the third diatessaron species, which extends from *c′ sol fa ut* to the acute *f′ fa ut*. This [fifth mode] is the sixth species in the diapasonic order, which is called Lydian. Four initial tones—the graves *f fa ut* and *g sol re ut*, and the acutes *a la mi re* and *c′ sol fa ut*—are proper for the fifth mode, and it is ended regularly on the grave *f fa ut*, as expressed in this example:

Pre- ci- bus et me- ri- tis   be- a- ti Bla- si- i mar- ti- ris

de- fen- de nos de- us   ab om- ni ma- lo gu- tu- ris.

The *Euouae* of the fifth mode is begun on *c′ sol fa ut*, that is, on the fifth above the final tone of the antiphon, whose psalmody, begun in unison with the final, proceeds with the notes *fa la fa,* as written in this passage:

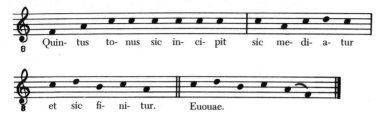

Quin- tus   to- nus   sic in- ci- pit   sic me- di- a- tur

et   sic   fi- ni- tur.   Euouae.

Likewise the versicles whose responses end on the grave *f fa ut* and begin on *c′ sol fa ut* are assigned to the fifth mode. Their modulation in the "Gloria patri" proceeds in this way:

Glo- ri- a   pa-   tri   et   fi- li-   o

et   spi- ri-   tu-   i   san-   cto.

*C*hapter thirteen   The Tonal Structure of the Sixth Mode

The modulation of the sixth mode is formed from the third diapente species, which was also ascribed to the fifth mode, and from the third diatessaron species, which extends from the grave *c fa ut* to the grave *f fa ut.* This [sixth mode] is the third diapason species, arranged between the grave *c fa ut* and the acute *c′ sol fa ut;* they call it Hypolydian. Four initial pitches are assigned to it as proper—namely, the graves *c fa ut, d sol re, f fa ut,* and the acute *a la mi re*—and it is ended regularly on the grave *f fa ut.* Its format is perceived in this musical example:

San   cte   He- ras- me   mar- tir   in-   cli-   te

fun- de pre- ces ad do- mi- num   no- stra pro sa- lu- te.

When, moreover, an antiphon ends on the grave *f fa ut* and its *Euouae* commences on the third above the final, that is, on the acute *a la mi re,* the sixth mode must be designated. Its psalmody is begun in unison [with the final tone of the antiphon] proceeding with the syllables *fa sol la,* as follows:

Sex- tus   to- nus sic in- ci- pit   sic me- di- a- tur

et sic fi- ni- tur.

Similarly, too, the versicles of responses in the sixth mode are begun on *a la mi re,* which is the third tone above the final of the preceding chant. Notes most appropriate for intoning the "Gloria patri" are selected in this way:

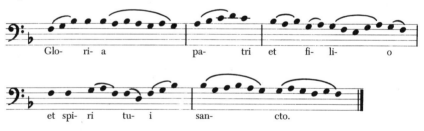

Glo- ri- a   pa- tri et fi- li-   o

et spi- ri tu- i   san-   cto.

Chapter fourteen The Structure of the Seventh Mode

The melodic structure of the seventh mode is formed from the fourth diapente species, extending from the grave *g sol re ut* to the acute *d' la sol re,* and from the first diatessaron species, extending from *d' la sol re* to the acute *g' sol re ut,* named the Mixolydian. The seventh mode possesses five proper beginning tones, namely, the grave *g sol re ut* and the acutes *a la mi re, b mi, c' sol fa ut,* and *d' la sol re.* There is also one permitted by ecclesiastical fiat: the grave *f fa ut.* The seventh mode is terminated regularly on the grave *g sol re ut,* as expressed in this modulation:

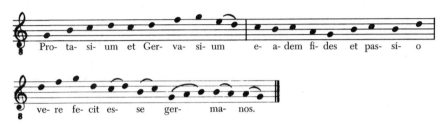

Pro- ta- si- um et Ger- va- si- um   e- a- dem fi- des et pas- si- o

ve- re fe- cit es-   se   ger-   ma-   nos.

An *Euouae* beginning on *d' la sol re* whose antiphon ends on the grave *g sol re ut* is customarily ascribed to the seventh mode. The ancients used to begin its psalmody on a fifth above the final tone of the antiphon, proceeding with the notes *sol fa sol.* Later musicians, however, often have begun psalmody of this mode on a fourth above the final, intoning the syllables *fa mi fa sol,* as is evident here:

Sep- ti- mus   Sep- ti- mus to- nus sic in- ci- pit   sic me- di- a- tur

et sic fi- ni- tur.   Euouae.   Euouae.   Euouae.

Further, there are also other endings for psalmody in this seventh mode which one will discover well illustrated in the Antiphonal itself. There exists still another psalmody of the seventh mode which Gregorians observe in connection with the antiphon "Nos qui vivimus benedicimus Dominum."[48] This psalmody terminates on the co-final [*d*], since it is brought about by acquired species. It is diminished by a single whole tone in the upper register, as is perceived in the subjoined example:

48. Cf. *Liber usualis,* p. 254, where Psalm 113 is framed by the antiphon "Sit nomen Domini" and cast in the *tonus peregrinus.*

Antiphon:

Nos qui vi- vi- mus be- ne- di- ci- mus do- mi- num.

Psalm:

In e- xi- tu I- sra- el de E- gyp- to do- mus Ja- cob de po-pu- lo bar-ba- ro.

Now this psalmody retains a melodic format quite similar in its beginning to the fourth mode on the mediant sixth because the antiphon is
mixed, comprehending the diatessaron species that is appropriate to it—
namely, the third species [C-D-E-F] with the third pitch as its final. Even
if they follow this antiphon with identical notes and clefs, Ambrosians employ a different psalmodic modulation: they begin on the co-final pitch of
the antiphon, that is, on the grave *g sol re ut*, where its diapente species
ends above, just the way they handle the other authentic modes, as follows:[49]

Antiphon: Psalm:

Nos qui vi- vi- mus be- ne- di- ci- mus do- mi- num.   In e- xi- tu

I- sra- el de E- gyp- to   do-mus Ja- cob de po- pu- lo bar- ba- ro.

Nevertheless, the most ancient Antiphonal made it perfectly clear that
this antiphon was first composed by the divine Ambrose with notes proper
to the seventh mode, where he shows both the seventh diapason species
and the Mixolydian itself to have been terminated on the grave *g sol re ut*
and also on its proper *confinalis d' la sol re*—a practice which he particularly employed in authentic modes—as is expressed in this passage:

Antiphon: Psalm:

Nos qui vi- vi- mus be- ne- di- ci- mus do- mi- num.   In e- xi- tu

I- sra- el ex E- gyp- to   do-mus Ja- cob de po- pu- lo bar- ba- ro.

49. For the Ambrosian version of this psalmody, see *Liber vesperalis*, p. 7.

We also set forth the same opinion on the antiphon "Nomini tuo da gloriam, Domino" which we Ambrosians sing with the psalm "In exitu Israel ex Egypto" at vespers on alternate Sundays.[50] For the most part our Ambrosians assign to the authentic mode shorter antiphons whose notes ascend from the final pitch by a ditone only, a practice which is demonstrated by this antiphon and psalm:

When the notes undergo only a trihemitone rise [*i.e.*, a semiditone or minor third] from the final pitch, however, a contrary point of view is held, for then they cast these chants in the plagal mold.

There are also some chants—the versicles of brief responses, for example, and also the responses themselves—whose notes are arranged so that they are raised by a certain amount from the final pitch and lowered in a like amount, for example, by a single pitch below the final and by a single pitch above the final. In such a case, if the note placed below is separated from the final by a wider interval—by the space of a whole tone, for instance—and the distance of the note above is narrower—that is, a semitone space away from and above the same final—the chants will be assigned, in my opinion, to a plagal classification. They are classified as authentic, however, when the upper note is a whole tone higher and the lower note is a semitone lower than the final. But when the distance of both the higher and the lower notes from that final is the same—when, for example, the lower note is depressed a whole tone below the final and the higher is raised a whole tone above the final—I feel that that chant or modulation must be assigned to its particular maneria; it is, after all, a sharer of both modes, that is, of the plagal and the authentic. We may properly call such a mode mixed or common.

Notes selected from the verses of nocturnal responsoria in the seventh mode with which the Gregorians attractively intone the "Gloria patri" follow:

50. *Liber vesperalis,* p. 7.

Chapter fifteen   The Composition of the Eighth Mode

The melodic structure of the eighth mode is formed from the fourth diapente species, which is also assigned to the seventh mode, and from the first diatessaron species, which extends from the grave *d sol re* to the grave *g sol re ut*. Since the lower tetrachord of the first mode [the Dorian] occupies the same ambitus [D-E-F-G], they say that the eighth mode becomes a sharer of the nature of the first. But the eighth mode enjoys no name in the order of the diapasonic modes, unless perhaps through logical extension of the idea, as was mentioned in Chapter 7, I call it the Hypomixolydian. The eighth mode possesses five beginning pitches—the graves *d sol re, f fa ut, g sol re ut,* and the acutes *a la mi re* and *c′ sol fa ut*—and it is terminated regularly on the grave *g sol re ut*, as this arrangement indicates:

Now it is clear from the prescribed beginning tones of the modes that the beginnings in plagal chants have not been allotted by ecclesiastical authorities to the fifth above the final, that is, where their diapente species end. In psalmody of the eighth mode the *Euouae* begins on *c sol fa ut*, raised, to be sure, by the interval of a fourth above the final pitch of the antiphon, whose psalmody is begun on that final and proceeds with the notes *ut re fa*, or on solemn feasts, with *ut re ut fa*, as is evident here:

From what has been said it is readily apparent that no psalmody is to be initiated on a pitch higher than that which coincides with the beginning of its *Seculorum Amen.* Besides, they execute ferial and lesser psalmody in a quicker tempo and more solemn ritual in a slower tempo. Thus the psalmody follows the mode of its antiphon, for the Greek *anti* is translated into Latin by *pro atque contra,* "for and against." They also say that in composition *antiphon* signifies equality. Hence an antiphon is like a modulation that is the equal of the psalm, or it is like a concert of one and the same mode set in that chant and its psalm. From the versicles of nocturnal responsoria in this eighth mode, the Gregorians evolve an agreeable "Gloria patri" modulation as follows:

In chants such as Alleluias and Sequences and very many in that category, church musicians are accustomed to intone one and the same vocable in a continuous, lasting passage. This the Ambrosians call by the common name "melody."[51] That is, while they are singing they are in mind and soul rushing along, as they say, to the Holy Trinity and the harmony of angels. These Ambrosians begin much of their psalmody in every

---

51. That is, the so-called *jubilus* or *neuma,* characterized by melismatic vocalization on a single syllable.

mode on that note on which the beginning of its *Euouae* is generally written, and they continue it with the same pitch up to the *Euouae* itself without the interpolation of any difference in pitch, and the ending of that
psalm tone accords with the notes of the *Euouae*. For, by the testimony
of Augustine, it is the ending to which everything is referred and whose
cause all other things become. Sometimes, also, in some psalmody (especially in the first mode) Ambrosians solemnly intone the beginnings and
mediations of the Gregorian rite; but Ambrosian modulations appended
to the endings of psalmody of this sort are made clear by these examples:

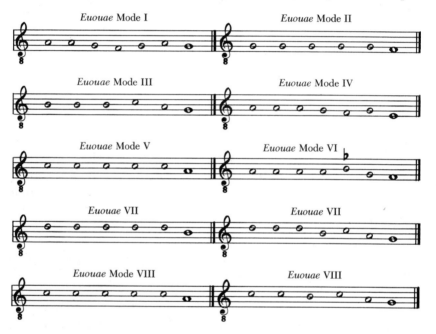

    There are, in addition, some melodies that are written with fewer notes.
For this reason, because of the obvious diminution, they are interpreted as
being imperfect since they are short of the usual range. If its *Euouae* does
not follow upon this kind of melody, one can scarcely determine whether
it is to be classified as an authentic or as a plagal mode. Hence some writers have based a decision in a case like this on certain pitches which become the determining factor.
    To the first maneria, in which the first and second modes are encom-
passed, they assign the grave *f fa ut* [as the critical pitch]; for the second
maneria, which governs the third and fourth modes, the grave *g sol re ut;*

for the third maneria, which the fifth and sixth modes inhabit, the acute *a la mi re;* for the fourth maneria, which contains the seventh and eighth modes, the acute *b mi.* This is accomplished in such a way that each critical pitch is, in diatonic sequence, a third higher than the final of its particular maneria. Thus the critical pitches of the first and second maneriae are higher than their finals by the interval of a semiditone, and the critical pitches of the third and fourth maneriae, in turn, are separated from their respective finals by the space of a ditone. The natural diatonic sequence of pitches requires this.

Hence, whenever in a melody of any maneria there are numerically more notes arranged above (that is, higher than the critical pitch), that melody is consigned to an authentic classification. On the other hand, if lower notes predominate, one considers such a melody plagal. But it is established that notes stationed on these critical pitches must not be reckoned with either mode. And yet, for the most part, even if in more prolix melodies—that is, those scored in very many notes—this truth becomes quite clear more often because of a criterion of this sort, such a technique is still unreliable in those cases that are expressed by a paucity of notes, as has been illustrated in the antiphon "Ubi charitas et amor."[52] In fact, in the opinion of most people, the authentic melody is disclosed by its own diapente species being repeated several times from its final upward, particularly when it is repeated as a single interval. On the other hand, they consider a plagal melody to be indicated by this kind of repetition of only a fourth upward from the final.

For brevity's sake, however, we leave it to each student to investigate for himself the "Gloria patri" melodies on the psalmodies of Gregorian Introits and on the antiphonal psalmody of the Ambrosians.

Book One of *The Practice of Music*
by Franchinus Gaforus[53] of Lodi
ends auspiciously.

52. The mixolydian antiphon sung during Vespers on Maundy Thursday at the ceremony of the Washing of the Feet is one of the earliest preserved chants, dating from the agape. See *Liber usualis,* p. 664; and *Early Medieval Music . . . ,* ed. Dom Anselm Hughes (*New Oxford History of Music;* London, 1954), II, 58.

53. Book I ends with one of many contemporary variant spellings of the author's name, which include Gafurius, Gaffurius, Gafurus, Gaforus, Gafforus, Gaphurius, and de Gaffuris. In the *Dodekachordon,* Glarean occasionally refers to Gafurius as Franchinus Laudensis, after his birthplace, Lodi.

BOOK TWO

OF *The Practice
of Music*

[THE
MENSURAL
SYSTEM]

Chapter one   Poets and Musicians Settled on a Short and a Long as the Measure of Time in the Voice

The movement of the voice in music, it is agreed, was set down in the preceding Book according to equal time values for the individual notes. Poets, and musicians too, paying judicious attention to this vocal movement, fixed on a short or a long as the measure of all time in the voice, using different symbols for the quantities of time involved. Thus they regarded all syllables as short or long. For a short syllable they assigned a measure of one unit of time and for a long syllable a quantity of two units of time. For duality is the first quantity that counts unity twice in succession. Thus the short syllable was discovered before the long, as Diomedes the Grammarian[1] says, for one comes before two. Of course, they believed that a syllable is short either on account of its own nature or by reason of a following consonantal sound, and they accurately perceived that a syllable is long either by nature or by position, or even by poetic license.

They also regarded certain syllables as common—when, for example, a syllable is short by its own nature or a liquid follows a mute. Then a syllable was regarded neutrally, that is, sometimes as a short and sometimes as a long, as *tenebre* and *patris*. This is inferred from many examples among Greek and Latin poets. They constructed, to the accompaniment of the lyre and cithara, every type of verse by a combination of different feet. Described in Book I of the *Theorica,* this will be more fully explained in the *De harmonia* [IV, 10], when I shall discuss the earliest authors of rhythms.

---

1. Diomedes was a Latin grammarian and author of a *De arte grammatica* (fl. late fourth-century A.D.). The important early typographer Nicolas Jenson printed Diomedes' text on grammar in Venice in 1478 within a volume containing several shorter tracts by other Roman grammarians (Phocas, Caper, Donatus, Agraetius, and Servius). Because Diomedes' book was highly esteemed as a teaching tool, it was reprinted in 1495 and 1500 and used in the educational system alongside Quintilian's *Institutio oratoria.* Gafurius here refers to the section in Diomedes' textbook on the rhythm of the different poetic feet (commencing on two unnumbered leaves before signature *h*), in which a foot is defined as follows: "Pes est sublatio ac positio duarum aut trium ampliusque syllabarum spatio comprehensa."

All types of verse are known to have been arranged in different feet, the feet being made up of different units of time. I shall mention the quantities of some of them.

The dactyl contains three syllables, the first long and the other two short, as in the words *armiger* and *principis*. Hence it consists of four units of time. The spondee also has four units of time, arranged in two long syllables, as *felix* and *aestas*. The iamb, called the quick foot, has three units of time arranged on two syllables, the first short and the last long, as in *pias*. The trochee is clearly the reverse of the iamb. It also includes two syllables in three units of time, the first long and the second short, as in *musa*. The anapest, the opposite of the dactyl, is called antidactyl by the Greeks, since it consists of three syllables, the first two short and the last long, as in *pietas* and *Erato*. The pyrrhic consists of two short syllables, such as *miser* and *pater*. Three short syllables are assigned to the tribrach, as *dominus*. Three syllables are allotted to the amphibrach, the first short, the second long, and the third short, as *carina*. The cretic or amphimacer comprehends three syllables, the first long, the second short, and the third long, as in *insulae*. The bacchius consists of three syllables, the first short and the other two long, as in *Achates* and *Ulixes*.

Especially appropriate for lyric verse, the proceleusmatic has four short syllables, as *avicula*. The double spondee was fashioned out of eight units of time in four long syllables, as *oratores*. The choriamb consists of four syllables, the first long, the following two short, and the last long, as *armipotens*. They fashioned the double iamb in four syllables, the first short, second long, the third short, and the fourth long, as *propinquitas*. The epitrite, which Diomedes calls *Hippius,* occurs in four ways. The first type, it is clear, was arranged in four syllables containing seven units of time, the first short and the other three long, as *sacerdotes*. The second epitrite also contains four syllables, the second short and the other three long, as *conditores*. Four syllables are assigned to the third epitrite, the third syllable short and the remaining three long, as *Demosthenes*. The fourth epitrite is made up of four syllables, the fourth short and the first three long, as *Fescenninus*.

Certain of these and other feet are considered to be simple, like the spondee and the iamb; certain others, like the double spondee and the double iamb, are considered to be compound. Diomedes himself, as well as Aristides in Book I of his *Musica,*[2] and Augustine better in Book II [8] of

2. Aristides Quintilianus was a Greek theorist of the first and second centuries A.D. and author of a *De musica* in three books whose translation into Latin Gafurius com-

the *De musica*, are known to have outlined the rhythmic nature of all of these feet.

Musicians themselves have assigned to the quantities of sound certain characters as their own appropriate names. With these they can compose every song in a diversity of the time units expressed, much like the way that verse is made up of many feet.

Physicians agree that the correct measure of a short unit of time ought to be matched to the even beat of the pulse, establishing arsis and thesis as equal to that which they call diastole and systole in the measurement of each pulse. Nevertheless, it is clear that in the pulse of sick people, who are the physician's responsibility, diastole and systole undergo an increase or change in unequal proportion. The Greek word *diastole* means "dilation" or "expansion" in Latin translation; *systole,* on the other hand, means "contraction." Poets, moreover, have arsis and thesis, that is, rise and fall in their metrical feet. Arsis and thesis provide the basis for the existence of these metrical feet. They use them in recitation so that the verse can strike the ear and caress the mind with a more pleasing sound.

Even though it is possible to find arsis and thesis in the feet whenever poetry is composed, nevertheless it is the apt and smooth conjunction of words which makes them exceedingly clear and assists in graceful articulation. An interweaving of words suitable for delivery in one or another fashion, according to the various kinds of verse, is made, so that the very texture of the verses reveals the feet, which run swiftly, as races are run, and with a fixed order of the verbal connections, unveils the smooth, spontaneously flowing rhythm.

Rhythm, in the opinion of Aristides, consists of units of time in space.[3] As to what time is the unit for the measurement of motion and rest in articulation, I accept the short unit of time. But in the treatise which Bede wrote on form and meter, he interpreted rhythm as measured composition conceived not by metrical theory but rather by the number of syllables according to the judgment of the ear, as are the verses of the vernacular poets. Rhythm, moreover, seems to be quite similar to meter. In fact, rhythm all by itself, without meter, is impossible; for meter is theory and measure, while rhythm is measure without theory.[4] Yet generally you will

---

missioned. Aristides' *De musica* is available in Greek and Latin translation in Meibom, II, 36 ff.

3. Meibom, II, 31.

4. Except for nominal changes in case and word order, this Latin passage was extracted from the *De arte metrica* of the Venerable Bede. See *PL,* XC, 173, under the sectional heading "De rhythmo" (xxiv).

even find proportion in rhythm on some occasion, not because the control of an artist has been observed, but because the sound and the movement itself bring it about. The vernacular poets necessarily compose rhythm in a rustic manner, while the rhythms of the learned poets are fashioned in accordance with the rules of art.

The Greeks assert that rhythm consists of arsis and thesis and of units of time which some people call free or empty. Aristoxenus said that rhythm is time divided into any units which can be brought together numerically.[5] According to Nicomachus, rhythm is the regulated synthesis of units of time.[6] But it is not our province to prescribe rules and canons for everything that relates to this sort of structure and invention. We leave to the poets matters which are properly theirs. Yet I would have poets pay closest attention that they may attain this elegance in their poetry. Let us, nevertheless, add examples in the event that more information is desired here, and let students make the transition to other cases by easier inference from one example to another.

The heroic hexameter loses most of its elegance whenever the second foot ends a part of the thought; it jars less if the thought ends on the third foot with a monosyllabic word. It closes most creditably and pleasingly on the first, fourth, or fifth foot with a part of the thought, keeping the verse from being made clumsy or stumbling when the thought is cut off, as in the case of the well-known line[7]

5. Gafurius' knowledge of Aristoxenus probably derives from Boethius and Bacchius. *Cf.* Bacchius' *Introductio,* in Meibom, I, 22, where in answer to the question "Quid est rhythmus," Aristoxenus is reported to have replied: "Tempus divisum in unoquoque quod rhythmum suscipere est." For an account of Aristoxenus' rhythmic theory, see C. F. Abdy Williams, "The Aristoxenian Theory of the Rhythmic Foot," *The Musical Antiquary,* II (1911). See also G. B. Pighi's Italian translation of Aristoxenus' *Rhythmica* (Bologna, 1959).

6. Nicomachus' definition of rhythm is also cited in Bacchius' *Introductio.* Again it was Boethius who contributed the weight of Nicomachus' authority to the strong mathematical orientation of Renaissance music theorists. A neo-Pythagorean, Nicomachus of Gerasa (second century A.D.) stressed the intimate interrelationship of music and number. His *Harmonices manuale* is printed in Meibom, I, 1–41. For an interesting sidelight on the semantic aspects of rhythm and meter, see Curt Sachs, "Rhythm and Tempo: An Introduction," *The Musical Quarterly,* XXXVIII (July 1952), 384–98.

7. This is the concluding dactyllic hexameter of Pyrrhus' famous speech to the Romans on the exchange of war prisoners, as reported, according to Cicero, by the epic poet Ennius. See Cicero's *De officiis,* I.xii, tr. Walter Miller (Loeb Classical Library, 1928), p. 38. The fifth word of the Latin line is in error. It should read *cum* rather than *hoc.*

> Dono ducite; doque volentibus hoc magnis dis.
> [I give and present them. Take them. The great
>   gods' blessings attend you.]

In addition, this example has a spondee in the fifth foot which hurts the ears more. Variety of metrical feet, where spondees are tempered with dactyls in alternation, also confers something to this scheme.

Further, it is useful to notice that heroic verse ending on a trisyllable appears to increase in power; on a monosyllable, unless that word is an enclitic, the hexameter breaks. Heroic verse is terminated badly on a polysyllabic word, better on a bisyllabic word. A too frequent concourse of vowels, and most especially the repetition of the same sound and the same letter and syllable, must be avoided and shunned. Since dissonance and sibilance offend the ears, they also hinder harmonious delivery and render it less pleasant. This same thing must be considered in every type of verse, for it is easy for anybody at all to see the difference in these two pentameters:

> Icareosque canes herculeasque feras
> [Icarus' dogs, Hercules' wild animals]

and:

> Sunt famuli tres mulae duae equi totidem
> [There are three slaves, two mules and the
>   same number of horses.]

and the Sapphics:

> Ad fori curris geminum sedile
> [You run to the twin seat of the forum.]

> Non tua haec spectacula cede Musis
> [Yield to the Muses these spectacles that
>   are not yours.]

and these Asclepiadeans:

> Odi divitias vulgus et arceo
> [I hate riches and ward off the throng.]

> Nec movit corybantes semeles puer
> [Nor does Semele's child rouse the Corybantes.]

Therefore, from what has been said, it is clear that if the juncture of the words has been carefully arranged, arsis and thesis can manifest their power more satisfactorily, so that a verse can deliver, sustain, and pour itself out without any contortion, almost by itself.

Chapter two   Various Characters of the Ancients and Their Measurement

Musicians promulgated the measurement of sounds in various characters by division and decree. The measurement is twofold. One, which consists in the continuous quantity of a sound, they ascribe to time. It is clear that this measurement was instituted for each character by the authorities themselves, not only on the basis of logic, but also by the arbitrary decision of the one who established it, a procedure which was also customary for the Pythagoreans, who laid equal stress on the dictates of authority and the instruction of pure reason. The other measurement consists in the intervals or distances of sounds, which are determined by reason alone in accordance with proportional measurement, as, for example, on musical instruments [monochords].

Therefore, measurement of time is the setting down of the quantity of each character, considered in two ways, to be sure. First, according to the basic classification of musicians, we measure the essential temporal value of the individual notes (we are using "characters" and "notes" interchangeably). Secondly, we classify the quantities of characters by "accident" [*i.e.*, by their nonessential traits], a fact which also results in a twofold consideration: first according to the accidents of these written characters—for example, alteration, imperfection, diminution, division, and so on—and secondly by those accidents of the different proportions—whatever the commensurability—which will be fully delineated in Book IV of this work.

Hence it is clear that this figurable or mensurable discipline has been designed with essence and with accidence. Notes and rests use essence in particular quantities—in mode, tempus, and prolation—but what happens to these notes beyond these three essential measurements is ascribed to accident, and accidents can neither be necessary nor intrinsic, as Aristotle says in Book I of the *Posterior Analytics.*[8]

Every mensurable description in notes or in rests (which show omitted mensurable sounds) is written either by a sign or by a canonic inscription. The Greeks used the following different rhythmical figures: a breve of one unit of time they represented by ⎯ ; the minor long, which they called double-time, this way: ≃ ; the long of three units of time thus: ⎣ ; the long of four units of time thus: ⎣⎦ ; the long of five units of time thus: ⊔⊔ .

They signified arsis by attaching a point to each character, like this: ⎯. ≃. ⎣. Every character without a point indicated thesis. They also expressed the consonant intervals—for example, diatessarons, diapentes, diapasons, ditones, semiditones, and other consonances adapted to harmony —in certain characters which we have decided to omit for the sake of brevity as both out of place with and foreign to present practice.

Our musicians used to express the breve note, that is, one unit of time, as a blackened square, in this way: ▪ . The long, that is, two units of time, they expressed as a square with a stem descending or ascending on its right side of a length equal to four sides of its square, in this way: ▐ . But because of the deformity resulting from this excessive length, some persons made the stem issuing from the square note equal to only three lengths of the sides of its square, like this: ▐ . Others arranged the stem in a length equal to only two sides of the square, like this: ▐ .

The long of three units of time was expressed in a similar shape by a square and a stem, but with a third of the square-shaped body not blackened, like this: ▐ or this: ▐ . They signified the long of four units of time as a blackened quadrangle with the square doubled in width, as follows: ▬ . This they called a double long. Finally, the triple long was presented, three times the width of the square and considered to hold the value of six units of time, like this: ▬ .

There were also some who included in a single character several longs shown by separate stems, like this: ▬▬ . Later musicians, subverting the description of these characters, wrote these notes empty, bringing together many square breves in a single form, thus: ⊓⊓⊓ . They also wrote the long together with breves and breves with longs in a single form, in this way: ⊓⊓⊓⊓ .

8. See Boethius' translation in *PL,* LXIV, 720 *passim.*

Although such notational characters have passed into disuse, it was desirable to discuss them briefly so that the more recent styles may be understood more easily by everyone.

Chapter three   A Discussion of the Five Essential Characters

A character is the representation of a sound either actual or omitted. We call a sound actual when it is a fixed measure that can be sung or articulated. An omitted sound is one which by its very silence is considered to be a fixed measure of time. Characters of actual sound are the notes themselves; the omitted sound is expressed by rests.

Moreover, of the notes, some are breves, some longs; for just as with syllables, shortening and lengthening are known to be natural attributes of the sounds themselves. Accordingly, musicians first traditionally made the breve note with a square shape like this: ▪ , which, since it consists of a measure of one time, they call tempus. The long they signified by a square also, with a stem on the right side jutting upward or downward from the square. They drew the stem in a length equal to the four sides of the square, like this: ◗ . Hence it was also called a double breve. But for the most part, music copyists draw a reasonable length for this stem without regard to any proportion. Since poets in their treatment of meter established a measure for long syllables like a larger limit in the quantity of sound—that is, which no other measure of time might at any point exceed —musicians have called this long note mode.

Then, dividing the square of the breve diagonally into two equal parts with right angles above and below, musicians assembled the semibreve, which they called prolation, assigning to it half the quantity of the breve, in this way: ◆ ◊ .

Finally, modern musicians have correctly ascribed a measure of one unit of time to the semibreve, comprehending within the sound of each semibreve diastole and systole. And since diastole and systole, or arsis and thesis, which are opposites and are in fact the smallest measure of the pulse, are considered as the measure of a single unit of time, they divided the semibreve, arranged in the full measure of one unit of time, into two equal parts so that in sound, as in the measure of the pulse, one part contains a unit of time equal to diastole and the other a quantity equal to systole. To this they assigned a shorter duration in sound, naming it "minim," and they draw it as a semibreve character with a stem attached to one of its angles, generally upward, in this way: ♦ ♀ .

The breve note, moreover, since it originally consisted of one unit of time, and the long, which formerly consisted of two units of time, are called the most basic elements in the time scale of mensurable sound. Their quantities are equivalent to the proportionable parts of a whole tone, for according to Aristides and Anselm, the tone is divisible into proportionable enharmonic dieses.[9] In like manner the long note is divisible into four semibreves, and the breve into four minims. Hence the quantity of a minim occupies one fourth of a breve, as if it flowed out of one of the four angles of the breve-square, or as some prefer, out of one side of the breve-square.

Every single thing is perfected by the least of its kind, such as unity itself, by means of which, since it is the least, every number takes its increase and also by means of which a breakdown of all numbers into itself is accomplished; and every line also increases by just a point—one at a time, of course—and the length of every line decreases clear down to the edge of the point itself. Thus it is clear that the minim note completes or perfects every single measure of musical time. Since in prolation the minim is constituted as the principal part of the semibreve, the minim has been called a unit of prolation.

Now, if I may make use of Franco's opinion, the smallest unit of musical time is not named for the smallest thing there is, but rather for "that which is minimum in the fullness of voice."[10] Aristides also seems to assert this in Book I of his *Musica* with the words: "Indivisible and minimum time

9. Anselm of Parma, *De musica*, III, ed. Giuseppe Massera (*Historiae musicae cultores*, XIV; Florence, 1961), p. 159.

10. This is one of Gafurius' infrequent references to the medieval theorist, Franco of Cologne (c. 1250 A.D.). Franco's observation on minimal time to which Gafurius here refers appears in the *Ars cantus mensurabilis*, V (in Couss., I, 120b; and also in Gerbert, III, 5, where the work is attributed to Franco of Paris). The remark had wide currency among theorists, and it is not surprising to find it also in Marchettus' *Pomerium*, ed. Joseph Vecchi (*Corpus scriptorum de musica*, VI; American Institute of Musicology, 1961), p. 78.

is that which is also called a sign."[11] He calls minimum time the least amount which is comprehensible to our senses, but he calls it a sign for the reason that it is indivisible. In geometry too they call indivisibility a sign. Furthermore, this indivisibility takes the place of unity.

Finally, in the tenors of their motets musicians have introduced a double long containing four units of breve time, in a way that is not unlike the spondee, which consists of two longs. Since this double long exceeds the other notes both in quantitative value and in shape, they call it the maxima. It is represented in this way: ◻ . They denominate this maxima the major mode because its duration of musical sound is greater than that in the other notes. Along the same line of thought, the maxima is compared to the proslambanomenos chord [A], which, on account of its very slow vibrations caused by the greater length of its string, yields a sound lower than the other chords of the Perfect System. In the same way the rest of the notes can easily be analogized to the other chords.

But since the four units of breve time can be patterned in various ways, musicians believe that this maxima corresponds to various feet of four units of time. When you consider one long and two breves in the maxima, you will make it sound quite a lot like the dactyl; if two breves and one long, the anapest; if four breves, it will accord with the proceleusmatic.

Hence there exists a series of notes in this order: minim, semibreve, breve, long, and maxima. Some authorities, however, make the order retrograde, from maxima to minim. If we compare these same notes to the theoretical order of the consonances, the minim will take the position of a whole tone; the semibreve, a diatessaron; the breve, a diapente; the long, a diapason; and the maxima, a double diapason.

Chapter four   The Shorter Notes

Next, a later generation proposed a minim note diminished by certain subdivisions for a more graceful melodic ornamentation similar to the division of a whole tone into its constituent parts. They divided the minim

11. See Aristides' *De musica,* I, in Meibom, II, 32, where the technical term "sign" is borrowed from geometry to indicate a mark or point "without parts."

into two equal parts corresponding to a measure of time, which, according to Prosdocimus, they call major semiminims.[12] Tinctoris, on the other hand, considers minims to be in duple proportion, represented, indeed, as minims having the end of the stem turned off to the right, like this: ♪ or as minims but with the body blackened, in this way: ♦ . Further, they divide such an empty minim with its stem turned back into two equal parts, which they call minor semiminims but which are written with the body blackened, in this way: ♪ or empty with the stem turned back toward the right and with the character of the number 2, like this: ♪ . Tinctoris, however, calls them "minims drawn in quadruple proportion." On the other hand (and this view is more pleasing to us), many have interpreted the first such subdivision—the adjacent parts of the minim, that is—as seminims, as though they were disjunct and separated minims. Further, they name the primary parts of such seminims semiminims because of their shortened measure of time and quantity. And so the seminim will follow the minim as a major semitone does a whole tone, and the semiminim will look back to the minim like a minor semitone to the whole tone.[13]

A third, most diminished particle of a minim, which Tinctoris wished to be named a "minim in octuple proportion," some call a minimum semiminim, some a comma. We have decided that it should be called a diesis, which is the smallest harmonic particle in the division of a whole tone. Many represent this as a blackened seminim with the tip of its stem turned back to the right, and in addition, with a stroke turned back from its lower angle, in this manner: ♪ , but since the appearance of this note is quite deformed in comparison with the other diminutions of this sort, we write it blackened, turning back the tip of the stem toward the left, in this manner: ♪ . For the right side is superior to and more perfect than the left in the manipulation of such notes.

There are some who have passed on a tradition of different forms for

---

12. Prosdocimus de Beldemandis, early *quatrocento* authority on Italian mensural notation, wrote, among other tracts, *Tractatus practice de musica mensurabili ad modum Italicorum* (Couss., III, 228–47). Like Marchettus before him, whom he criticized, Prosdocimus was a professor of philosophy at the University of Padua.

13. These remarks point up the lack of standardization in the form and nomenclature of these smaller note values. What Gafurius called a seminim, Prosdocimus called a major semiminim and Tinctoris called a minim in duple proportion. Tinctoris' rather cumbersome phrase does not appear in any of his extant writings, but Gafurius may have heard him suggest the idea when they were both living in Naples. Gafurius' designation of the first two binary subdivisions of the minim as seminim and semiminim certainly causes some confusion because of the similarity of the terms.

these notes, including Franco, Philip of Caserta, and even Johannes de Muris and Anselm of Parma in the third session of his *Musica*.[14] They produce a long with an ascending plica and also a breve appendaged on either side. Again, Anselm postulated a major, minor, and mean breve. He designated the major breve by a square with a stem descending from its left side, like this: ⊟ . He expressed a minor breve as a square with an ascending stem on the left, like this: ⊟ and the mean breve as a square without a stem, like this: ⊡ . He also described the major semibreve as a square with two stems, one ascending and one descending, both on the right side, as follows: ⊟ . The minor semibreve he described as a square with two stems on the left side, like this: ⊟ . He designated the mean semibreve as a square with a stem drawn through the middle of the square both upward and downward, in this manner: ⊟ and by a similar method he designated various other notes. The representations of these notes have fallen into disuse because modern musicians have decided they are better rejected than approved.

Chapter five   Ligatures

A ligature is the combining of simple notes in a certain order by means of suitable graphs.[15] There are four notes which can be tied to-

14. Philip, or Filippo, of Caserta was a composer-theorist with whom Gafurius was acquainted in Naples, c. 1478–80 and the author of a Neapolitan treatise on mensural notation, *Tractatus de diversis figuris*, which is printed in Couss., III, 118–24. A copy of this tract was made by Gafurius' teacher, Bonadies, and is preserved in the Codex Faenza 117 of the Biblioteca Communale in Faenza.

Johannes de Muris (c. 1290–1351) advocated an orderly scheme of precise mensural relationships in his *Ars nova musicae* (printed in Gerbert, III, in two parts: *Musica theorica* [pp. 255–83] and *Musica practica* [pp. 292–301]). The desire to study de Muris in depth prompted Gafurius in 1499 to compile his *Glossemata* "on several parts of de Muris' *Theorica* and *Practica*." This autographed, unedited document is preserved in Codex H 165 inf. (16v–22r) of the Ambrosian Library. (See n. 24, Book IV, below, for another work also based on de Muris.)

For Anselm's discussion, see *De musica*, III (Massera ed., pp. 198–99).

15. The definition of a ligature given here echoes the definition given by Franco in

gether: the semibreve, breve, long, and maxima. Just as a simple note that is subject to being tied can be bound to another, so also a tied note or one joined to another can be untied and separated into the form of a simple note, except for the semibreve. The semibreve is recognized to be out of place as the lead simple note of a ligature. The exception to this occurs when semibreves in ligatures are drawn in a single oblique shape, and this representation of them is not at all consistent with notational simplicity.

Therefore, some ligatures are set down in a single form, like this:

others in several different graphs, as follows: . Furthermore, some of these ligatures are ascending, others descending.

The ligature is called ascending when its second note is higher than the first, as here: . Nor does it matter if several notes in such a ligature descend. Ascent and descent in ligatures are considered to be governed by the initial advance in motion between the first and the second notes.

A ligature is said to be descending when the first note is higher than the second, in this way: .

As to the beginnings of ligatures, some are said to be with propriety, some without propriety, and some with opposite propriety. Every ascending ligature whose initial note has no stem ascending or descending is said to be with propriety, as in this example: . Likewise, every descending ligature whose first note has a stem descending—that is, attached to its left side—is said to be with propriety, as follows: .

Moreover, every ligature with propriety makes its first note a breve. Accordingly, they err who make a long the first note of an oblique form in an ascending ligature, in this way: .

According to Franco, propriety is the ordered disposition and arrangement assigned by leading authorities to the initial notes of ligatures in plain chant.[16] Thus every ligature in plain chant possesses propriety only. On the other hand, ligatures without propriety and with opposite propriety are never appropriate for the notes of plain chant, inasmuch as, differing essentially from the ligature with propriety, they produce notes that are diverse both in name and in quantity, something which is by no means

---

Ars cantus mensurabilis, VII (Couss., I, 124a) and picked up by Marchettus for his *Pomerium* (Vecchi ed., p. 186).

16. Franco, *Ars cantus mensurabilis,* VII, in Couss., I, 124.

allowed in plain chant, where musicians have set down their notes in equal temporal value.

Every ascending ligature whose initial note has a stem descending from its right side was said to be without propriety, as here: ♪ ♪ ♪ . Also they call every descending ligature whose initial note had no stem a ligature without propriety, as here: ♪ ♪ ♪ ♪ ♪ . Every ligature without propriety yields a long as its first note.

Furthermore, every ascending or descending ligature whose first note had a stem ascending on its left side is said to be with opposite propriety, as here: ♪ ♪ ♪ . And every ligature with opposite propriety always makes its first note a semibreve. It makes the second note a semibreve too, not on its own account, but because of its sequential position, for a single semibreve is not acceptable for a ligature; two, however, are joined together most properly.

It is clear indeed from the foregoing that the long, breve, and semibreve are the only notes which qualify most satisfactorily as beginning notes of ligatures. But the maxima, which is uniformly represented by a shape that is always long and quadrangular, is never varied by a diversity of quantity; it is conceded to be appropriate for initial, medial, and terminal notes of ligatures, as here: ♪ ♪ ♪ ♪ .

For the final notes of ligatures, however, the phrases "with perfection" and "without perfection" are known to be relevant. Every ligature, whether ascending or descending, is declared to be with perfection when it has as its final note a square directly above the penultimate note, as follows: ♪ ♪ ♪ ♪ , or when its final note is diagonally above the penultimate with a stem descending on its right side, as follows: ♪ ♪ ♪ , or when it has a square shape below the penultimate, as follows: ♪ ♪ ♪ . Musicians have established a long for this final note in such ligatures.

On the other hand, every ligature, ascending or descending, is said to be without perfection when it has its final note in an oblique shape above the penultimate, in this way: ♪ ♪ , or in a square shape without a stem diagonally above, as follows: ♪ ♪ ♪ , or below the penultimate in an oblique shape, like this: ♪ ♪ ♪ ♪ . Musicians themselves have held that the final note of this ligature is always a breve. Thus it is clear that a long and a breve can be stationed not only at the beginning but also at the end of ligatures. But the semibreve cannot be stationed at the beginning or the end at all except in a ligature of opposite propriety. In that case only two semibreves may be joined together; then the first and final notes are called semibreves, as here: ♪ ♪ ♪ ♪ .

There is no essential difference between the middle notes of ligatures, however, since all are alike in quantity. Hence, it is necessary to select only one name. Franco, Anselm, and musicians in general hold that all middle notes are breves.[17] They think falsely who argue that a middle note is a long, as here, for example: . The long merits a position only at the beginning and end of ligatures; the semibreve in the initial and middle position—when, that is, more than two notes are joined in a ligature of opposite propriety—but at the beginning and at the end if there are only two semibreves. As has been brought out in the preceding discussion, however, the breve occupies an appropriate position as a beginning, middle, or final note of ligatures.

Musicians have nowhere been accustomed to tying the minim note in a ligature.

Finally, since simple notes suffer accidents—alteration, imperfection, for example, and the like—they undergo the same type of modification in these ligatures too.

Chapter six Rests

A rest, which the Greeks call a time of silence, is a character showing an artistic cessation of song which signals singers to refrain from singing. Musicians established the rest for suitable repose and for the restoration of the voice after laborious soaring, and also for a sweetness to the melody. For just as a preacher of the divine word or an orator often soothes a restless audience by a kind of jest and makes them more attentive and well-disposed, so a singer of songs who intersperses some rests among the notes holds the attention of his audience for the remaining parts of his song.

The character of the rest is a certain line or stroke drawn through a space or spaces or part of a space; it is not added to a note but is entirely apart from the notes. The ancients employed four rests for their songs, which, since they represent the measure of omitted sounds, assumed the

17. Franco, *Ars cantus mensurabilis,* VII, in Couss., I, 124; and Anselm, *De musica,* III (Massera ed., p. 182).

names of these notes. Of these rests one is a breve, one a long, one a semi-breve, and one a minim.

In the notation of vocal music the breve rest is a stroke drawn from a line to an adjacent line, encompassing the distance or space in between. The long rest, that is, one of the duration of two breves, is a stroke encompassing two whole spaces of three lines. There is also a long rest of three units of time, which, touching four lines at its extremities, occupies three entire spaces. They call this long rest perfect because with its silence it passes over three equal units of time or the duration of three breves.

In the quantities of such characters the number 3 is deemed perfect, first, by reason of its priority, because it demonstrates innately the first even binary number, which they regard as feminine, plus the first odd number, which is called masculine; and by the union of first one and then the other of these two, the other numbers are created. Secondly, all their different parts produce that same number 3, for the aliquot 1 and aliquant 2 yield the number 3.[18] Thirdly, the harmony in these first three numbers is arranged in natural succession, as Augustine says in Book I of his *Musica,* for the number 3 is made up out of 1 and 2 and no number intervenes naturally between them, something which does not happen among the other numbers; for 2 and 3 do not make 4 precisely, and the numbers 3 and 4 do not yield the number 5 precisely, the number which naturally follows them. It is the same for the other numbers. Fourthly, the number 3 has ternary equality, for in that number beginning, middle, and end are set down equally. Thus we acknowledge the Holy Trinity in the Supreme Deity. Finally, by reason of mutual aggregation, this same number 3 multiplied by 2, or the number 2 by 3, gives rise at once to the number 6, and mathematicians proclaim 6 to be perfect in its aliquot parts.

A rest larger than that of three units of time is not figured in with the other notes of a song; it signifies, rather, the end of a composition. Therefore, when according to the arrangement of the composer it is necessary for two or three rests of perfect longs such as these to be figured in—that is, when there is a silence of six or nine units of time—two or three rests of the three-space type, or more, are to be written down, according to the discretion of the composer.

18. Aliquot: "contained an exact number of times in something else—used as a divisor or part (5 is an aliquot part of 15); opposed to *aliquant.*" Aliquant: "being a part of a number or quantity but not dividing it without leaving a remainder (5 is an aliquant part of 16)." (*Webster* III.)

The breve rest generally occupies the value of three semibreves in its period of silence. Musicians associate this with the perfect breve, calling it then perfect time.

The semibreve rest is a stroke adhering to some one line and descending to the middle of an adjacent space. There are also those who have chosen to keep silence for a third part of one unit of time if the rest comprehends only one third of a space, and in addition, two parts of a unit of time when the rest occupies two thirds of this space, but modernists disagree with this. They believe that two contiguous semibreve rests more correctly comprehend two thirds of a perfect breve, a practice which contemporary musicians observe.

The minim rest is a stem attached to a line ascending to the middle of the neighboring space. I call the space or interval a distance or an incomposite vacancy of two lines, for this rest possesses a mensurable quantity of half of a semibreve.[19] Frequently this rest possesses a mensurable quantity of one third of the semibreve since, to be sure, perfect prolation governs the semibreve itself. But if you care to rest for two thirds of this semibreve, musicians agree that two contiguous minim rests should be written. Indeed, in this case it is easy to see that a semibreve note and its rest are resolvable into three minims. This is ascribed to perfect prolation. Likewise with those two semibreve rests in a contiguous arrangement, singers immediately recognize that the breves exist in accord with that ternary division which belongs to perfect time.

More recent musicians write the seminim rest, which was unknown to ancient musicians, as a minim rest ascending with the tip bent to the right. This has half the duration of a minim. However, the semiminim rest, a character which no composer uses, would have to be formed just like an ascending minim with the tip bent to the left. This possesses half the duration of a seminim rest.

Indeed, it is clear that in the consideration of notational characters, the left side is inferior to the right, for when you attach a stem to a square breve note on its right side, descending or ascending, you will observe in that spot the clearly defined long, but if the stem adheres to its left side, descending or ascending, a breve or semibreve will result.

19. Thus the analogy is made from the incomposite minim rest to an incomposite interval of a second. Presumably Gafurius would regard a semibreve rest as composite in the same way that a composite third is made up of two incomposite seconds.

These, therefore, are the written forms of these rests:

| Perfect | Imperfect | Breve | Semi- | Minim | Seminim | Semiminim |
| Long | Long | | breve | | | |

Chapter seven   Mode

Mode is the rule or the order of a quantity in a long that is assigned when the whole long is divided into its neighboring components. Some say, however, that mode is the measurement of breves in longs and of longs in maximas. As in other things also, mode is always to be observed in notes according to the measure of time and the number of the notes themselves. Some think that this word "mode" derives from "measured modulation." Others believe it comes from "measuring off," since it produces diverse modal movements by the varied treatment of units of time. I understand units of time as breve notes. In fact, it was mentioned earlier that in poetic theory a long is equal to two breves.

Thus since duality is an even and feminine number, as Pythagoras believed, the binary conception of notes was regarded as imperfect but the ternary and masculine as perfect, for males excel females in the state of perfection. Therefore, the mode is imperfect when a long contains only two units of time or two breves. Ancient writers of music used to represent imperfect mode by means of two points imprinted in a quadrangular figure, as follows: ⊡ . The mode is perfect, however, when there are three breves accommodated in the long. It was designated as follows, with three dots arranged in a square: ⊡ .

More recent writers call this treatment of the long the minor mode in comparison with mode when it occurs in the maxima. On the other hand, the ancients postulated a single mode—that is, of both the maxima and the long—as if when perfection is computed one cannot be constituted without the other. Later musicians decided that in the perfect minor mode, for the sake of ease and convenience, a rest of three units of time, which is present in the long, must be placed at the head of the piece, as a reminder, so to speak, that three breves are contained in a long. They say, however, that the imperfect mode of the long is shown merely by the representation of this long note all by itself.

Every long note belongs to some minor mode. They assign it to the perfect minor mode if the sign of perfection, that is, a rest of three units of time, precedes it. But with the sign lacking, as if the treatment occurred by depriving it of its dress—dress being more seemly and more perfect than deprivation of dress—they wished this long to belong to the minor imperfect mode, conferring only two breves upon it.

They wished the major mode to be contained in the double-long note, which they believed to be imperfect because the double long comprehends only two longs. Since no sign of perfection is attached to it, this character, in fact, is named the maxima of the major imperfect mode. With two rests of three units of time added, which we have called perfect long rests, they decided that the major perfect mode is present in the maxima note.

It was certainly not incongruous to designate the minor perfect mode with a single rest of three units of time and then put down two such rests for the recognition of major perfect mode; for two are greater in quantity and temporal measure than one and necessarily indicate a mode larger than the one which a single rest alone indicates. Moreover, the maxima itself contains three longs. If such a long contains three breves, the maxima will accommodate nine breves or units of time. All musicians agree, according to Anselm, that at the most nine units of time of this type can be contained in one character; this is a duration which a singer can hardly exceed in one breath.

It is clear that the ternary arrangement of longs is a combination of a ninefold formation of its units of time with very definite evidence of perfection. For the number 3 is the first side of oddness, which, multiplied by itself, results in its own odd square, that is, the number 9. If you divide this by 3, it is at once converted into 3's. Not without justification did Ausonius with incredible excellence describe such a ternary treatment to Symmachus in *A Riddle Of The Number Three.*[20] In his mass *Dixerunt discipuli* Eloy, most learned on the modes, signified the major perfect mode with those two rests of perfect longs, and further, indicated perfec-

---

20. A discussion of this riddle occurs in one of a series of epistles written by the Gallic poet Decimus Magnus Ausonius (c. 310–94 A.D.). See *Ausonius,* XVI, tr. Hugh G. Evelyn White (Loeb Classical Library, 1919), I, 359–69. Much esteemed by his contemporaries, as well as by his correspondent, the prefect Symmachus, Ausonius became a Roman prefect in 378 and under Gratian attained the consulship the following year.

tion of the minor mode by means of a single rest of three units of time.[21] Dunstable also used these rests in the same way in his tenor "Veni sancte spiritus," as follows:[22]

Many composers are accustomed to write these long rests as essential and indicial in compositions. I say the rests are essential when there are as many breves to be omitted among the notes of another part (for example,

21. Eloy d'Amerval was a French poet and composer, a contemporary of Josquin. His mass, scored *a 5* and based on the antiphon, "Dixerunt discipuli," (*Liber usualis* [Tournai, 1939], p. 1748), is noteworthy for its polytextual technique. See Gustave Reese, *Music in the Renaissance* (New York, 1954), p. 263.

22. The three-note ligature in this Dunstable excerpt presents a somewhat unusual problem in mensuration. If numerical values of 1-1-3 are assigned to the respective notes of the breve-breve-long combination, the values are transformed into 1-2-6 by two successive alterations. First, the value of the second breve is doubled in order to attain a ternary perfection in conjunction with the first breve. Then, the two breves, having jointly achieved a state of perfection, compel alteration of the long following, thereby consummating a second, all-embracing perfection of the entire ligature. See Willi Apel, *The Notation of Polyphonic Music, 900–1600* (Cambridge, Mass., 1942), p. 124, where this ligature is shown in the original, black notation of the Old Hall MS. For a transcription of the entire four-part isorhythmic motet which Gafurius cites, see John Dunstable, *Complete Works,* tr. and ed. Manfred F. Bukofzer (*Musica Britannica,* VIII; London, 1953), pp. 88–89.

Dr. Andrew Hughes, whose edition of the Old Hall MS. is in press as part of the A.I.M. CMM series, has kindly pointed out that the B-flat key signature in the Dunstable excerpt as presented by Gafurius as well as the particular arrangement of the three long rests do not occur in any sources of the Dunstable motet known to him. Professor Hughes suggests that "we may postulate a different source known to Gafurius and not to us." It is possible also that Gafurius edited the excerpt when he was preparing the *Practica.*

Gafurius' purpose here was to demonstrate the double function of three long rests placed at the head of a composition; that is, to show that they indicate the major perfect mode and that they are essential, ordinary rests in their own right.

the highest part) as there are incomposite spaces between the lines of these rests. I say the rests are indicative, however, when two such long rests signify the perfect major mode or when a single one signifies perfect minor mode. This is manifestly demonstrated in the tenor part quoted above, "Veni sancte spiritus." Generally, moreover, the rests that are not figured in are set down as indicative only, when, that is, they precede a sign of tempus—namely, a circle or semicircle written at the beginning of a composition. For, in that case, those two rests of three units of time merely announce the major perfect mode; a third rest would announce the minor. Tinctoris also shows this in the tenor of his motet "Magistralis."[23] He has proved adeptly that he delights to compose other difficult songs, and it does not matter that these three rests are drawn together within the same spaces of the lines or in different ones. Further, indicative or incommensurable rests of this type are written down in this tenor, as follows:

23. Two motets by Tinctoris are extant—"O virgo miserere" and "Virgo dei throno"—and may be seen in the Mellon Chansonnier (46v–47r, 154v–155r) in the Yale University Library. Neither shows this type of time signature. Tinctoris' motet "Magistralis" is presumed to be missing.

Anyone will readily see the quantities of all the maximas and longs to be considered in any mode whatever in this very clear example:

Chapter eight   Tempus

Musicians have wished tempus to be understood as the quantity ascribed to breve notes. Tempus is twofold: perfect and imperfect. Perfect tempus ascribes three semibreves to a breve note, and this is indicated by means of a circle written at the beginning of a composition. Musicians believe that by the use of a circle, a ternary, perfect division of this breve is indicated, for within its circumference beginning, middle, and end are present as equals. Another reason, which is more pleasing to me, is that in the number 6, which is perfect, that well-known, spherical, circular circumference is recognized to be produced naturally in accordance with its distance from the midpoint, which they call the center. If the center is distant from the circumference by only a finger's breadth, then that circumference will be measured by a quantity of six fingers. Hence mathematicians call the compass itself a sextant.

There are also those who show the perfect ternary division in breve notes, by means of two rests of semibreve value written at the beginning of a composition. To be sure, they count these in together with the other subsequent notes, as follows:

One can readily perceive by this that a rest of one breve, divisible into three equal parts, belongs to perfect tempus, and that its two semibreve rests are thirds of it. But when one happens to arrange two semibreve rests of imperfect tempus, many assert that a single breve rest is more appropriate, unless, I add, one of the two preceding semibreve rests was figured in with an antecedent [semibreve note] and the other with a subsequent one, and conversely. Some also see a perfect division of tempus in music in three blackened breve notes, that is, accidentally imperfect by virtue of the coloration.

Imperfect tempus, however, separates a breve note into two semibreves, for they derived "semibreve" from *semis,* which is half, and "breve" on the grounds that it produces one half the value of the breve.

Further, employment of a semicircle signifies such a binary resolution of breves in music. Nor should you regard this semicircle as a half circle but rather as an imperfect circle, for it represents an imperfect half. With this semicircle they wished to express imperfect tempus in breve notes, not, certainly, to confer on each single breve note one half the quantity of perfect tempus, which is a semibreve plus a half, but rather two thirds of this perfect tempus like an imperfect division of tempus. To be sure, one can observe this fact mathematically, because this semicircle governs precisely two thirds of the circumference of the circle. This is shown most effectively by the figure of an equilateral triangle inscribed within the circumference of a circle, in this way: ⊖. It is true that writers and copyists of songs are not accustomed to notice this, since they draw this semicircle in a size either equal to, more than, or less than half the circle. Illustrations of perfect and imperfect tempus are set down quite clearly in this example:

Moreover, they err who call a semibreve of imperfect tempus major because it comprehends half of a breve, and who regard as minor that part which contains a third of a perfect breve since each semibreve figured in the same prolation is always equal to another semibreve. And it is not inconsistent, since the one possesses half and the other a third of a breve note, because these breves are arranged in dissimilar quantity. Several authorities, however, strongly maintain that perfect and imperfect quantities of these notes are expressed with the characters of the numbers 3 and 2, with a circle preceding the numerals when it is perfect in numerosity or with a semicircle if it is imperfect.[24] Subsequently, they treated the rest of

24. The signs for perfect and imperfect tempus are indicated by *O*'s and *C*'s, respectively, in the text which follows.

the perfects with the character 3, the imperfects with the character 2. If the composition were in perfect major mode made up of both the perfect minor mode and perfect tempus, it would be recognized by the signature O33. If, however, the composition is in perfect major mode together with imperfect minor mode and perfect tempus, it appears this way: O23. Furthermore, perfect major mode and perfect minor mode and imperfect tempus is indicated by the signature O32. But when they score a composition in imperfect major mode and in perfect minor mode and imperfect tempus, they set this signature before the music: C32. If, however, it is in the imperfect major mode together with the imperfect minor mode and perfect tempus, they write this signature: C23. In this way they variously write individual signatures for the individual quantities of the notes.

When they set down only two signs, they wished minor mode and tempus to be understood, as for example, the perfect minor mode and perfect tempus in this way: O3, and perfect minor mode and imperfect tempus in this way: O2. There are also those who not only indicate perfect or imperfect tempus by the characters of the numbers 3 or 2, but treat even sesquialter or duple proportion in semibreves. In the same way they show imperfect minor mode and imperfect tempus with the two signs C2, and imperfect minor mode and perfect tempus as C3. But we think we should censor these signatures for the above-mentioned quantities since, in the words of the Philosopher, "it is useless to do by means of more what can be done with fewer." If the perfect major mode is distinguished from the imperfect by means of a single sign, that is, by two rests of three units of time, the imperfect mode is shown with no sign at all, but only by its note. By the same token the minor perfect mode is shown by means of a single sign, namely, by a single rest of three units of time, like a kind of dress. The imperfect, as if by deprivation, is treated by nothing but a representation of only its own note. It is clear that the different characters ought to stand, not for different quantities of the same name, but rather only for the perfect modes. Hence it is that since ancient and modern musicians assigned a circle and semicircle to perfect and imperfect tempus, we segregate them from the modes in our discussion.

Again, some believe, without justification, that the characters 3 and 2 produce sesquialter and duple proportion. In order to remove all doubt, I dissent from this in Book IV, Chapter 1, on logical grounds. I regard duple and sesquialter proportion as alien to the quantities of minor mode or tempus. Further, musicians desired that the perfect quantities of the notes, written down in a certain continuous quantity, be indicated in accord with geometric principle. For the point, circle, and line are the first and fore-most concepts in geometry. Since a point is the smallest thing and the be-ginning of a continuous quantity—just as unity is among numbers and a sound is in music—and since a circle and line are formed by the aggrega-tion of points, the point is known to signify a certain power of perfection in continuity, for, as was brought out in Chapter 3, each thing is perfected by the least of its genus. Hence, in order to indicate the perfect quantity of smaller notes, which they call prolation, musicians have themselves de-cided that it should be represented by means of a character for each unit of time. To the circle, since it is a perfect figure, they assigned perfect tempus, as was said, in breves. Then it became traditional to compute the perfect minor mode in longs by means of the rest of three spaces hereto-fore explained. Finally they show the perfect quantity of maximas mathe-matically by means of two rests of three spaces, since the major mode is contained therein.

Chapter nine   Prolation

Prolation is the essential quantity allotted to semibreves showing the division of the whole into its nearest parts. It preserves a partition quite similar to the other essential quantities. One kind of prolation pro-vides for a ternary division of the semibreve into three minims. This is called perfect prolation. The other kind of prolation is binary, whereby only two minims are assigned to each semibreve. They call this division imperfect.

There are some who call such a ternary, perfect prolation major and binary prolation minor. I do not like this since both prolations would be considered as belonging to a single note, that is, to the semibreve. One semibreve is not dissimilar to another semibreve, as the maxima, for in-stance, is to the long. In the long and maxima the major and minor modes are recognized to exist separately. Nevertheless, it pleased several of the ancients to assign such major and minor prolation to semibreves and min-ims respectively. They wrote major prolation in semibreves divisible into minims and minor prolation in minims divisible into seminims. They wrote the minim in three equal figurable parts, as Anselm shows.[25] They called prolation major when it was constituted in semibreves and ascribed minor prolation to minims. Modern musicians, however, have omitted the ternary division of the minim and write the minim and its particles in a binary division only.

It was customary to show perfect prolation by a point inscribed within the sign of tempus. Imperfect prolation, lacking such a point, is easily recognizable. Several authors have been accustomed to express perfect prolation by means of two contiguous minim rests counted in with the notes of the composition. There are also those who hold that a point of division placed before or after a minim note, or between two minims, is a sign of perfect prolation; that since it applies the minim, to which it is attached, to the nearest semibreve, the minim note must be figured in ternary division when computing perfect prolation. But even if such a point does indicate a ternary computation of minims, still the number 3 is generally affixed to minims in perfect prolation, so that that point of division would not be necessary to indicate a ternary computation.

For example, when I arrange three semibreves or three minims in a composition—remembering that in perfect prolation every semibreve contains three minims—and when these three minims are computed together, a point of division is certainly not needed in that place. Therefore, if a perfect semibreve were the best and only sign of perfect prolation, the point of division would be inadmissible. It is not sensible to use a sign that stands for one thing in front of another sign that stands for the same thing.

Thus it is clear that a point placed inside the sign of tempus has been assigned by authorities to perfect prolation; the point without the sign of tempus still indicates prolation.

One can readily understand that neither the major mode without the minor nor the minor mode without tempus can occur in composition. Therefore these signs show the perfection of both mode and prolation, as though they were garments. When those signs are omitted, the notes by themselves bring imperfection into effect.

Otherwise, perfect and imperfect tempus are customarily indicated by means of a circle and semicircle respectively, so that perfect prolation can be notated by means of a point inside either one. Prolations of this type are demonstrated by these examples:

25. *De musica,* III (Massera ed., p. 170).

Chapter ten   The Parts of Notes

Of the parts of notes, one is called an adjacent part, one a remote part, one more remote, one most remote. The adjacent part is that note into which the whole is reduced first of all, as a long with respect to a maxima, a breve with respect to a long, a semibreve with respect to a breve, and a minim with respect to a semibreve. A remote part is that note between which and its whole a single intervening note falls in natural order, such as a breve with respect to a maxima, between which only a long resides, or a semibreve with respect to a long, between which only a breve is interposed, or a minim with respect to a breve, which only a semibreve intercepts. The more remote part is the note between which and its whole two larger notes are arranged in natural order, as a semibreve with respect to a maxima, which, if a frame is imagined, enclose a long and a breve in between. The most remote part is that between which and its whole three larger notes naturally reside, as, for example, a minim with respect to a maxima, between which a long, breve, and semibreve fall in natural sequence.

The same principle is also applicable to subdivisions of the minim and its individual notes. From such a standpoint it is clear that the maxima note is always the whole and the diesis always the partial, and the other six notes—long, breve, semibreve, minim, seminim, and semiminim—wholes and partials. But since those three diminished notes [seminim, semiminim, and diesis], subdivisions of the minim, do not admit of a ternary division, we propose no smaller note beyond the minim for imperfectible

treatment. According to modern writers the minim concludes ternary division. Thus accidents are ascribed only to the first five notes in mensural
music.

Chapter eleven   The Imperfection of Notes

With respect to the imperfection of notes one is passive only, one
active only, and some are both passive and active.

The only passive note is the maxima. Although this note can be imperfected in many ways by different notes, it never imperfects any note, for
on no occasion does it precede or follow in music a note larger in quantity
than itself to which it can be applied as an imperfecting third part.

Two things must be noticed in general. First, an imperfecting note will
always be smaller than the note it imperfects. Secondly, the note to be
imperfected must always be considered in its perfect numerical quantity,
or at least, the part of it that is imperfected must always be considered in
its perfect numerical quantity. Anselm, in Book III of his *Musica,* grasped
this very well in a sentence which reads: "Furthermore, the quantity of
withdrawal is a third of the value denoted by the note from which it is
subtracted because these notes establish a ternary division of the measure."[26]

Imperfection, therefore, is a reduction, at most, of one third of the
whole in accordance with its ternary arrangement, which I have previously
considered in this volume.

When notes are arranged in music according to a binary and imperfect
quantitative computation, however, musicians generally adorn them with
a certain point of augmentation. Because of this point of augmentation,
the quantity of each single note increases by half. Hence they acquire a
ternary division which makes them equal to perfection itself.

One note, the minim, is active only. Even though it may imperfect other
notes—semibreves in perfect prolation, for example—yet, because it does
not itself permit a ternary division of its own quantity, the minim can
never be imperfected by another note.

26. Massera ed., p. 174.

A note which can both imperfect and be imperfected is both active and passive. There are three such notes: the long, breve, and semibreve. Each of these notes can imperfect a larger note and can, in turn, be imperfected by a smaller. Every imperfectible note can be imperfected either by a part preceding only, by a part following only, or in both directions. Thus a note having a third part that cannot be divided into three equal parts—a semibreve of perfect prolation, for example, whose third part is a minim not susceptible to ternary resolution—can be imperfected by one part only.

Moreover, every note which is imperfected by the detachment of its abstracted third part is said to be imperfected as to the whole. But when it is imperfected through the reduction of an abstracted third of its adjacent part, it is said to be imperfected as to the adjacent part by its remote part. In the same way a note can be imperfected by a more remote part as to its remote part and by a part most removed as to its more remote part, as, for example, a maxima note by a minim in perfect prolation.

To make a generalization: musicians have maintained that every note preceding one like itself and arranged in perfect quantity is always perfect and can never be imperfected by reason of the reduction of an abstracted part. The imperfectible note, therefore, will necessarily be written in front of a larger or smaller note.

There are, moreover, three things that show an imperfectible note to be imperfect: numerical imperfection, division by a point, and the coloration of notes. As to the first sign of imperfection: however often smaller notes are written, before or after a larger note, in a number less than or more than three, so often is the larger note imperfected by the smaller note nearest it (unless this note was previously reduced by others) or by the nearer remote or more remote parts, or by both adjacent and remote parts, and so on in various ways, as is clear in this tenor:[27]

27. This is the first of thirteen polyphonic examples appropriated by Glarean for use in his *Dodekachordon*, this example appearing in III.ix.208 (Basel, 1547; Microcard facsim., Sibley Library, Rochester, New York). Unless otherwise indicated, all references hereinafter are to this edition.

Unlike others, the Swiss scholar graciously acknowledged his source. Glarean remarks: "I know that many excellent men of our time have written about the adage [from Dorian to Phrygian], among whom, however, two must be especially revered, whom I never mention without prefatory remarks of esteem, namely Franchinus and D. Erasmus of Rotterdam, the former my teacher through the written word, the latter through the spoken word, [to] whom I confess to be under as great an obligation as anyone whatever!" (*Dodecachordon*, tr. Clement A. Miller [American Institute of Musicology, 1966], II, 129).

In this tenor, as is apparent, the first breve imperfects the following long by a part preceding as to the whole because it is its adjacent third part. The first semibreve imperfects the preceding breve by a part following as

to the whole. Moreover, the two minims situated between the breve and
the long imperfect the breve by a following part as to the whole, which,
even if its parts are remote, since they are equivalent to its adjacent part,
are recognized to produce the effect of a single adjacent part. The long
following both those minims is imperfected by the first breve as to the
whole by a following part. The first breve at the sign of perfect tempus
and perfect prolation is imperfected by a part following as to the whole,
that is, by the adjacent part, and also as to its part, by a remote part, to be
sure, which is one third of that adjacent part.

Further, an imperfectible note can be imperfected by a part preceding
and a part following at the same time—that is, when only one third of its
adjacent part is in front of it, similarly, one third of another adjacent part
follows after it. Then it is said to be imperfected as to the parts. Thus, according to the method of musicians, these notes can be imperfected in
several ways, as is clearly proved by this tenor:[28]

28. Glarean, *Dodekachordon*, III.ix.209.

In the tenor above, the first semibreve imperfects the following long by a part preceding as to the adjacent part, for that semibreve is a third of the adjacent part of the long. The following semibreve likewise imperfects that long by a part following as to the adjacent part of the long. The first breve, which is written at the sign of perfect tempus and perfect prolation, is handled in the same way, for it is revealed to be imperfected by its remote parts, namely minims, as to the two adjacent parts, both by a part preceding and a part following. The first of the two longs in the ligature is not imperfected because "a note before one like itself cannot be imperfected." The second long is imperfected by a part following as to the whole, that is, by the adjacent part, which is the breve. That imperfecting breve is also imperfected by the subsequent semibreve as to the whole.

Again, it must be borne in mind that "a note before one like itself can never be imperfected." This rule applies to like notes which are separated by another note in between them and which are also entities, but not to units within a whole, since notes which are units—two breves of perfect tempus, for example, considered within a long of the imperfect minor mode—can then be imperfected even in a case where there is a breve before a breve. This happens when a note is imperfected as to both parts, by a part preceding and by a part following, as is clear in the long of the tenor above, which is diminished by a part preceding and a part following by two semibreves that are abstracted. It also occurs in the breve of perfect tempus and perfect prolation, which is imperfected by those two surrounding minims. For if a like note preceding one like itself and considered as a unit could not be imperfected, there would never be a note imperfectible by a part preceding as to its adjacent part or as to its remote part, a fact which anyone can readily observe for himself.

Moreover, a single minim must not be permitted to imperfect another note except in a setting of perfect prolation. Gulielmus de Mascandio[29]

___

29. Mascandio or Mascaudio are versions of the name of Guillaume de Machaut (c. 1300–1377). Machaut's improper use of a minim to imperfect a breve of perfect tempus and imperfect prolation was first brought to light by Johannes de Muris, his

arranged a breve of perfect tempus and imperfect prolation imperfected
by a single minim, but this is absurd, for a note is customarily imperfected
either (1) by its third part, as, for example, a long of minor perfect mode
by a breve, or (2) by one third of its half, as, for example, a long of imperfect mode and perfect tempus by a semibreve, or (3) by a third of its third
part, as, for example, a breve of perfect tempus and perfect prolation by
a single minim.

There are also those who think a breve of perfect tempus and perfect
prolation may be imperfected by two minims, sometimes preceding, sometimes following, either way. But unless these two minims imperfect the
aforementioned contiguous breve as to the whole—of which these minims,
by alteration of the second minim, are the third adjacent part—as occurs
in the following tenor and in many compositions, it is not permitted. Nor
is it permitted—because it is in little use—unless the first minim imperfects the first single semibreve and the second minim imperfects the third
unit semibreve by abstraction.

When a note that is divisible into three ternary parts is imperfected by
a part preceding and by a part following by remote parts as to the adjacent parts, then it is claimed that the first unit adjacent part is imperfected
by a part preceding as to the whole and the third unit adjacent part by a
part following. But the second such unit retains its perfection, a situation
which can be seen in the first long of the preceding tenor surrounded by
the two semibreves.

But if its two remote parts precede this kind of note, which is divisible
into three adjacent thirds, and one remote part follows it, then it is said to
be imperfected as to all its adjacent parts. For example, when there are
two minims in front of a breve of perfect tempus and perfect prolation
and a single minim follows, then the first of the two minims imperfects
the breve as to the first adjacent part, the second as to the second, and
the minim following imperfects that breve as to the adjacent third part.
I add that if the two preceding minims imperfect as to the whole that
breve whose third part they are, through alteration of the second minim,
then the following minim will imperfect that breve as to the adjacent third

compatriot and contemporary. In Gafurius' *Glossemata* (see n. 14, Book II, above)
the section on alteration, based on Part Two of de Muris' *Ars nova musicae,* discloses
a rubric consisting of the name Gulielmus de Mascandio and a freehand drawing of a
hand with a disproportionately long index finger pointing graphically to the error.
Had de Muris been the transgressor he would have amplified the rubric to include an
hoc falsum est or some equivalently terse note of reprobation.

by a part following and the second adjacent part is perfect. Thus, by such a reduction, that breve, containing nine minims in its entirety, relinquishes four minims of its normal value.

By a similar consideration several authorities agree that the larger note is diminished by one third of itself, which they call imperfect as to the whole, then also by a third of the adjacent part, that is, as to the part, and also again by a third of the second adjacent part as to that part. Moreover, they imperfect it as to the remote parts in such a way that a part larger and greater than half the quantity of that note is withdrawn by reason of this imperfection. For example, if I abstract a perfect breve from a long in perfect minor mode, perfect tempus, and perfect prolation, which contains twenty-seven minims, then of course I abstract a third part of it, taking away nine minims. Then I abstract a semibreve, or a third of its adjacent part computed in three minims, and again the other semibreve, a third of the other adjacent part embracing three minims. Here too, I abstract four minims from those four remaining semibreves, so that out of the twenty-seven minims which that whole long rightfully contains, nineteen would be taken away by the abstraction of reducible parts. An example of such complicated imperfection, however, has hardly come forth into light and practice, and we maintain that it is better avoided than employed, because imperfection is the abstraction of one third of the whole or less, and a third which must then be applied in order to make up a ternary division of quantity.

Nature leads to this result: that when we remove a third of any total, two parts remain. Therefore, every note in its perfect quantity—arranged, that is, in a ternary aggregation of its related parts—if it is imperfected by the abstraction of one third, must necessarily exist imperfect and adhere to a binary division as though it were a substitute for an imperfect quantity.

An imperfect note, however, divisible into only two perfect adjacent parts, is said to be imperfected as to both parts by a part preceding and by a part following—that is, when one remote part has preceded it and one has followed it. Likewise, when two remote parts that imperfect a note not only precede it but also at the same time follow it, whether they appear as simple and disjunct or as ligatures, the first imperfects the first imperfectible part, the second the second. This is a fact which many writers profess in compositional notation, and it can be very clearly observed from the tenor given here:

In this tenor the first long is imperfected by a part following as to both adjacent parts by the two ligatured semibreves that follow. The first of these semibreves imperfects the first unit breve by a part following, and the second semibreve imperfects the second unit breve. The second long is imperfected by a part preceding as to both its adjacent parts by the two preceding semibreves. The first of these imperfects the first unit breve by a part preceding, the second the second. The third long is imperfected by a part preceding and by a part following as to both its adjacent parts, for the preceding semibreve imperfects the first unit breve by a part preceding, and the following semibreve serves to imperfect the second unit breve by a part following. The fourth long is perfect as to both its adjacent parts because it stands in front of one like itself that is not a unit, although it belongs to the imperfect minor mode. The fifth long is imperfected by a part following as to both its adjacent parts joined together, by a semibreve and the two following minims. The first semibreve imperfects the first conjunct breve by a part following, and the two minims, which add up to the value of a semibreve, imperfect the second unit breve similarly by a part following. But the first breve that follows the sign of imperfect tempus and perfect prolation is imperfected by a part preceding and by a part following as to both its adjacent unit parts. It is clear that the first of these unit parts is imperfected by a part preceding, the second by a part following. Furthermore, the following breve is imperfected only by a part following as to both parts by the two subsequent minims, the first of which imperfects the first unit part and the second of which imperfects the second by a part following.

As to the second sign of imperfection. Whenever a point of division is placed next to some note, whether for its own sake only or for itself and another or others, then that note imperfects the preceding or following larger note, if it can be imperfected. This is shown in this tenor:

In this tenor the third breve is imperfected by a part following as to its whole. The point of division placed after the first semibreve indicates this. That the fourth breve is imperfected by a part preceding as to the whole is clearly indicated by the point of division placed before the two minims that precede it. But the point of division that is written between the two semibreves inserted between the final breves indicates that the fifth breve is imperfected by a part following and the sixth breve by a part preceding. If, however, the larger note preceding or following the smaller note to which the point has been added is not subject to imperfection, then the smaller note is led back or transferred to the first note, where it can be applied in the regular way as a ternary factor.

The same interpretation also holds when a smaller note without a point precedes a larger note which cannot be imperfected. In such a case this smaller note will be transferred in order to perfect a previous place by ternary computation. This is shown in the tenor example here:

In this tenor the point placed between the third and fourth semibreves shows that the fourth semibreve must be figured with the third breve of the following ligature. This is because it can be added neither to the first nor to the second note on the ground that a like note before one like itself cannot be imperfected, as has been explained. For the same reason, the semibreve that precedes the final three disjunct breves without a point is escorted to and imperfects the third breve.

The same interpretation will also be made when a point of division is added to some breve in relation to longs in the perfect minor mode, and to some long in relation to maximas in the perfect major mode, and also to some minim with respect to semibreves in perfect prolation. If any of these notes occur without a point, they must be conducted to more distant notes that are receptive to such imperfection.

What should be said when four semibreves have been arranged between two breves of perfect tempus? I say that according to the ancients the first of these semibreves is transferable and must be counted in with the preceding breve which it imperfects by a part following as to the whole. This is especially true when the breve following the four semibreves is perfect, that is, when it is punctuated by a point of perfection or situated before a note like itself. Otherwise, if that breve is imperfectible (that is, if it can be imperfected) then the first breve preceding the four semibreves will be perfect on its own account, and the fourth semibreve will imperfect the following breve by a part preceding as to the whole. Nevertheless, for the purpose of removing doubt, I recommend that such a preceding breve, perfect on its own account, ought to be written with a point of perfection, unless a point of division is placed between the third and fourth semibreves. The example of the tenor here proves this point:

In this tenor the first breve is imperfected by the first semibreve because the second breve cannot be imperfected. The third breve is imperfected by a part following as to the whole by the first semibreve following it. The fourth breve is perfect. The fifth breve is imperfected by a part preceding as to the whole by the semibreve just before it. The sixth breve is perfect because it is in front of one like itself. The seventh breve is perfect, written with a point of perfection. The eighth breve is imperfected by a part preceding as to the whole by the preceding semibreve. The ninth breve is perfect because it stands in front of one like itself. The tenth breve is perfect because three semibreves taken between that breve and the point of division follow it in ternary purity. The last breve is imperfected by a part preceding as to the whole by the semibreve preceding it; the point of division placed before that semibreve indicates this.

The same interpretation must be observed in regard to four minims which are interposed between two semibreves of perfect prolation, and in regard to four breves written between two longs of the perfect minor mode. If, however, a single minim and one semibreve follow immediately upon a breve of perfect tempus and imperfect prolation, then that breve cannot be imperfected as to the whole by its adjacent third part which follows it immediately because that adjacent following part, a semibreve quantity, to be sure, is separated into dissimilar parts incapable of union, namely, into a minim and a half of the following semibreve [*i.e.,* a minim here equals a half rather than a third of a semibreve]. The tenor here shows this:

As to the third sign of imperfection [coloration]. Whenever a note in a perfect, ternary accumulation of quantity is filled in, it is imperfected by one third of its normal value, and its third part, similarly blackened, must follow. The coloration of the second note confirms the single reduction that is being made. It does not matter whether the one third that is reducible precedes or follows the larger note, which is, so to speak, its whole, immediately or mediately, provided that, for the sake of perfecting the numerical relationship, the reduction is redirected to that larger note. The smaller part is always referred to the larger part as if to its own whole. This is perceived in the tenor part here:[30]

30. Glarean, *Dodekachordon*, III.ix.210.

When three like notes are colored, with one or another note intervening or one after the other, the first unit part of the second note is taken back to the first; the second is applied to the third subsequent note, a colored one, in order to complete the ternary division.

There are also those who color half the body of a long note. They regard the final breve which is included in it to be imperfect by its subsequent third part. Even if it has an empty space in part of its area and is colored in another, still in my opinion that long should not be allowed to signify this, because the state of being empty and the state of being filled in are by nature wondrously antipathetic to each other. They do not show one and the same thing. I would prefer that both of these breves, the empty and the colored one, be written with separate bodies. Nevertheless, this matter does not require the most abstruse argument because in the opinion of composers it is very evident indeed that these are related to each other.

In addition, notes which have been set down indicating imperfect quantity are generally written filled in. Musicians are wont to make them equal to sesquialteral diminution, as will be described in Book IV, where sesquialter proportion is discussed quite fully. But if a single such note or only two of them are written in this coloration, they are lessened by half their normal quantity as though they are in a primary or duple proportion. My teacher, Bonadies, proposed this, and it is a rational approach.[31]

It was the practice among ancient musicians, furthermore, to write all notes consisting of essential quantities colored. The notes, however, which were imperfected accidentally they notated as empty.

Chapter twelve The Point

A point is the smallest, indivisible quantity of any continuum. We define the point more appropriately, however, as that certain smallest sign which is placed accidentally [as a nonessential property] either before, after, or between notes, the beginning of a continuous quantity indeed, just like the beginning of a line or a circle.

The point is twofold: there is a point of division and a point of perfection. The point of division is one which is placed either before or after some note and neither augments nor diminishes it, but rather indicates that it is to be applied to and counted in with a preceding note or a following note in order to perfect a ternary division among the notes. This happens, to be sure, in two ways, namely mediately [indirectly] or immediately [directly]. A note is said to be figured with and applied to a preceding or following note mediately by means of a point when this point, placed before or after any note, isolates the note. It is not to be figured in at all with the nearest note or with the notes preceding or following. It is fitting

31. Gafurius' teacher was the author of a *Regulae cantus* and some musical compositions, one of which, a "Kyrie," survives in the Bonadies codex, also known as the Faenza MS.117. The recently discovered Bonadies codex, besides being an important repertory of early fifteenth-century keyboard music, contains some later additions made by Bonadies in 1473 and 1474, assorted treatises by Hothby, Caserta, de Muris, and others, and some contemporary vocal compositions as well. See *An Early Fifteenth-Century Italian Source of Keyboard Music,* facsim. of the Codex Faenza, Biblioteca Comunale, 117, ed. Armen Carapetyan (American Institute of Musicology, 1961); and Dragan Plamenac, "Keyboard Music of the 14th Century in Codex Faenza 117," *Journal of the American Musicological Society,* IV (1951), 180–201.

that this be called a point of transportation or transposition, since it trans-
ports the note to which it is attached to be counted in with notes farther
away. It is said, however, to apply immediately when the note itself to
which the point has been added is counted in with the nearest note or
notes. I call this properly a point of division. It is shown in this tenor:[32]

In this tenor the point added after the first semibreve subsequent to the
first breve indicates that that semibreve must be applied to the breve in
order to perfect the temporal quantity. But the point in front of the semibreve immediately preceding the second breve causes that semibreve to be
figured in with the second breve in order to perfect the ternary division of
time. The point placed in front of that semibreve which immediately precedes the three breves in consecutive order, however, shows that that
semibreve must be transferred to the last of these breves and that it has to
be counted in with that last breve in order to perfect the ternary division
of time. The semibreve cannot be applied to the first breve or to the sec-

32. Glarean, *Dodekachordon,* III.iv.199.

ond breve, for a like note before one like itself cannot be imperfected. The point that is written between the two semibreves placed between the two breves, however, is a point of division and confirms that the first semibreve is to be applied to the first breve and the second semibreve to the second breve. It must also be noticed that a point of transportation requires that the note to which it is added must be transferred, not to the notes before, but to the notes after it—that is, to the first location it can get. There are some who encircle such a note that is to be transported with two points, one on each side, as is perceived in this tenor:

Accordingly, a point of division is applied only to notes set down in their perfect quantities. Hence, when it is added to a long, it will perfect the major mode; to a breve, the minor mode; to a semibreve, tempus; to a minim, prolation. Such a point, however, does not apply to a maxima because no larger note is written to which the maxima may be joined as a third constituent part.

The point of perfection is one which, when placed after some note, perfects it, rendering it divisible into three equal parts. This point, too, is con-

sidered in two ways. The first way occurs when it is applied to some note
which is arranged in its perfect quantity, for then even if it could be imperfected by a smaller note preceding or following it, the point causes the
note to continue in its own perfection, and therefore it is called a point of
perfection. The second way occurs when it is placed after some note which
has been arranged in its imperfect quantity, for then it is recognized to
augment that note by exactly half of its normal quantity. For this reason
they call it a point of augmentation. Since it embellishes the note with a
ternary division, making it equal to a perfect note, it presumes to claim
for itself a kind of perfection. Hence they also call it a point of perfection.
This is discerned in the accompanying tenor.[33]

In this tenor the point added to the first breve causes it to persist in its
perfection. If it were not perfected by the point, it could be imperfected
by a third of itself, that is, by the dotted minim plus the subsequent seminim. The point added to the third breve accomplishes the same thing.

33. Glarean, *Dodekachordon*, III.iv.200.

But the point added to the second breve at the sign of imperfect tempus causes its augmentation by half of its normal quantity, showing that it can be resolved into three equal parts. The point added to the third semibreve at the same sign effects the same thing, for it augments it by a full half of its normal quantity, making it subject to ternary division. For this reason it is said to be equivalent to a semibreve of perfect prolation.

The same result is obtained in respect to both maximas and longs when such a point is added. Arranged in their perfect quantity, the notes will maintain their own perfection; in imperfect quantity, however, they will undergo augmentation.

Generally the point both of division and augmentation is considered as one and the same thing. For example, when it is placed after a semibreve immediately following an imperfectible breve of perfect tempus, and directly thereafter a single minim and two semibreves follow in some combination or other, then this point both counts the semibreve in with the breve and also augments it by half of its value. Hence such a point is commonly called both a point of division and a point of augmentation.

Thus a point placed in front of notes can indicate division only, but placed after notes both division and perfection. There are some people with whose permission I would like to say this: a note embellished with a point of perfection cannot undergo perfection either of a third or of any other part of itself, since perfection and imperfection are mutually opposites, and the Philosopher does not permit opposites to coexist in the same subject.[34]

Chapter thirteen   Alteration

According to Johannes de Muris, alteration in mensural music is a doubling of the normal value in accordance with the type of note.[35] It is

34. Aristotle, *Topics,* II.vii, in *The Works of Aristotle,* tr. W. A. Pickard-Cambridge (Great Books of the Western World; Encyclopaedia Britannica, 1952), I, 158.

35. Except for a nominal change in word order, de Muris' definition is substantially the one which appears in Gafurius' *Glossemata,* II ("Sequitur practica musicae Joannis de Muris doctoris parisiensis") under the subheading "De Alteratione" (Ambrosian

called alteration as though it were the action of another. It occurs, to be
sure, among notes aranged in their perfect quantity, and also in imperfect
quantity when they are adjacent parts of their own perfect whole (a semibreve, for example, of imperfect prolation in perfect tempus and a breve
of imperfect tempus in the minor perfect mode, and so on).

A minim is altered in order to perfect the division of perfect prolation.
A semibreve is altered to perfect the division of perfect tempus. A breve
is altered to perfect the numerical integrity of the minor perfect mode.
The long is customarily altered to complete the ternary treatment of the
major perfect mode. However often only two minims are found between
two semibreves of perfect prolation or between two measured values of
these two semibreves—between two semibreve rests, for example, or between a semibreve and a rest, or between a rest and a semibreve—the
second minim is always altered so that it becomes equal to the value of
two minims, unless a point of division is placed between them. The same
thing occurs when two semibreves are surrounded by two breves of perfect tempus or by their [equivalent] quantities, or when two breves are
found written between two longs of the minor perfect mode or their quantities. Likewise, when two longs are written between two maximas of the
major perfect mode or between their figured quantities, the second is always altered, unless, as mentioned before, a point of division is interposed.
This is clearly shown in the tenor here:[36]

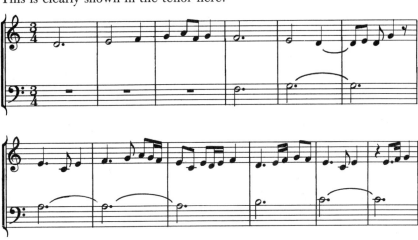

Library, Codex H 165 inf., f. 20r). In his *Tractatus alterationum* (Couss., IV, 66–70)
Tinctoris used an almost identical definition of alteration.

36. Glarean, *Dodekachordon*, III.x.212.

If, however, a particular rest and a note comparable in value are placed between two larger notes, as was said before, then either the rest precedes the note or the note precedes the rest. If the rest precedes the note, that note is altered. But if the note should precede the rest, no alteration occurs, since the second is always altered, and not the first, and a rest can by no means be altered.

Still there have been some who have imputed alteration to rests. Every school of musicians condemns this. There are two excellent reasons why alteration is assigned, not to the first of two notes, but to the second. The first reason is that in an interval of a sounding string divided into two equal quantities, the proportion will always be greater in the second part than in the first, as though out of deference to the ending, to which they are accustomed to ascribe the larger and more perfect part. Arithmetic mediation clearly proves this. When the undivided diapason interval is dissected on a chordotone into two equal differences [of the terms], the first, lower part will contain the epitrite fourth, the second the hemiola fifth [4:3:2].

The second reason is that the first of two such notes—semibreves, for example—can be changed into another form to the extent of taking on twice its normal value, for it can be denoted as a square note. Then it would be called a breve, to which the second semibreve might then be attached in order to complete the ternary division. Thus, it is better to write the breve note as a square when it is imperfected by a subsequent semibreve than to alter the first semibreve. The second such semibreve is altered because, in addition to the fact that it increases by twice its quantity, it cannot assume another shape. If the breve receives a square shape, it will be equal not only to the value of two but also of three semibreves, because then a like note before one like itself results, which cannot be imperfected. This is a fact which each individual singer can readily observe by himself.

It should also be noticed that when two like notes, simple or in ligature, imperfect some larger note as to both parts, the only parts into which that note is resolvable, they are not subjected to alteration; that is, the second of these is not altered. But if two smaller notes imperfect as to the whole the larger note, which is resolvable into three perfect or ternary parts of which they are a third, the second of these will then be altered, as is revealed in this example:

In the tenor shown here, the second semibreve following the first long is not altered because both these semibreves do not imperfect that long as to its whole like an adjacent part. This is because that long is in the imperfect minor mode. They imperfect it rather as to both parts. The second of these two semibreves, written before the two ligatured breves, is altered because the second is in between the value of a breve divided and a breve [undivided]. The second of those two minims immediately following the first breve at the sign of perfect tempus and perfect prolation is altered because both these minims imperfect the breve as to the whole, that is, as to a third of its ternary part, which is commonly called adjacent.

Finally, Johannes de Muris asserts that an altered note is imperfected by a part preceding.[37] We think this must be contradicted, since an altered note is never divisible into three parts, and it is true that a like note can never be imperfected by one like itself.

Chapter fourteen   Diminution

Diminution in mensural music is the abstraction of a certain quantitative value from the notes themselves. It is generally indicated by musicians in three ways. The first way is by canon, the second by proportion, the third by means of a short stroke.

Diminution is treated canonically when the values of notes decline and are changed in measurement according to a sentence of canonic rule that is written in—by this instruction, for example: "Let a maxima be a long, a long a breve," and so on. Then the maxima is removed in favor of a long, the long is discarded in favor of a breve, the breve in favor of a semibreve, the semibreve in favor of a minim. By this technique, diminution is customarily also accepted in a contrary sense, namely, by this canon: "Let a breve be a maxima, a semibreve a long, a minim a breve," and so on in various ways which are relegated to the arbitrary arrangement of musicians. But this type of diminution is improperly employed because it produces an effect of augmentation rather than of diminution. Hence we call diminution the variation of mensurable quantity in relation to the primary scheme of notes; or stated another way, at any rate, diminution is a variation of the normal, basic quantity dictated by the shape of the note.

Diminution is effected by proportion when it is constituted with appropriate numerical symbols signifying a definite proportion. This diminishes the notes themselves according to the design of the proportion that is set down. Again, this diminution is improperly employed when a proportion of minor inequality is obtained, for then, granted that the notes receive an augmentation of quantity, still it is customarily called diminution in a contrary sense, not unlike the case of the grove of the Grammarian which

37. Gafurius noted his censure of de Muris' assertion in the margin of the *Glossemata:* "Hoc falsum est quia similis [ante] similem imperfici not potest; nec potest ipsa imperfici quia non est divisibilis in tres aequas partes" (Ambrosian Library, Codex H 165 inf., f. 20v).

lacks light and the fishpond which is without fish.[38] We have assigned our fourth book, on mensural theory, to such proportional diminution.

Diminution set forth by a short stroke is shown in the accompanying illustration of mensural notes by means of a stroke cutting the sign of tempus. This is appropriate for proper temporal measurement but is not suitable for the notes themselves, for by such a sign the value itself is diminished, not the number of notes. A breve of perfect tempus, whether produced by diminution or in its original state, always contains three semibreves, and perfection is upheld. In the same way, too, a breve of imperfect tempus is known always to possess two semibreves, even if it is subjected to diminution, a fact which is noted in the example here:[39]

38. There is a pun between *lux* and *lucus* which does not come through in English translation. The Latin reads: "nec secus quam lucum grammatici quae luce careat . . . ," *lucum* referring to the grove in which the peripatetics held their classes. In this connection, the Aristotelian Theophrastus (see n. 13, Book I, above) left a will which was brought to light by the eccentric Greek philosopher, Diogenes, and which conveys the notion of the garden as an ancestor of the modern college. Classical scholars used to be associated with the groves in which they taught rather than with the lamp, with which we have symbolized professors since the Middle Ages— not unlike the Grammarian's Park in the dark.

39. Glarean, *Dodekachordon*, III.viii.206.

Since duple proportion is a more familiar technique and much easier than other proportions both in its division and performance, singers are more often accustomed to follow duple proportion more readily than they do diminution by a short stroke, which is its equivalent.

C*hapter fifteen*   Syncopation

Syncopation in mensural composition is the referral of a note back beyond its own larger note or notes to one or more other notes with which it belongs in counting.[40] Syncopation occurs in composition whenever the music proceeds by means of several notes in passages of diminshed note values considered together, no matter whether their quantitative arrangement is binary or ternary. This can be comprehended very clearly in this tenor:

40. As presented here, syncopation must be construed as the temporary displacement of normal binary or ternary patterns brought about by the intercalation of one or more larger note values or comparable rests. This concept thus suggests a dislocation in rhythmic continuity that is metrical rather than accentual in character. The smaller note values are "parts" related (as in Ch. 11, Book II, above) to the intervening larger notes. When more than one of these larger notes separates the normal group-

Composers are in agreement that a minim note must not be transferred beyond a breve rest by syncopation but only beyond a semibreve rest, and that rarely. Similarly, a semibreve note ought rarely to be transferred back beyond a breve rest and never beyond a long rest. They recommend that the other notes be treated in the same fashion. Still, many of the more recent composers of music disagree with this. Not only do they conduct a semibreve note beyond a breve rest by means of syncopation, but they even cause that same semibreve to be transferred by syncopation beyond a long rest, which is still more removed, making similar transferences for the other notes.

If some things which you perhaps believe are necessary both for ecclesiastical and mensural instruction seem to be omitted here, consider that this is done on purpose. I rely on the diligence of my readers—who, I believe, will ignore nothing which pertains to this discipline—to study my books industriously. It is difficult for things that are known not to be left out by people, of course, to whom the whole matter, or much of it, is very well known.

Book Two of *The Practice of Music*
by Franchinus Gaforus
felicitously ends here.

---

ings of its smaller notes, the "referral" [*reductio*] of the smaller note has the effect of reinstating, theoretically at least, the regular binary or ternary patterns. This is accomplished by the introduction of a point of division, specifically referred to in this instance as a "point of transportation" (see Ch. 12, Book II, above). It is interesting to note that the terms *transportatio, syncopatio,* and *reductio*—points of division—have been used interchangeably to signal the presence of syncopation.

BOOK THREE

OF *The Practice*
of Music

[THE
ART OF
COUNTERPOINT]

$\mathcal{C}$*hapter one*   Counterpoint and Its Basic Species

On the authority of Bacchius, the genus of harmonic music is a universal phenomenon exhibiting inner diversity and containing species[1] or forms of various musical combinations which we call counterpoint—the concordant harmony, as it were, of mutually related sounds set note against note, and vindicated in practice. Even if it is based on definite rules, yet counterpoint may be adjudged to be most beautiful to the degree that the use for which it has blossomed forth is the more noble. Counterpoint, therefore, is the art of manipulating musical sounds in proportionable dimension and temporal quantity, for music consists of pitches, intervals, and durations.

Now, one sound is prosaic, that is, the way in which we utter and deliver orations; one sound is prosodic, the way we recite poetry according to arsis and thesis; and another is modulated sound, which occurs when we perform something in harmony by means of natural voices or on instruments. These modulated sounds inhabit fixed intervals in fixed dimension; the prosaic sounds are undefined; while prosodic sounds are a kind of mixture, as it were, of both.

Some intervals—equisones [octaves]—are framed by their outer pitches in duple dimension; some—consones [fifths]—in *hemiola* [3:2] and [fourths] in *epitrita* [4:3] dimension; some are a mixture of both equisones and consones in triple and quadruple dimension; and some—the smallest interval, indeed—in sesquioctave [9:8]. On the other hand, some intervals are confined within their pitch extremes in an indefinite and irrational dimension. We shall present a more detailed treatment of this in our *De harmonia*.

Guido also writes about irrational intervals as follows: "Even though they join sounds together in singing, nevertheless, the ditone, semiditone, and semitone admit of no division."[2] Since the Pythagoreans, in particular, assigned every harmonic manipulation either to the multiple or to the

---

1. Bacchius, *Introductio artis musicae*, in Meibom, I, 19.
2. Guido of Arezzo, *Micrologus*, ed. Jos. Smits Van Waesberghe (*Corpus scriptorum de musica;* American Institute of Musicology, 1955), p. 116.

superparticular, those intervals which are not part of the first three multiple proportions in the harmonic system and do not belong to the first two superparticulars are called irrational and indefinite. Incomposite thirds and incomposite sixths, however, from whose extremes concordances issue and which can be called irrational consonances notwithstanding, are suitable intervals for this discipline.

There are three types of conjunct sounds which in a certain harmonic sense are agreeable to the ear. Some conjunct sounds are so composed in relation to each other that they are detected as suitable by the ear alone, as for example, the incomposite third and the incomposite sixth. Some intervals are not only agreeable to the ear but also seem to convey a sensation of sameness, as for example, the incomposite fifth and the incomposite twelfth; while other intervals are so endowed that they seem to the ear to effect a single sound although they are constituted of different sounds, as for example, the incomposite octave and double octave.

Briennius calls those sounds which are agreeable to the ear alone *emeles*, or "pleasing," those which share in a sameness of sounds symphones, and those which seem identical homophones or antiphones. On the other hand, Boethius, agreeing with Ptolemy, calls the first of such conjunct sounds which in the judgment of the ear are suitable for composition emeles; but he calls the symphones, derived from a superparticular computation, consones, as though they were sharers in similitude, and those which stem from the multiple and seem the same he calls equisones.[3]

In the art of counterpoint, time itself has indeed brought about a refinement among all these intervallic combinations, so that the antiphones or equisones have been named the perfect species of counterpoint, the emeles the imperfect, and the consones the intermediate. This refinement, to be sure, was advanced by Franco too, and it is also evident from the following pronouncement by Guido: "No sound harmonizes perfectly with its own fifth, and no two sounds, except the octave, yield a perfect concordance."[4]

Furthermore, although vocal compositions are varied, the art of counterpoint is finite. Its mandates are not arbitrary and various but general and

3. Briennius, *Harmonicorum libri tres*, II.ii, in John Wallis, ed., *Opera mathematica* (Oxford, 1699), III, 401–5; Boethius, *De institutione musica*, I.viii, ed. Gottfried Friedlein (Leipzig, 1867).

4. Guido, *Micrologus*, Van Waesberghe ed., p. 113. It is a striking coincidence, considering the numerous manuscripts available during the Renaissance, that Gafurius' quotation here is almost word for word the one given in Van Waesberghe's edition.

well-defined. For even though it happens that the techniques and diversity
of composition are infinitely varied, still the art of counterpoint does not
differ from other arts whose mandates are finite and universal; it is limited
to a few mandates, although the particular individual applications may
reach to infinity, as Anselm declares.[5] Accordingly, in this discipline, even
though the musical symbols increase in variety and number—there being
no confusion on account of the additions, since by means of them the
several parts of an artistically arranged composition can be performed in
their proper rhythmic values—nevertheless, vocalists commit them to
memory more easily and advantageously.

Thus the discipline of counterpoint provides conjunct sounds which are
concordant by means of the proportional measurement of intervals. But
since intervals are a kind of silent bridge from sound to sound, they are,
according to Bacchius, not audible but rather intelligible.[6] This is why the
divine Plato, in Book VII of *The Laws*, believed that every harmony, when
skillfully ordered, even though lacking in sweetness of sound, is better by
far than one which is without order.[7]

Chapter two   The Nature and the Naming of the Contrapuntal Species

The species or elements of counterpoint in instrumental music and
in vocal harmony necessarily result from the properly proportioned combination of low and high sounds out of which harmonic music arises. Although this combination does not occur in the unison, which is simple and
of a singular nature, nevertheless, because it contributes a degree of augmentation to the other consonances (for they are derived from it just as
unity contributes to numbers or a point to a line) musicians, treating the
unison as unity, have unanimously included it among the concordances.
Moreover, musicians have bestowed names on the concordances, depend-

5. Anselm of Parma, *De musica*, III, ed. Giuseppe Massera (*Historiae musicae cultores*, XIV; Florence, 1961), p. 193.
6. Bacchius, *Introductio*, in Meibom, I, 17.
7. *The Dialogues of Plato*, tr. B. Jowett (New York, 1937), II, 557.

ing upon the number of sounds in each of the combinations arranged in
the diatonic genus. Thus they call the ditone, which consists of three
sounds, a third; the diapente, made up of five sounds, they name a fifth;
the diapente plus a whole tone, in six sounds, they call a sixth; the diapason, demonstrable in eight sounds, they call an octave; and so forth for the
other combinations.

Some of these concords are simple or primary, namely those found
among the seven basic, distinct sounds, as for example, the unison, third,
fifth, and sixth. Some are replicate, or secondary—such as the octave,
tenth, twelfth, and thirteenth—for these, conceived in duple dimension,
sound similar to the primary consonances. The octave, for instance, sounds
equal to the unison, the tenth to the third, the twelfth to the fifth, and the
thirteenth to the sixth. The other consonances are twice-reproduced or
tertiary, as for example, the double octave, seventeenth, nineteenth, and
twentieth. Thus the double octave sounds like the unison and octave, the
seventeenth like the third and tenth, the nineteenth like the fifth and
twelfth, and the twentieth like the sixth and thirteenth.

Some of these concords support a mean consonant pitch; others do not.
Of those supporting a mean consonant pitch, the intervallic distances between upper and lower extremes in some is closer; in others, more open.
Such a combination will affect the nature of the harmony to the degree
that the mean interval of these extremes is wider and variable. But if a
single pitch is the mean, however variable it is—for instance, in that species which they call the third to which only a second pitch furnishes the
mean—yet because of its simplicity it is far removed from the nature of
harmonic sweetness. In fact, they rank the third first in the order of conjunct and concordant sounds, as if it were the first of the concords to depart harmoniously from the simplicity of the unison, just as the number 2
is first away from unity itself. But those combinations of sounds which contain no mean pitch in diatonic arrangement do not conform to the law of
counterpoint, as, for example, the whole tone and semitone.

Now a third is arranged in two ways, that is, as a ditone and as a semiditone. Granted, when a third is ditonic, it may be transmuted into the
form of a semiditone by the subtraction of a semitone. When, however,
the interval is semiditonic, it may be converted into the interval of a ditone
by the addition of a semitone. Nevertheless, the actual concord and also
its natural name are said not to change. When the interval is ditonic they
call the third major because of its larger size. When it is semiditonic the
third is called minor. Because of this variation and its uncertain dimension,

authorities have decided that this third should be called the vagrant imperfect species of counterpoint, and yet that minor third, which they call a semiditone or trihemitone, is an harmonious distance.

From the permutation of the diatonic genus into the chromatic, the ancients, with nature as their guide, carefully selected from each tetrachord the concord with the largest incomposite interval. For this reason some call the minor third chromatic. On the other hand, they call the ditone the incomposite enharmonic third, because, as has been mentioned in Book I, Chapter 3, it encompasses the widest incomposite interval of an enharmonic tetrachord. I shall treat these matters in more detail, however, in the *De harmonia* [I, 3]. Thus, from the variation of this third, which is brought about either by the subtraction or the addition of a semitone, it is clear that a definite permutation of one genus into another is effected.

Now the fifth, which is produced by a perfect diapente made up of three whole tones and a minor semitone in sesquialter dimension [3:2], possesses a mean pitch concordant with its extremes. It is composed of the first two simple species, that is, of a minor third and a major third, constituted in harmonious mediation. Hence it yields a sweeter harmony in its extremes and adheres, by a kind of imitation, so to speak, to harmonic mediation. Indeed, if such a mean pitch is transposed by the interval of a hexachord [sixth] higher, it will enclose the higher mean between those extremities in harmonic mediation and perfect the composite equal-sounding diapason [octave]. Therefore, since the diapente comprises the larger, principal interval of this harmonic complex, these fifths as arranged in the diatonic genus in sesquialter proportion bring about a more pleasing, sweeter species of counterpoint.

The sixth is named from its six tones arranged diatonically. It is imperfect because it cannot be measured rationally on the chordotone. (The chordotone is a string which comprehends all the consonances arranged in musical proportions.) It happens that the sixth, made up of four whole tones and a minor semitone, is varied and diminished by the subtraction of a major semitone [apotome], although it does not sacrifice its particular sonority nor its name.

One sixth is called major, the other minor. The major sixth is made up of a diapente and a whole tone. The minor sixth, however, is made up of a diapente and a semitone. Hence, by such a variation, we can call the sixth a vagrant species just like the third. The sixth possesses a single harmonious mean which is a third up from the lower extreme and also sounds as the root of the diatessaron above. While the diatessaron consonance is dissonant, even if it is classified as a simple species, nevertheless, when it is joined to a concordant mixture, it produces an harmonious mediation with its extremes, as though it were close to and a sharer of harmonic mediation. Generally, however, such a mediated sixth—when, that is, its mean sounds the ditone third to the lower extreme—requires that that mean pitch be lowered the tiniest bit. This is something we are taught by experiment on instruments.[8] By a certain adjacency of sound the fourth is tempered a little toward participation in the sweet fifth, while the major third is inflected downward a little in the direction of the minor, sweeter, semiditonic third. So it is not incongruous to name the third and the sixth as imperfect, vagrant concordances; in a certain way they are each sharers of one and the same method and movement.

As for the octave, it is clear that the equal-sounding diapason is formed out of five whole tones and two minor semitones in duple measurement on the chordotone. The octave is the perfect species of counterpoint and the first, in fact, that is formed in harmonic mediation. For harmonic mediation is known to be drawn in the proportion in which the longer string, emitting the lower sound, governs the shorter string, which yields the highest sound, an octave; and the same proportion exists between the interval, or difference, of the longer and mean strings, which is a diapente, and the difference that is the interval of the mean and higher strings, which makes up the diatessaron.[9] Again, the larger interval, which is expressed in larger numbers, contains the larger consonance—that is, the diapente—and the smaller interval, fashioned from smaller numbers, supports the smaller consonance—that is, the diatessaron. This is indeed characteristic of harmonic mediation, as I shall demonstrate in the *De harmonia* [III, 5].

Thus it is clear that the mean is a constituent of harmony, as Peter of Abano, the Interpreter, testifies in the Twelfth *Musical Problem.*[10] Hence,

8. Here Gafurius acknowledges the need to temper the sizes of each of the incomposite intervals which make up a composite major sixth in order to accommodate the sense of auditory pleasure, attesting his awareness of the practical world of music about him. He attained his objective by the simple expedient of lowering the mean by the distance of an 81:80 (Didymic) comma. Thus Pythagoras' 81:64 major third was diminished into the "sweeter" 5:4 interval, while the fourth was expanded into a 27:20 interval, approaching the "sweeter" fifth.

9. In the harmonic proportion 6:4:3, for example, the ratio of the difference between the first two terms (2) to the difference between the second and third terms (1) is identical to the ratio of the outer terms: that is, 2:1 = 6:3.

10. Peter of Abano, *Expositio problematum Aristotelis* (Venice, 1482), XIX.xii. This is but one of several solutions to this twelfth musical problem.

since the equal-sounding diapason is the first and smallest consonance which is mediated harmonically, Aristotle himself in the Eighteenth *Musical Problem* asserts that it is the only one to sound pitches perfectly together.[11] In addition, between its lowest and mean pitches, the octave supports an intermediate concord, namely, either the major or minor third, which, since it was expedient to do so, was touched on earlier in our consideration of the fifth. Thus the octave mediated harmonically is that first, simple harmony from which all musical harmonization blossoms forth in a more pleasing and sweeter modulation.

The tenth, which is octave to the third, partakes of the nature of the third. It is imperfect and vagrant, since it is minor by the subtraction of a semitone and major by the addition of a semitone. The tenth does not admit a mean sonorous pitch between itself and the octave because it is the first species issuing from it, like the simple third from the unison. The tenth supports three intermediate sonorous concordances: a third, a fifth, and an octave. Even if these concordances do enclose a harmonic complex between the first, lowest pitch, the fifth, and the octave, nevertheless, by the admixture of the vagrant, imperfect species (of the third, that is) to the lower pitch and also the sixth arranged between the fifth and the higher tenth, they weaken the harmonic consistency and render it less pleasing. For anything that is arranged well and correctly suffers alteration of its very nature when it supports something that is deformed and incongruous.

The twelfth, sounding equal to the fifth, consists of eight whole tones and three minor semitones. It is made up of a diapason and a diapente. Since it possesses a single octave mean pitch—supporting, that is, a duple and sesquialter dimension—it finds repose in an harmonic mediation conceived in the triple proportion of both its extremes and differences. This fact is proved by the numbers 12, 6, 4. If I write the number 12, which attaches to the longest, lowest string, *G ut,* and the number 6 for its octave, *g sol re ut,* and then the number 4 for the twelfth, *d' la sol re,* the terms extreme to each other and the differences between them are controlled by one and the same proportion. As 12 to 4 makes a triple proportion, so the difference of 12 and 6, which is 6, governs the difference of 6 and 4, which is 2, in triple proportion. Likewise, there exists a larger proportion in the larger numbers and hence also a larger consonance, and a smaller proportion in the smaller numbers, which, as we mentioned earlier, is a characteristic of harmonic mediation.

11. Aristotle, *Problems,* XIX, tr. W. S. Hett (Loeb Classical Library, 1936), I, 389.

The twelfth also supports a fifth arranged between the root and octave in harmonic mediation, to which fifth the twelfth is octave. But if you interject a third as well as an octave to this third, which is tenth to the root, the beauty of this harmonic entity will be suspended because these are dull-sounding, irrational intervals.

The thirteenth imitates the nature of the sixth, inasmuch as it is the distance of an octave above. It is imperfect and vagrant: minor, to be sure, by the subtraction of a semitone and major by its addition. Furthermore, it is mediated harmoniously by a third, sixth, octave, and tenth infecting the sweetness of the harmonic complex.

The double octave, equivalent in sound to the disdiapason, contains ten whole tones and four minor semitones. It keeps for its very own all the potency and nature of harmonic melody, for it sustains and governs the seven diapason species of the harmonic system. For this reason antiquity ascribed the arrangement of the fifteen basic sounds to the most perfect system.

When this double octave is arranged in the mediation of a single string, the division of its great length into two equal dimensions of equal-sounding diapasons is recognized as belonging to geometric proportion. The larger number governs the mean by the very same proportion by which the mean approaches the smaller number. Once more, the difference of the larger number and the mean to the difference of the mean and the smaller number is judged by the same standard, which is characteristic of geometric proportion. For instance, when I write the number 16 for the longest string of the chordotone, whose lowest sound is *G ut,* I assign to its octave, *g sol re ut,* the number 8, and likewise for its double octave, which is the acute *g′ sol re ut,* I write the number 4. By this technique 16 to 8 effects a duple proportion that establishes the equal-sounding diapason; and 8 to 4 similarly yields a duple proportion. Furthermore, the difference of the larger terms, which is 8, in relation to the difference of the smaller terms, which is 4, likewise produces a duple relationship. The sounds themselves must be understood by means of the proportionate terms of these strings. The intervals of the sounding strings must be understood by the differences of those terms. Just as the terms are in duple relationship to each other, so the lower and larger interval is in duple relationship to the smaller and higher.

In the same way the double octave supports the concords of the fifth and the twelfth mediated harmonically and sweetly. When the third and tenth pitches are interposed, however, this type of very sweet harmony falls upon the ears clouded and tainted.

The seventeenth, sounding equal to the third and tenth, is double octave to the third and octave to the tenth. It is vagrant and imperfect, emulating the sonority of the third itself, and it is mediated harmoniously by a third, fifth, octave, tenth, twelfth, and double octave.

The nineteenth sounds like a double octave to the fifth and an octave to the twelfth. It supports a third, fifth, octave, tenth, twelfth, double octave, and seventeenth harmoniously mediated.

The twentieth sounds like an octave to the thirteenth and like a double octave to the sixth, and supports many mean pitches harmoniously: the third, sixth, octave, tenth, thirteenth, double octave, and seventeenth. In fact, those intervals which go beyond the double octave, since they exceed the expanse of geometric mediation, are in a certain way ill-sounding and weak and somewhat destitute of the nature of proper sonority.

The rest of the conjunct sounds affect the sense of hearing unpleasantly when their extreme pitches are sounded simultaneously: for example, the second, the simple fourth, the seventh, and those which sound as compounds of these simple intervals. Hence they are segregated from the elements of counterpoint because they occupy no stable position in music except in a very rapid passage of temporal measure.

Chapter three   The Eight Mandates or Rules of Counterpoint

Musicians have distinguished the ways in which the elements of music follow one another in eight rules.

The first rule is that the beginning of each composition is undertaken by perfect concords, either on a unison, octave, or double octave, or even on a fifth or a twelfth. Even if the latter are by no means perfect, still they are included with the perfects because of their sweeter sonority. Yet this first mandate is not obligatory but rather discretionary, for perfection in all things is ascribed to endings, not to beginnings. Hence most musicians begin compositions with imperfect concords, as is attested to by these examples:

The first musical example here begins on a third, the second example on a sixth, the third on a tenth. Even if these intervals are imperfect elements of harmony, nevertheless, they are recognized to be congruous and harmoniously appropriate for such beginnings.

The second rule is that two perfect species of the same kind cannot be constituted in composition ascending or descending together in consecutive parallel motion. For example, two unisons, two octaves, two double octaves, or even two fifths or twelfths (which, even if they are not perfect, still, on account of the suavity they share, are enumerated with the perfects, observing their rules and mandates) cannot be written in consecutive parallel motion. This rule is not discretionary but mandatory, rejecting every exception. Still some authorities have thought that two fifths ascending or descending in parallel motion can be intoned, provided that they are tuned in different quantities and intervals, that is, from a perfect fifth to a diminished one by the subtraction or defection of a semitone: for example, by proceeding from the interval between *A re* and *e la mi*, or between proslambanomenos and hypate meson, and then in consecutive parallel motion ascending to the interval between the grave *B mi* and *f fa ut*, or between hypate hypaton and parhypate meson. This is, in my opinion, incorrect.

No one doubts that a fifth diminished by a semitone is incongruous for composition, for such a diminution is particularly obvious. For this reason, harmonic mediation does not permit a series of diapente species to be evolved from proslambanomenos in diatonic arrangement. Nevertheless, this fifth, as organists maintain, permits the diminution of a small, concealed, and somewhat vague quantity which these organists call temperament.[12]

The third rule is that at least one imperfect concord—a third, for example, or a sixth, or some such type—has to be set between two perfect concords of the same kind ascending or descending, in contrary or similar motion. In the same way several imperfects, similar and even dissimilar, such as two, three, or four thirds and one or more sixths, are properly arranged between two perfects of the same kind, as the present example shows:

12. This remark may be one of the earliest adumbrations by a theorist on the con-

Furthermore, counterpoint containing a single discord—a second, fourth, or seventh, for example—between two perfect concords of the same kind ascending or descending in parallel motion is not allowed. It is not allowed whether that discord is written as a more diminished note, like a seminim or semiminim or even a minim, or whether it imitates a temporal note of larger quantity such as a semibreve or breve, for if an open and obvious discordance is not fit for counterpoint, it cannot occupy a place in lieu of an imperfect concordance. For this reason also a discord that is concealed by speed can by no means be substituted for such an imperfect concordance.

The fourth rule is that several perfect and dissimilar concords ascending or descending can be produced in succession in counterpoint, as, for example, a fifth after a unison or after an octave, an octave after a fifth, and others in the same way, as is evident in this harmonization:

The fifth rule is that two perfect, similar concords can be constituted in counterpoint following one after the other in immediate succession provided that they proceed in dissimilar and contrary motion, so that if the first voice of the two octaves ascends, the second descends, and conversely. Likewise, when two fifths succeed each other immediately, the first is ef-

cept of temperament. In effect, it anticipates the meantone system advocated by the blind organist Arnold Schlick in his *Spiegel der Orgelmacher und Organisten* (Heidelberg, 1511). Schlick's fifth measures one fourth of a syntonic comma (the Didymic 81:80 comma), smaller than the 3:2 fifth of Pythagoras. (See R. Kendall, "Notes on Arnold Schlick," *Acta Musicologica,* XI [1939].)

fected by thesis [descends], and the second is effected by arsis [ascends], or conversely, as this example proves:

In the contrapuntal arrangement above, the first note of the cantus (that is, of the higher part) is an octave above the tenor, but the second note of the cantus is an octave below the tenor because it is lowered by an octave and the tenor is raised by an octave. Also the first semibreve of the contratenor is raised a fifth above the tenor, and the second semibreve is raised a fifth above the cantus. Likewise, the final semibreve, or penultimate note, of the contratenor is lowered a fifth down from the tenor. The final note of this contratenor, the long, is raised also a fifth above the tenor, a technique which occurs in almost all compositions.

The sixth rule is that in counterpoint the parts of a song—tenor, cantus, and contratenor—ought to be in contrary motion to each other; when the cantus ascends, the tenor descends, and conversely, and the contratenor behaves similarly in relation to one or the other of these parts. This is an arbitrary rule, however, for very often the notes of a tenor, ascending or descending, follow the notes of the cantus in parallel motion. The same movement takes place in the contratenor. This happens especially when the parts of the song are in canon to each other with identical motion and notes, as this piece demonstrates:

The seventh rule is that when we seek a perfect concordance out of an imperfect one, at the end of a song perhaps or at the end of some part of its harmony, it is necessary that the voices converge in order to reach the nearest perfect concordance by means of the different motions of both parts. For example, when tenor and cantus sound a major sixth, that is, a diapente plus a whole tone, both then proceed in contrary motion. The tenor descends one pitch and the cantus similarly is raised one pitch to the octave, which by the deliberate contrariness of the motion is nearest to that sixth, and the voices meet there. It is a characteristic of the major sixth to move across to the octave, of course.

On the other hand, the minor sixth resolves frequently on a fifth by oblique motion, that is, with one voice of the counterpoint stationary and the other moving. It also progresses to the octave in contrary motion. Furthermore, when cantus and tenor sound the third, they resolve on a unison when the first contrary movements are made. Widening out in contrary motion, both progress to the fifth. This is easily demonstrated by this harmonization:

In this example cantus and tenor, on a third with the first semibreve, progress to a unison on the second semibreve. From the fourth semibreve, which sounds the minor third, they resolve in contrary motion on a fifth with the fifth semibreve. From the fifth semibreve to the sixth semibreve, they are converted into a minor sixth by a single movement of the cantus, the tenor remaining stationary. Proceeding then to the seventh semibreve, a motion of the cantus alone with the tenor stationary effects a fifth. With the eighth semibreve also by means of a single upward movement, the tenor stationary, it attains the minor sixth. From here, when both of these move by contrary motion, each one moving an interval of one whole tone, they are mutually dissolved and establish the ninth semibreve on an octave adjacent to the sixth. From the eleventh semibreve, similarly ensconced on a sixth, they proceed by contrary motion to the equal-sounding octave with the twelfth semibreve. Among the other progressions also it is fitting that a similar procedure should be employed.

The eighth and final rule is that every composition ought to be concluded and terminated on a perfect concordance—on either a unison, as was the custom of the Venetians, on an octave, or on a double octave. This is a practice which every school of musicians observes more frequently in order to achieve harmonic mediation, for according to the Philosopher the end of every single thing is perfection.

Chapter four   Which Discords Ought to Be Permitted in Counterpoint and Where

We think we must explain briefly which discords ought to be admitted in counterpoint. In counterpoint a normal semibreve occupying a full measure of time, in the manner of a pulse throbbing evenly, cannot support a discord, as teachers of the art have maintained. Similarly they also do not permit a breve note as a discord, for when it is marked, such a discord corrupts the nature and the sweetness of the harmony. But when a discord is concealed by means of syncopation and by the very rapidity of a passage, it is permitted in counterpoint. This occurs in almost all composition when we engage an imperfect concord out of which, by the contrary motion of the voices, we advance directly to the perfect concord nearest to it. At that time a minim or even a semibreve which immediately precedes the imperfect concord will be a discord. That is, it will be either a second when it issues out of a third into a unison, or a fourth when it evolves into a fifth, or a seventh when it resolves into the equal-sounding octave. Consequently this type of syncopated discord is concealed, causing no blow to the ear. It is evident in this example:

In this harmonization the first minim of the cantus produces a second with the tenor—manifesting a discord, to be sure—and the second minim of the cantus similarly is most noticeably a fourth, discordant with the tenor. To these I would rarely concede admittance, for their discordancy is marked, even though the minim occupies only half the time of a semibreve and steps quickly. Still, several composers, such as Dunstable, Binchois, Dufay, and Brassart,[13] did permit such a discordant minim and semibreve. The penultimate semibreve of the cantus, however, which is separable into two minims, makes its second minim a seventh, discordant with the penultimate semibreve of the tenor, but it is concealed under the guise of syncopation. You will find the same thing in the penultimate semibreve of the contratenor, which, when you divide it into two minims, will show the second of these minims as a fourth, discordant with the final semibreve of the tenor but concealed. Accordingly, it is necessary that such a minim and also the discordant semibreve be allowed in counterpoint.

13. Of these leading composers of the Burgundian School (first half of the fifteenth century), only the chanson specialist, Gilles Binchois (c. 1400–1460), is represented in the Milanese codices, which were prepared under Gafurius' supervision. A "Te Deum a fauxbourdon" from the pen of Binchois is preserved in Codex 2269 (118v–121r).

Besides the syncopated type there is also hidden discordancy in counterpoint: that which is included and made obtuse among the several concordant parts of a composition. Moreover, if a semibreve diminished in duple
proportion, and a breve in quadruple, and others similarly situated, have
a temporal value equivalent to a minim note, even if they are discords,
they can be tolerated in counterpoint.

Chapter five   The Agreeable Sweetness of the Fourth

The discord which arises out of four conjunct sounds in succession
sounding the diatessaron consonance is permitted in two places in counterpoint.

First, when a tenor and a cantus sound an octave to each other, then the
middle part, which is called the contratenor, arranged above the tenor on
a fifth which is compounded out of three whole tones and a semitone, will
be a fourth or a diatessaron below the highest pitch, which makes an
equal-sounding octave to the lower. Such a fourth between a contratenor
and a cantus will concord extremely well because it is harmonically mediated, as the accompanying harmonization discloses:[14]

14. At bar 3 the original contratenor produces a series of consecutive dissonances
with the cantus which is completely at variance with Gafurius' customary handling of
the dissonance. It seems reasonable to substitute the rhythm ♪♪♩ for ♪♪♩ on the first
beat of the contratenor.

In this harmonization the first note and also the final note of the contratenor cause a fifth to stand above the tenor and a fourth below the cantus
consonant to each part in harmonic mediation.

Secondly, when tenor and cantus proceed by means of one or more
sixths, then the middle voice, the contratenor, will always occupy the
fourth below the cantus, always maintaining a third above the tenor. Musicians call this kind of counterpoint *fauxbourdon*. In it this middle contratenor quite frequently follows the notes of the cantus, proceeding at an
interval of a fourth below it; it is often observed by musicians in the performance of the psalms. And so such a fourth, arranged between a contratenor and a cantus, even in semibreves, breves, and longs, is accepted as
harmonious in counterpoint. This technique is aptly demonstrated in the
following harmonization:

It is evident from the above harmonization that all the notes of the contratenor are lowered from the notes of the cantus by a fourth and raised
from the notes of the tenor by a third, rounding off a sixth from tenor to
cantus. But when the notes of the contratenor are distributed a fifth above
the notes of a tenor, then the tenor together with the cantus enclose an
octave or a diapason symphony in harmonic mediation. Hence such composition is recognized as harmonious.

Chapter six   Why the Fourth is Concordant Between a Middle and a Higher Sound and Discordant Between a Middle and a Lower Sound

The interval of a sixth mediated by a third above a tenor harmoniously supports a fourth between the middle and high terms because a fourth, arranged between those two concordant though imperfect intervals (the third and sixth) is obscured by these intervals in the way that smaller things are obscured by larger ones. Even so, this fourth is recognized to have been evolved both from art and from nature.

Higher sounds are generated by swifter vibrations. Thus they are weaker than lower sounds, which slower vibrations produce, as we have explained in Book II, Chapter 1 of the *Theorica.* Thus weakened by that velocity, the discordance of the fourth is concealed in the upper register. On the other hand, when a fourth is conceived in lower sounds, then its presence is pronounced, and it returns an unhappy sonority to the ear on account of the slowness of the vibrations. Our Boethius in Book I of his *Musica* asserts this to be characteristic of lower sounds. Slowness naturally requires more time for itself than rapidity. Hence there can be more discordancy in lower sounds, and consequently the discordance is more obvious, an idea which Aristotle treats in the Twenty-first Problem of the "Harmonics."[15] Among such lower sounds, therefore, counterpoint does not tolerate the discordancy of such a fourth.

Chapter seven   The Conformity and Diversity of the Third and the Sixth

It is evident that the first imperfect concords of the simple variety, the third and the sixth, are evolved by manipulation of the equal-sounding octave in an alternate movement of the voices. When two sounds have

15. Aristotle, *Problems,* XIX, Hett ed., I, 391–93. Gafurius undoubtedly gleaned his

been arranged an octave apart—tenor and cantus, for example—if the cantus is lowered by a sixth, a third will emerge at that point, raised above the tenor. When in such an arrangement of an octave one transposes the lower pitch a sixth higher, he will also arrive at a third under the cantus, major or minor in accordance with the natural diatonic progression of whole tones and semitones.

In amplification of this I say that the mean pitch [the fifth], arranged in the harmonic mediation of an octave, generates both of these intervals by a single, oblique movement to the extremes. When the mean pitch is lowered by a third, it will produce a third to the lower pitch and a sixth to the higher. When, however, this mean pitch is raised a whole tone or a semitone, it will prove to be a third to the higher voice and a sixth to the lower. Moreover, when the cantus is lowered from the octave by a major or minor third, it will be transformed at once into a minor or major sixth. Likewise, when the tenor sounds an octave below the cantus and ascends by the interval of a third, it will prove to be a sixth to the cantus. This technique may be recognized by diligent examination of this excerpt:

One should also notice that if one species or concordance is produced by the raising or lowering of another, one constituent will be major and the other minor. For example, a major third raised from the tenor or lowered from the cantus leaves a minor sixth, and vice versa, since in the perfect octave only five whole tones and two minor semitones are compre-

---

information on acoustics from Peter of Abano's *Expositio,* but his discussion of the dual nature of the fourth may have been arrived at independently.

hended. It is clear, therefore, that in the manipulation of an octave, a third is easily generated from the motion of a sixth, and a sixth issues from the motion of a third. Since both are imperfect, they seem somehow to preserve one and the same nature and propriety.

We said in Chapter 3, in regard to the seventh rule, that a third to a unison and to a fifth, and a sixth to an octave move most fittingly by contrary motion. They are more ineptly treated in oblique motion. Hence it is clear that a third which, by contrary motion from it, is encircled by two adjacent, perfect concordances—that is, by a fifth and a unison—is sweeter than a sixth. For the sixth, even if it is surrounded by an octave and a fifth, does not proceed to these two concordances by contrary motion; it is converted into a fifth by oblique motion. It goes to the octave, however, by two contrary movements, as is evident here:

Furthermore, the sixth shares more of the fifth than of the octave because it is closer to the fifth and contiguous to it: no middle voice intervenes between a fifth and a sixth. Between a sixth and an octave, however, a seventh pitch is naturally arranged. Thus the sixth, more remote from the octave, shares more of the nature of the fifth, and since the fifth is some distance from the perfection of the octave, the sixth, partner of this fifth, obtains a more imperfect sonority than the third which, like a mean to extremes, shares the perfection of both the fifth and of the unison. As has been said, this third in its first, closer advance, is known to resolve by contrary motion both on a fifth and on a unison, to which the perfection of the octave is plainly ascribed. The subjoined representation of notes demonstrates this as follows:

Chapter eight   The Naming of the Pitch Extremities in Concordances

There are also those who discuss the extreme pitches of concordances in terms of the various names of the vocal syllables. They say that when the tenor articulates *ut*, the cantus on a unison will similarly intone *ut*, on the third *mi*, on the fifth *sol*, and *la* on the sixth in each hexachord. But on an octave the cantus itself will sound *ut* the same as the tenor, and according to the same system they believe the rest must be similarly named.

Even though we have described this method in our *Flos musicae*,[16] nevertheless we believe that there is no law that this system has to be observed, because it is not the equality nor the diversity of syllables but rather the disjunct extremities of the sounding terms with their particular intervals that define the concordances. When the tenor intones *ut* on G *ut*, the cantus will not only be able to articulate *ut* at the octave, according to Guido's diatonic system, but *sol* and *re* on the grave g *sol re ut* as well. Every syllable arranged on the grave g *sol re ut* sounds a perfect octave to G *ut*, the diapason consonance.

Similarly, one can readily unite all the concordances with the second pitch as far as a nineteenth in the Guidonian scale. When the tenor rests on A *re*, the cantus will be able to intone *fa* and *ut* on the third, that is to say, on c *fa ut*, and *la* and *mi* on the fifth on the grave e *la mi*. And *fa* on f *fa ut* on the minor sixth, and *la*, *mi*, and *re* on the perfect octave on a *la mi re*, and likewise *sol*, *fa*, and *ut* on the tenth on c′ *sol fa ut*. And *la* and *mi* on the acute e′ *la mi* on the twelfth, and *fa* on the acute f′ *fa ut* on the thirteenth, and *la*, *mi*, and *re* on the superacute a′ *la mi re* on the double octave, and *sol* and *fa* on the seventeenth on c″ *sol fa*, and on the nineteenth *la* on e″ *la*. This is very clearly perceived in the accompanying table of correlations.

And there will be similar treatment for the rest of the concordances in turn, not, of course, by the placing of a single syllable on each part [tenor and cantus], but rather by mutually proportioned sounds in their proper intervallic dimensions.

16. See p. xx above.

Table of Correlations

			G ut	A re
e″	la		20th to G ut	19th to A re
		tone		
d″	la sol		19th to G ut	
		tone		
c″	sol fa			17th to A re
		semitone		
b′	mi		17th to G ut	
		apotome		
b♭′	fa			
		semitone		
a′	la mi re			15th to A re
		tone		
g′	sol re ut		15th to G ut	
		tone		
f′	fa ut			13th to A re
		semitone		
e′	la mi		13th to G ut	12th to A re
		tone		
d′	la sol re		12th to G ut	
		tone		
c′	sol fa ut			10th to A re
		semitone		
b	mi		10th to G ut	
		apotome		
b♭	fa			
		semitone		
a	la mi re			8ve to A re
		tone		
g	sol re ut		8ve to G ut	
		tone		
f	fa ut			6th to A re
		semitone		
e	la mi		6th to G ut	5th to A re
		tone		
d	sol re		5th to G ut	
		tone		
c	fa ut			3rd to A re
		semitone		
B	mi		3rd to G ut	
		tone		
A	re			Unison
		tone		
G	ut		Unison	

Chapter nine   How the Various Elements of Counterpoint Are Arranged by the Alternate Raising and Lowering of Species

I do not think it is inappropriate to explain more precisely how the elementary species of counterpoint are customarily commingled in music.

When the cantus occupies a third with the tenor and the voices are manipulated in contrary motion, they will resolve at once on a unison. And from that third, by contrary motion again, they leap forward to a fifth. But when the cantus, positioned a third above the tenor, is raised by one pitch, and the tenor is lowered by a fifth, then jointly they will perfect an octave. Conversely, when the tenor, arranged on an octave with the cantus, is raised by a fifth and the cantus is lowered by one pitch, they will find their way from the octave in a more graceful transition to the third.

One can also proceed very well by contrary motion from an octave to a sixth, and from an octave to a fifth by the single motion of the cantus lowered by a fourth, or of the tenor raised by a diatessaron. But from a sixth one easily reaches a third with the pitch of the organizing voice [cantus] lowered by a fourth, or when the pitch of the tenor alone is raised by a fourth. For it is the composer who invents the higher part of a composition.

Similarly from a third also the cantus raised by a fourth will give a sixth as answer to the tenor; but if the tenor, when arranged on a third with the cantus, should be lowered by a fourth, it will depart from the cantus the same distance of a sixth. These matters are clearly set forth in this harmonization:

When you try to proceed with the other contrapuntal elements, you will perceive the same relationship of a tenth to an octave which we have described for the third to the unison, and what we said concerning an octave to a fifth applies equally to the relationship of a double octave to a twelfth; what we said concerning a sixth to a third applies in like manner to the relationship of a thirteenth to a tenth, and likewise for the other species in the Guidonian system introduced above. Further, a concordance ascribed to perfection which the voices attain by contrary motion is sweeter and more delectable than one conceived in oblique motion. This is because when the various sounds proceed in contrary motion, each hastens to meet the other to mingle in concordant sweetness, and it is by this commingling that harmonious counterpoint is produced.

Chapter ten   The Notational Diversity of Sounds in Counterpoint

In counterpoint, musicians customarily select sounds that harmonize in various ways with the notes of plain chant—that is, with the tenor, which is the basic voice of the relationship. Sometimes they make the notes of the cantus or even of the contratenor equal in time to the notes of the plain chant, which are assigned to the tenor, by scoring note against note and by employing only semibreves in the arrangement. They call this simple or plain counterpoint because all the notes are arranged in equal temporal value, as is written in this harmonization:

Sometimes these same composers fit semibreves and minims and other more diminished notes to the notes of plain chant, arranging the notes of the plain chant in the time of semibreves. They call this broken or florid counterpoint, as here:

Sometimes they write counterpoint to the notes of the plain chant in a recurring pattern, putting two seminims after three single minims, as follows:

Again, composing with a variety of numerical values for the notes above the notes of the plain chant, they fashion the counterpoint in different rhythmic patterns, as is evident here:

Sometimes, also, they compose a lower accompaniment to the plain chant notes above. Accordingly, the conclusion must indeed be drawn that counterpoint can be fashioned by various notes and species or elements but always in keeping with the lawful mandates, a fact which we know must be entrusted to the judgement of arrangers and composers.

Chapter eleven The Composition of the Different Parts of Counterpoint

The counterpoint of compositions scored for three or four consonant parts is handled in this way: when tenor and cantus maintain an octave relationship to each other, the contratenor will concord most excellently and sweetly on the fifth above or the octave below the tenor. But if to these three conjunct parts you try to fit another part into the song, a contratenor acutus, you would set it on a third above the tenor, or in order to attain a still sweeter harmony, on a fifth. If you arrange it on a third above the tenor, it will concord on a tenth with the contratenor gravis; if you arrange it on a fifth, however, it will be a twelfth away from this baritone part. For the baritone, which the contratenor gravis is also called, is understood to be the lower part or register of a vocal composition. It is from *vari,* which means "low, heavy," with the *v* changed into a *b,* as if singing the lower part of the song. This technique is exemplified here:

In this example the first semibreve of the contratenor acutus, constituted on a third above the tenor, stands a tenth higher than the first semibreve of the baritone and a sixth below the first semibreve of the cantus. The first semibreve of the baritone is a double octave below the first semibreve of the cantus. And so out of each of these patterns good harmony is produced. The final semibreve of the contratenor acutus is a fifth higher than the tenor, distant from the final semibreve of the baritone by a twelfth, and a fourth below the final semibreve of the cantus, so that a harmonic concordance appears there. But when the baritone is dropped a fifth below the tenor and the cantus is a sixth or an octave above it, then the contratenor acutus, arranged on a third above the baritone, will harmonize. This is perceived in the first semibreve of the following example. Nevertheless, the harmony will be mediated more sweetly if the contratenor acutus is made to sojourn on an octave above the baritone, as is quite evident on the final note of this example:

But when the baritone inhabits the octave below the tenor and the cantus rests a third above the tenor, so that it stands a tenth above the baritone, the contratenor acutus can be established on a fifth above the baritone. The baritone will then be a sixth below the cantus and a fourth below the tenor, and so they will maintain a mutually harmonious relationship. This fact is lucidly shown by the first and last notes of this example:

It is clear from the foregoing reasons and examples that each part in a composition is related to the other parts by their different movements according to the rules and elements of counterpoint, that is, so that each part may correspond harmoniously with the individual parts of the composition and none will anywhere lead to a full dissonance, except to the dissonance of the fourth, which accords sweetly in higher and middle inter-vallic combinations, as has been mentioned in Chapter 5.

The sixth is generally discordant in the lower register on a full, fixed pitch unless its pitches resolve immediately on an octave by contrary motion, a fact which we leave to be investigated by the judgement of the ear. A similar discordance of a thirteenth is also conspicuous in the lower register. We believe that the reason for this is that owing to the length of time spent in the lower register, the harshness and dissonance of imperfection fall more openly upon the ears, wounding them.

Thus the contratenor acutus and the tenor itself ought always to be concordant with the baritone, so that when the contratenor acutus is an octave above the baritone, the tenor will be arranged a fifth or a third above the baritone. But if the tenor is introduced an octave above the baritone, then the contratenor will mediate the interval of this octave on a third, or more sweetly on a fifth. In either case, in the variety of the diverse species of the parts of a composition, one part is mingled with another in modulation and notation. Likewise, the baritone may ascend a fifth above the tenor when the cantus sounds an octave to the tenor. In that event, the contratenor [acutus] will be concordant when it is arranged a third above the tenor. It will then diverge from the baritone a third below, and from the cantus a sixth, as is perceived on the last note of the example below. Likewise, when the cantus sounds a tenth above the tenor, then the baritone will take a pitch a fifth above the tenor, and the contratenor acutus preferably will introduce the octave above the tenor. This fact is clearly observed in the first note of this harmonization:

When one wishes to add a quintuple or fifth part concordant with these four, one should take care to join this fifth part first to one and then to another of the parts by means of diverse species in accordance with the rules and mandates of counterpoint.

Chapter twelve   Similar Perfect Concordances Permitted in Succession in Counterpoint

It seems necessary to consider how many perfect species of the same kind may be constituted as stationary voices in composition.

With regard to this, several stationary octaves and several stationary fifths are suitable in counterpoint, and even several of the other perfect species are frequently arranged in a stationary context. But if there is a progression from a perfect concordance of tenor and cantus or of any part with another to a perfect concordance ascending or descending like itself, and there is a rest of one minim interposed in one of these parts of the composition, I feel it must by no means be praised. For when the very small intermission of a minim of silence is inserted, the progression is heard as two similar perfect concordances ascending or descending in parallel succession. For example, when tenor and cantus are arranged on an octave, if the cantus itself, which is settled on the octave, rests for a minim and the tenor is not resting, or even if the tenor is resting for the same length of time, then it is not proper for a second octave to follow immediately upon the preceding because of the parallel ascent or descent of the diverse sounds. The minute portion of time interposed, as we mentioned before, is the basis for my objection. This is obvious in this example:

In this example all the initial notes, which are located on an octave, are properly arranged because they are stationary, even with a semibreve rest interposed. The fifth minim of the cantus, which proceeds directly after the minim rest to an octave with the tenor, is not permissible, however, because of the lower octave immediately preceding it. There are some authorities who do not permit two similar perfect concordances ascending or descending consecutively even with a semibreve rest between them, although several disagree with this because a semibreve rest occupies a full measure of time.

Two or more semibreve rests will mediate fittingly two similar perfect, consecutive concordances, ascending or descending, whether they are introduced in the tenor, cantus, or even in the contratenor or baritone. Moreover, why do we think we must believe those who argue that composers should not sound more than three semibreve unisons in a composition? They argue that the cantus should not appear to have been converted into the tenor and conversely the tenor into the cantus. This, in our opinion, is indeed ridiculous.

Very often, composers of songs notate the tenor and contratenor in more diminished notes and the cantus in longer notes. More recent composers use this practice, which is very clearly evident in the example at hand:

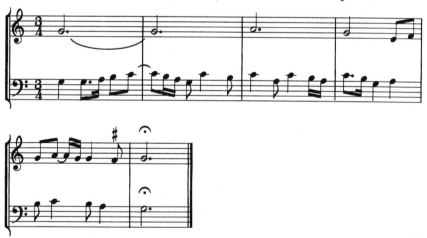

There is also a certain very famous progression of notes in counterpoint —that of the baritone accompanying the notes of the cantus by moving with similar notes at an interval of a tenth, while the tenor harmonizes with each of the parts, a procedure which Tinctoris, Gulielmus Guarnerius, Josquin des Prez, Gaspar [Weerbecke], Alexander Agricola, Loyset, Brumel, Isaac, and other eminently delightful composers frequently observe in their compositions.[17] This technique is also perceived by consideration of the following harmonization:

17. Gafurius gives here a veritable dean's list of Renaissance composers of the Franco-Netherlandish School. Josquin des Prez, Gaspar Weerbecke, Alexander Agricola, Loyset Compère, Antoine Brumel, and Heinrich Isaac were all more or less exact

Chapter thirteen   The Counterpoint of Musica Ficta

Let us pursue briefly the fictive, or chromatic, species of counterpoint, which are detected from the division of individual whole tones on the strings of the monochord. These species, which are produced by chromatic measurement, demonstrate colored compositions, which are also called fictive. Such an arrangement is necessary for the perfection of the harmonic system, not only as a means of tempering the harshness of the diatonic genus in the direction of more sweetness, but also of seeking the perfection of several consonances on the diatonic chordotone.

We proceed in a threefold way in the consideration of musica ficta: according to the measurement of the chromatic genus, according to the description of the mixed genus, and according to the division of the enharmonic genus. These are all said to be condensations and embellishments of the diatonic genus. We have decided to present the measurements of these genera mathematically, however, in the *De harmonia* [II, 1 *et seq.*].

In Guido's diatonic system musica ficta is shown by a single whole tone interval where the B-*molle* hexachord employs the fourth chord degree *fa*, dividing the whole tone distance between *a la mi re* and b-*mi*, or between mese and paramese, after the fashion of the conjunct tetrachord [A B♭ C D]. They are also accustomed to designate the notes that divide such whole-tone intervals with the sign of the rotund B [B-flat] and to articulate them by the syllable *fa*. Quite frequently many articulate *sol* a semitone interval below *la*, especially when there is a progression beginning with the notes *la sol la* on *a la mi re* and also ending on it, as in the "Salve Regina." This is also the case between *sol* and *fa* beginning and ending on g *sol re ut* with the passage *sol fa sol* the way the Ambrosians are accustomed to perform it. It is not the syllable *fa* which makes the semitone

---

contemporaries of Gafurius. With the exception of Isaac and Brumel, each served the Sforzas shortly before Gafurius' assumption of duties at the Duomo of Milan in 1484. Josquin is reported to have been associated with the Duomo as late as 1479. Most heavily represented in the Milanese Codices are the compositions of Gaspar and Loyset. One composition by Brumel, his *Missa l'homme armé*, was written into Codex 2268 (191v–203r). From evidence available it is reasonable to assume that Gafurius had a direct relationship only with Tinctoris and Guarnerius.

but rather the dimension of the semitone interval itself, circumscribed by
two sounds.

When, therefore, you seek this fictive progression in the hexachords of
Guidonian tradition, you subtract a major semitone from the higher notes
of individual whole tones, describing them with the syllable *fa* and the
rotund B by using the technique of permutation. In this way, a whole tone
may be transformed into a semitone.

Many authorities assign such a semitone pitch to each of the whole tone
intervals. In fact, when *mi* is converted into *fa*, they write B-flat in place
of B-natural. When *fa* is changed into *mi*, however, they put B-natural in
place of B-flat. When you change *mi* into *fa* on the grave *e la mi*, *fa* will
be set a major semitone lower, and its hexachord will begin on the grave
B fa.[18] But if you transform *fa* into *mi* on the grave *c fa ut* by making it
a major semitone higher, this hexachord will begin on *A re*. On the other
hand, when you convert *mi* into *fa* on the grave *B mi* by changing it into
a major semitone lower, you will begin this hexachord on the acquired *F
fa ut*, a whole tone below *G ut*. Thus it is not incongruous to classify such
a compositional technique "acquired" music.[19] Throughout the rest of the
notes [chord degrees] of the system you can produce a like conjunction of
acquired hexachords. You can easily discover by means of these musica
ficta both acquired species of consonances and acquired whole tones.

There are also those who, by the imposition of the sign ♯, desire that
the note to which it is added be lowered by the smallest interval of a diesis (the diesis is half the interval of a minor semitone defined by its two
pitches). This is characteristic of the enharmonic genus.

Thus in the handling of musica ficta, counterpoint proceeds by the same
mandates which we have set forth and is woven together by the same concordances, as can be observed in this arrangement:

18. The Latin here reads *B mi*, but this is obviously an error and has been cor-
rected to read *B fa* in translation. With E♭ as *fa*, the acquired hexachord must commence on B♭.

19. Thus, by the process of musica ficta three new hexachords are acquired in lowering the pivotal note the distance of a major semitone or apotome:

	B♭-hexachord			A-hexachord			F-hexachord	
	mi	= *fa*		*fa*	= *mi*		*mi*	= *fa*

Chapter fourteen   False Counterpoint

False counterpoint occurs when two singers proceed together on the dissonant extremities of conjunct sounds. Major and minor seconds, for example, and also the major and minor fourth, seventh, and ninth are of this type. They are almost entirely removed from the logic and nature of sweet harmony.

Our Ambrosians employ this technique in the solemn vigils of the martyrs and in several chants of the mass for the dead, claiming that it was established by the divine Ambrose as a kind of mourning song by which the Church deplores the bloodshed of its martyred saints and the judgement of the dead. This is inconsistent, for I have never found that it was celebrated by the mellifluous Ambrose: as Guido says, when he wrote ecclesiastical chants he labored marvelously for sweetness only. Was it not recorded that the simple modulation of the second, fourth, and sixth modes is appropriate for sadness and lamentations? It is preferable to believe that this false counterpoint was introduced by some composers who were smothered by spitefulness at not knowing music, as is attested by the judgement of Guido himself: "Many techniques are in use and not held in restraint by rule, since music has for a long time fallen into disuse while envy and inertia are destroying all study."[20]

The pattern of false counterpoint, which the Ambrosians call sequence, is this: a single singer intones the notes of the plain chant in a higher voice, and two or three, in unison with each other, accompany the notes of the chant on either a second or a fourth in a fixed order, which, since it is inconsistent with all the logic of modulation, I am loath to describe. Sometimes they begin such an accompaniment on a unison with the plain chant, proceeding thereafter by seconds and fourths until the end, or up to a certain terminal point where unisons are appropriate. Generally they begin on a second or fourth and always end on a unison.[21] Such a progression is indicated by the [first] example at hand:

Discordant Litanies of the Dead

20. Guido's reproachful verses, like the better known trochaic "Musicorum et cantorum magna est distantia...," may be found in *Guidonis versus de musica explanatione* (*PL*, CXLI, 405).

21. For a short historical account of this strange "expressionistic" practice, which was in vogue in Gafurius' time, see E. T. Ferand, "The 'Howling in Seconds' of the Lombards," *Musical Quarterly*, XXV (1939), 313–24.

Chapter fifteen   How a Singer Ought to Behave When He Performs[22]

Finally we are led to propose to young singers for the purpose of instruction and admonition that in performing they should not project their voices with an unusual and unsightly opening of their mouths, or with an absurd loud bellowing when they strive after melodies, especially in the divine mysteries. They should also spurn excessive vibrato and voices which are too loud, for they are not compatible with other voices similarly pitched. In short, because of their own continual instability they cannot maintain harmonious proportions with the other voices.

It is likewise fitting for one voice to be adjusted to another—a tenor to a cantus, for example—so that one may not be obscured by the other and succumb to its excessive clamor. When the voice of the tenor reaches up to the high cantus, one can readily consider in how many singers' voices the cantus may proportionately blend with this tenor. For the most part the tenor voice lies below the cantus in duple dimension, but when it is lower, it appears slow and powerful because of the longer time [*i.e.,* slower vibration] inherent in it. But the cantus voice, in a smaller space of time, is rapid and weak. Hence the low voice must sustain the upper voice as the strong sustain the weak, and not overpower it by its volume. It is

22. In the 1496 table of contents, Chapter 15 of Book III is entitled "De Regimine et Modestia Modulantis" ("Concerning the Discipline and Deportment of the Singer"), but here in the body of the text this chapter bears the variant title "Quo-modo se Regere debet Cantor dum Cantat."

not the confused and overshadowed sounds that produce harmony but rather the extremes and means mutually united in harmonic proportion. Furthermore, in performance the voices of the baritone and high contratenor conduct themselves in like manner to each other and to the other parts.

They call the tenor, which supports the cantus and is supported by the baritone, the basis of the relationship; for, while holding a median position, it is surrounded by the high cantus and the lower baritone. Thus, harmoniously, the other parts observe, heed, and venerate the tenor. It draws the harmony of both parts to itself and confers of itself on the others. Nor is it fitting that the tenor be broken up by chattering notes of small diminution because it upholds concordances with the other parts on individual notes. It will produce more discords than concords with the other parts by those diminished notes; hence it falls unsweetly upon the ears of those present.

Also an extravagant and indecorous movement of the head or hands reveals an unsound mind in a singer. The hand or head does not produce harmonious sounds; a well-modulated voice produces them. Those who sing imprudently are for the most part displeasing to those whom they expect to please. This was the principal reason why Guido himself, when he forsook florid, mensurable song, devoted himself to ecclesiastical modulation. For he says concerning these people, a fact which I painfully report, "In our times among all men singers are fools."[23]

Moreover, let the composer of music strive to adapt the melody in its sweetness to the words of the song, so that when the words concern love or a longing for death or some lamentation, he will articulate and arrange doleful sounds so far as he can, as the Venetians are wont to do. I believe it amounts to this in the last analysis: that the song be arranged in the fourth, sixth, or even the second mode, since these modes are more gentle and are known to produce this kind of effect easily. But when the words describe indignation and reproach, it is appropriate to emit rough, harder sounds, which generally are written in the third and seventh modes. Words of praise and modesty seek somehow the median sounds and are appropriately assigned to the first and eighth modes. But I have determined to describe the characteristics and powers of these modes in full in our *De harmonia* [IV, 1 *et seq.*].

23. Guido, *De ignoto cantu,* in *PL,* CXLI, 413. See also the opening lines of Guido's *Prologus antiphonarii sui,* in Gerbert, II, 34–37; and in English translation in Oliver Strunk, *Source Readings in Music History* (New York, 1950), p. 117.

Finally, let the composer of songs beware of arranging the tenor or baritone in a composition stationary throughout all its notes. For a stationary voice cannot harmonize proportionably with another part in attaining a perfect concordance by contrary motion. Therefore it does not fall in the category of a concordance which caresses the hearing. Such a sound is brought about on instruments like the bagpipe, which in the vernacular they call a *piva,* and according to Aristotle it is called *vernare,* and among the common *bordonizare,* or droning. No change occurs in it by raising or lowering, and hence no delight arises. But when the droning part is lowest, it sustains the very high and rapid sounds of this bagpipe, since it has been said that high sounds are supported and fortified by lower ones. They call a bagpipe *piva* from its very shrill sounds which always seem to cry "pi vi." In the elucidation of the Tenth [Musical] Problem, Peter of Abano asserts that *vernare* is "a sustained pitch, partaker of neither rise nor fall."[24]

It is fitting also that a cithara or lyre player use the tones of the lyre in order to bring out the harmony arising from its melodious strings and make his tones harmonious with its tones in alternating variety—for example, either by intoning the tenor with his stringed instrument and the cantus with his own voice, or conversely. Or he may even contrast the narrow intervals of one with the broad intervals of the other, or the speed of one to the slowness of the other, or highness to lowness, in such a way that simultaneously and together they deliver up a unified harmoniousness, a technique which, it is known, must be observed both in accordance with artistic method and in accordance with the teachings of the divine Plato in the seventh book of *The Laws.* Plato says: "The whole variety of rhythms must be adapted to the tones of the lyre."[25]

Book Three of *The Practice of Music*
by Franchinus Gaforus of Lodi
felicitously ends here.

---

24. "... extensum esse sonum nullius intentionis" (*Expositio,* XIX.x). Peter of Abano's interesting multiple-choice solutions to the tenth musical problem are not available in Hett or in other modern translations of Aristotle's *Problems.*

25. Jowett ed., II, 567.

BOOK FOUR

OF *The Practice
of Music*

[PROPORTION
IN MENSURAL
MUSIC]

C*hapter one* The Definition and Differentiation of Proportion

According to Euclid proportion is a fixed reciprocal relationship of two quantities of like genus in any dimension.[1] Some proportions are rational, others irrational.

A rational proportion is the reciprocal comparison of two commensurable quantities, whether they are in disjunct or continuous arrangement. In a disjunct proportion, such as 6 to 4, and in similar numerical relationships, a common divisor—some common measure uniting both terms exactly—is given. The number 2 multiplied by 3 makes 6; multiplied by 2, however, it makes 4. Hence the number 2 is called the common measure of both terms. In a continuous proportion, however, such as a three-foot line to a two-foot line, a half-foot, when considered as a fractional divisor, can serve as a common measure for both terms. In weights, too, there is proportion: in a quantity of nine ounces to a quantity of six, a three-ounce weight is recognized to be the common measure of both. Euclid in the introduction to Book X calls such quantities sharers.[2]

An irrational proportion, on the other hand, is the mutual relationship of two incommensurable quantities, as for example, the diagonal of a square to its side.[3] Of these two quantities no common divisor is found which measures both quantities exactly. Campanus and Albertus proved this most impressively in their work on proportions by their presentation of Proposition 7 from Euclid's Book X.[4] Euclid calls these incommensurable quanti-

1. Euclid, *Elementa geometriae*, v, Diffinitio 3, tr., with commentary, by Johannes Campanus (Venice, 1482).

2. Euclid, *Elementa*, Introduction to X.

3. The irrational number $\sqrt{2}$, arrived at by the Pythagorean theorem, is the length of the diagonal of a square whose sides are one unit long. (See Philip J. Davis, "Number," *Scientific American* [September 1964], pp. 52–53.)

4. Campanus, or Campano da Novara, was an Italian mathematician, astronomer, and physician of the thirteenth century, noted for his commentary on Euclid. Gafurius was undoubtedly acquainted with his 1482 edition of Euclid, and in fact, owned a copy of the *Elements*, which he donated to the Church of the Coronation in Lodi in 1518 (see Alessandro Caretta, Luigi Cremascoli, and Luigi Salamina, *Franchino*

ties surds. In fact, such an irrational proportion is dissociated from arithmetical theory because unity, at the very least, is a common measure for all numbers. Mathematicians are in general accord as to this.

But considering irrationality from an harmonic point of view, so to speak, we have proposed in Book III, Chapter 2, of the *Theorica*—and not inaptly, I think—that those intervals which do not measure up to full consonances on the chordotone be called irrational intervals. For from their dimensions no perfect common denominator is recognizable, as we shall show in the *De harmonia* [III, *passim*]. Therefore, since arithmetic proportion depends upon number, geometric proportion upon surfaces, and stereometric proportion upon solids (some authorities assign this to geometric proportion), so musical proportion, a sister to these sciences, proceeds in a similar manner. As we have explained in Book V of the *Theorica*, music, with numbers acting as guides, disposes its pitches along a continuous sounding string. We shall treat the matter in more detail in our work *De harmonia* [II, *passim*], where we intend to describe proportion according to the different genera.

The function of numbers which is relevant here deals with sounds according to their progression in time. Hence we postulate a dual role for musical proportion: first, in the disposition of sounds by consonant intervals, which belongs to the domain of the theorist; and second, in the temporal quantity of these sounds according to the numerical value of the notes, a matter ascribed to the active or practical discipline.

No matter what genus is being considered, our discussion will adhere steadfastly to rational proportion, because in the terms of each proportion some kind of common measure, unity at least, is present. Very often, also, proportion is viewed in terms of powers, as Albertus and Giovanni Marliani attest in their work on proportion.[5] Many authorities even consider proportion in terms of places and divisions of time, as Plato does in his *Timaeus*,[6] and as every school of philosophy concurs, insofar, of course, as

Gaffurio [Lodi, 1951], p. 117).

Albertus de Saxonia (d. 1390), whose *De proportionibus* was published in Venice in 1487 and again in 1502 in Bologna, was a leading medieval mathematician and Aristotelian, as well as the first rector at the University of Paris. See *Neue Deutsche Biographie* (Berlin, 1953), I, 135.

5. Marliani, a Milanese mathematician and a contemporary of Gafurius, was revered by his contemporaries as "a marvel of scientific attainments." He was a highly paid professor of medicine and astrology at the University of Pavia during Il Moro's reign. See L. Collison-Morley, *The Story of the Sforzas* (New York, 1934), p. 182.

6. *The Dialogues of Plato*, tr. B. Jowett (New York, 1937), II, 17.

something is more than or equal to something else. This is a characteristic of quantity, as Aristotle bears witness in his *Predicaments.*[7] Hence it is necessary, first of all, that proportion be present in both disjunct and continuous quantity: in sounds, locations, temporal values, weights, and powers.

There is also the proportion of equality, the reciprocal relationship of two equal quantities, such as 2:2 and a two-foot line to a two-foot line. A proportion of inequality, on the other hand, is the reciprocal relationship of two unequal quantities, such as 4:3 and a three-foot line to a two-foot line. Some of these unequal proportions are said to be of major inequality, when, that is, a larger quantity is made equal with respect to a smaller quantity, such as 4:3. Other proportions belong to minor inequality, when a smaller quantity is equated with a larger quantity, such as 3:4. Accordingly, there will be a corresponding proportion of inequality in music, the temporal equation of a larger number of notes in distribution and articulation with a smaller number of like notes, or of a smaller with a larger number, as this example discloses:[8]

It is clear from the above definition of proportion, as it is also evident in the musical example, that all figures or notes are compared in some proportion or other to notes like themselves in name and quantity. Semibreves of minor prolation, for instance, are matched with semibreves of minor prolation, and breves of perfect tempus with breves of perfect tem-

7. Aristotle, *In categorias,* II ("De quantitate"), tr. Boethius, in *PL,* LXIV, *passim.*
8. Glarean, *Dodekachordon,* III.xii.238 (Basel, 1547; Microcard facsim., Sibley Library, Rochester, New York).

pus. But if the proportion is arranged in some other way—if, for example, a sesquialter proportion is arranged in the higher voice of a composition counting three breves of perfect tempus with two breves of imperfect tempus arranged in the tenor part—you will perceive that such a sesquialter interpretation is absurd. These three breves of perfect tempus do not agree in quantitative value with two breves of imperfect tempus. For if you make a proportion of the parts of these breves which do not agree with each other in quantity—namely, nine semibreves of minor prolation to four semibreves of the same minor prolation—you will certainly not find a sesquialter relationship, which was indicated by the numbers appropriate to it, but a duple sesquiquarta [9:4] instead. The same thing will happen when you arrange to have three semibreves of major prolation equated with two semibreves of minor prolation according to the same sesquialter proportion, a fact proven by the example at hand:[9]

In order to remove doubt and indecision every proportion in a numerable arrangement of notes ought to be written with suitable numerical characters. If you designate a proportion by means of a single number— a sesquialter, for instance, by the number 3—this number 3 (and I should like to say this with the permission of certain people) might be compared not only to the number 2, with which it signifies a sesquialter proportion, but might be compared equally well to the number 1 for triple proportion, or to the number 4 for subsesquitertia. In the same way a composer could arbitrarily compare it with other numbers. Therefore, the terms of a proportion in music should be written down, so that the number for the group to be altered is placed directly above the term for the preceding group, like this: $\frac{3}{2}$. Or I might have said more clearly that the number for the notes to be diminished is written directly above the number for the preceding

9. Here Gafurius deliberately proves his point by negative illustration. This is the only musical example in the *Practica* in which the parts cannot be synchronized, where there is no fit.

group nearby to which it is to be reduced. Then the proportion as arranged in a composition will be clearly recognizable, so that when it refers to a preceding quantity in tempus or prolation, it will obey the natural interpretation of the proportionable numbers. So also, if, for example, a proportion is written among the notes of the higher voice scored in the quantitative value of the notes of another part—the tenor, as an illustration—then it will observe by imitation the same natural numerical scoring. Otherwise, the tenor and the upper voice would be arranged in disparate quantities. Among the remaining parts of a composition to be fitted together, the same method of treating proportions must also be used.

Chapter two   The Five Proportional Genera of Major and Minor Inequality

Proportion of major inequality proceeds in five ways: (1) either a larger number comprehends a smaller number several times exactly, and the proportion is called multiple, as 6:2, 4:1, and 5:1; or (2) a larger number comprehends a smaller number one time and in addition one aliquot part of the smaller number, and it is called *epimoria* or superparticular, as 3:2, 4:3, and 5:4; or (3) the larger contains the smaller once plus one aliquant part of the smaller number made up of several aliquot parts, and it is called superpartient, as 5:3, 7:4, 9:5, and 11:6; or (4) a larger number comprehends the smaller several times plus an aliquot part of the smaller and is called multiple superparticular, as 5:2, 7:3, and 9:4; or (5) a larger number possesses a smaller number several times and in addition one part that is not made up of one aliquot part but rather of several aliquot parts, and the proportion is called multiple superpartient, as 8:3, 11:4, 14:5, and 11:3. For there are five types of relationships, and they are the generic names of the proportions to which infinite species belong, as is evident in Book III of the *Theorica* and as we shall reveal in subsequent pages one by one.

Moreover, the effect of these proportions of major inequality is to diminish the notes to the value of those which precede them in composition according to the nature of the proportion, and thus a larger number of notes is equated with a smaller number of notes.

There are also five genera of proportions of minor inequality, in contrast to the aforementioned ones. They have the same nomenclature with the prefix *sub-*, as submultiple, subsuperparticular, subsuperpartient, submultiple superparticular, and submultiple superpartient. Of these, there also exist infinite species for whose names the prefix *sub-* is not inappropriate, as will be shown in succeeding pages. It is a property of these proportions of minor inequality to augment notes to the value of those which precede them, according to the nature and dictates of each individual proportion. Therefore, since such genera of minor inequality are opposite to the genera of major inequality, they exert the same sort of influence in a contrary manner. For the same science of opposites obtains. Submultiple is opposed to multiple, subsuperparticular to superparticular, and the others similarly. In summary, we maintain that the submultiple is opposite to the multiple genus because the effect which the one produces is voided by the succeeding opposite. This is verified by these number-formulae—1-2-1, 2-3-2, 3-5-3, 2-5-2, 3-8-3—in which the extreme terms are equal to each other.

Chapter three   The Multiple Genus and Its Species

The multiple genus occurs whenever a larger number, paired with and placed above a smaller number, contains the smaller number several times exactly—two, three, or four times, and so on. If the larger number contains the smaller one twice, the proportion is called duple, as 2:1, 4:2, and 6:3. This is the first species of the multiple genus, in which a larger number of notes is equivalent to a smaller number in such a way that each note of the larger number is diminished by half its quantity. It is indicated in music as follows—$\frac{2}{1}$ $\frac{4}{2}$ $\frac{6}{3}$—and may be observed in this harmonization.[10]

10. Glarean, *Dodekachordon*, III.xii.229.

If during the course of a composition a subduple proportion, the oppo-site of this duple, should follow it immediately,[11] with no sign of tempus interposed to obstruct its natural power, the duple proportion is at once destroyed, and the notes after it will be computed in accordance with their original numerical quantities, that is, the values in effect ahead of the sym-bol for duple proportion. This is because of the equality of the extremes arranged in these opposite proportions, as is proved by this example:[12]

11. Gafurius uses the Latin adverb *immediate* here in the sense employed by Bri-ennius in his explanation of *mediate* and *immediate* (*Harmonicorum libri tres*, III.iii, in John Wallis, ed., *Opera mathematica* [Oxford, 1699], III, 479–80). The term does not mean that the proportional signs are contiguous but that no sign of tempus or other proportion intervenes.

12. Glarean, *Dodekachordon*, III.xii.230.

Similarly, every proportion is voided whenever a sign of perfect or imperfect tempus is inserted after passages in proportion. Some composers
customarily represent duple proportion with the single cipher 2. Following
the reasoning given in Chapter 1 on sesquialter, this seems erroneous,
because a proportion is the weighing of two numbers in relation to each
other. Frequently, however, duple proportion is denoted in music by means
of a canon, without numbers, by the inscription "Diminished in duple,"
for example. Similarly, the other multiples are denoted by appropriate
canonic inscription.

Sometimes unequal proportion is indicated by means of identical signs
placed in the individual parts of a composition. If, for example, I notate
all parts of the score—cantus, tenor, and contratenor—with one and the
same sign of proportion right after a semicircle (which is the sign for imperfect tempus and the binary calculation of semibreves), I write the single
character of the number 2 for duple proportion, as is evident in this harmonization:

A harmonization of this type must be so handled that the notes of the
upper part are never matched with the notes of the tenor or contratenor,
or conversely, by means of a proportion of equality that is scored in the
one part and in the other with an identical sign. Instead, I think that the

quicker notes of each part in duple ought to be matched with like notes placed ahead of the sign of imperfect tempus, as though these notes were in proportion to preceding notes. This Ockeghem sets up in his chanson "L'Autre d'antans" as follows:[13]

Notwithstanding, I am distressed at the setting of a single number as an indication of a proportion. It has been previously mentioned that proportion cannot be constituted in less than two terms.

Triple Proportion

Triple proportion, the second species of the multiple genus, occurs when a larger number of following notes, paired with and placed above a smaller preceding number, is referred to and made equal to this smaller number of notes, comprehending the smaller three times exactly, as 3:1, 6:2, 9:3, and so on. In this proportion three notes are equivalent to one of the smaller number similar in name and quantity, in such a way that each of the three is diminished by two thirds of its normal value. It is indicated in music as follows: $\frac{3}{1}$ or $\frac{6}{2}$ or $\frac{9}{3}$, which the accompanying harmonization reveals:

13. This popular chanson is transcribed in *Trois chansonniers Français du XVe siècle,* ed. E. Droz (Paris, 1927), pp. 32–33. See also A. W. Ambros, *Geschichte der*

But if a subtriple, which is the opposite of triple proportion, is arranged among the figures or notes after the triple proportion, the triple will soon be destroyed, and the notes following this subtriple proportion will revert to the prior computation of the notes, that is, the way they were before the triple. This cancellation is also effected by individual opposite terms when they follow immediately upon one another, for the equality of the extremes is quite apparent, as it is set down in this example:[14]

Quadruple Proportion

Quadruple proportion, the third species of the multiple genus, occurs when a larger number of succeeding notes related to a smaller preceding number is equated with the smaller number and comprehends it four times exactly, as 4:1, 8:2, and 12:3. In this proportion four notes are computed

Musik, ed. Otto Kade (Leipzig, 1911), V, 12–13, where the chanson appears in modern transcription without text, except for the incipit "Lauter dantant." The original notation may be seen in the Mellon Chansonnier (p. 48), Yale University Library. The chanson is also cited by Tinctoris in his *Proportionale musices* (Couss., IV, 156).

14. Glarean, *Dodekachordon*, III.xii.231.

and equated with one note similar to themselves in both name and quantity, so that each note of the four is diminished by three fourths of its
quantitative value. It is represented in musical composition in this way:
$\frac{4}{1}$ $\frac{8}{2}$ $\frac{12}{3}$, the way it is expressed in this harmonization:[15]

When a subquadruple proportion is introduced immediately among the
notes, however, it causes an effect contrary to the quadruple proportion,
and the latter is at once consigned to oblivion, as is clear in this example:[16]

15. This fine example of a partial signature supports the dual-range theory; its cantus range from C to D (a major ninth) and its tenor from F to G (also a major ninth)
are a perfect fifth apart.

16. Glarean, *Dodekachordon,* III.xii.232.

Quintuple Proportion

Quintuple proportion, which is the fourth species of the multiple genus, occurs when a larger number of following notes comprehends a smaller number of preceding notes five times exactly and is equivalent in potency to this smaller number, as 5:1, 10:2, and 15:3. In this proportion five notes are equivalent in articulation and temporal value to one of the smaller number like themselves in both name and quantity, so that each one of these five notes is diminished by four fifths of its own value. The proportion is indicated in music in this way: $\frac{5}{1}$ $\frac{10}{2}$ $\frac{15}{3}$, as is here evident:

It will also have to be admitted that generally, even among the other proportions of major inequality of any one genus, each single note of the larger number ought to be diminished by as many portions of its quantity as there are units in the difference of the two terms. For example, inasmuch as the number 5 in relation to the number 1 produces a quintuple proportion, the numerical value of each unit comprehended in the number 5 will be five, so that each of these units may be separated into five diminished particles. But since the number 4 makes the difference of 5 and 1, the individual units of fives are equally diminished by four fifths of their normal value. Similar interpretation should be applied to the other species. Moreover, when a subquintuple is arranged in a composition immediately afterward, the subsequent notes will return to their former value, as is evident here:

Sextuple Proportion

Sextuple proportion, the fifth species of the multiple genus, occurs when a larger number of subsequent notes related to a smaller number of pre-

ceding notes comprehends it six times exactly and is equivalent to it both
in quantity and temporal value, as 6:1, 12:2, and 18:3. In this arrangement
six notes of the one are equivalent and equal to one similar to themselves
so that each single one of these six notes is diminished by five sixths of its
quantitative value. It is indicated in music in this way: $\frac{6}{1}$ $\frac{12}{2}$ $\frac{18}{3}$, and shown
in the following example:

If, however, a subsextuple proportion should be inserted immediately after
the sextuple, then the sextuple is voided, as is clear in this harmonization:

Septuple Proportion

Septuple proportion, the sixth species of the multiple genus, occurs when a larger number of succeeding notes contains a smaller number of preceding notes seven times exactly and is equivalent to it both in quantity and value, as 7:1, 14:2, and 21:3. In this way, seven notes are matched with one similar to themselves so that each of these seven notes is diminished by six sevenths of its value. It is indicated in music in this way: $\frac{7}{1}$ $\frac{14}{2}$ $\frac{21}{3}$. The composition below elucidates this proportion:

But if a contrary subseptuple proportion is placed immediately after the septuple, then the latter is destroyed, as is perceived in this composition:

Octuple Proportion

Octuple proportion, the seventh species in the order of the multiple genus, occurs when a larger number of subsequent notes comprehends a smaller number of antecedent notes eight times exactly and is equivalent to it in potency, as 8:1, 16:2, and 24:3. This proportion makes eight notes equal to one like themselves so that each of these eight is diminished by seven eighths of its value. It is indicated in music in this way: $\frac{8}{1}$ $\frac{16}{2}$ $\frac{24}{3}$, as is clear in this example:

When a suboctuple is placed immediately after the octuple, however, since it is opposite to this octuple, the octuple itself soon disappears, as is revealed here:

Nonuple Proportion

The eighth species of the multiple genus, the nonuple proportion, occurs when a larger number of following notes includes a smaller number of antecedent notes nine times exactly and is equated with it in quantity and temporal value, as 9:1, 18:2, and 27:3. Nine notes in this proportion are the equivalent of one exactly like themselves. Consequently each of these nine is diminished by eight ninths of its normal value. It is indicated in music in this way: $\frac{9}{1}$ $\frac{18}{2}$ $\frac{27}{3}$, as is evident here:

But if a subnonuple should immediately follow the nonuple, then the latter ceases to operate, as is perceived in this composition:

Decuple Proportion

Decuple proportion, the ninth species of the multiple genus, occurs when a larger number of following notes contains a smaller number of preceding notes ten times exactly and is equivalent to it in potency and value, as 10:1, 20:2, and 30:3. In this proportion ten notes are matched with one similar both in name and quantity so that each of these ten is diminished by nine tenths of its quantitative value. It is indicated in music like this: $\frac{10}{1}$ $\frac{20}{2}$ $\frac{30}{3}$, and is most clearly set forth in this composition:

A subdecuple proportion set immediately after a decuple, however, anni-
hilates and destroys it, as is evident in this example:

There are infinite species of this multiple genus which we relinquish to
the diligence of musicians for investigation.

Chapter four   The First Genus of Minor Inequality, the Submultiple, and Its Species

The submultiple genus, which is the first of minor inequality, occurs when a smaller number of notes, paired with and placed above a larger number, is related to the latter and comprehended within it several times exactly, as, for example, 1:2, 1:3, 1:4, 2:4, 2:6, 2:8, and so on. A smaller number is equated with a larger, so that the individual units of the smaller number submit to augmentation by as many particles of their own quantity as there are units making up the difference of the proportionate terms. For example, if I write a subtriple proportion with the numbers 3:9, since the number 6 makes up their difference, each unit of the number 3 will be increased by six thirds of its quantity. This also happens among all the genera of minor inequality. The species of this submultiple genus are infinite. The first is subduple, the second subtriple, the third subquadruple, the fourth subquintuple, and so on.

Subduple Proportion

Subduple proportion occurs when a smaller number of succeeding notes is contained in a larger number of preceding notes two times exactly, equivalent to it both in quantity and measure, as 1:2, 2:4, and 3:6. In this proportion each note of the smaller number is equivalent to and measured with two notes like itself in name and quantity so that it acquires twice its normal value. It is represented in music as follows: $\frac{1}{2}$ $\frac{2}{4}$ $\frac{3}{6}$, and is disclosed in this musical example:[17]

17. In this example, the subduple 4:8 proportion in the cantus relates retroactively to the "a la breve" notes preceding, so that breve and semibreve in the *tempus imperfectum diminutum,* ♩ and ♪ respectively, are transcribed as ♩ and ♩ in the subsequent subduple section.

Frequently it is the practice of musicians to indicate this subduple proportion by canonic inscription, when "It increases twofold" is written out.
I feel (and I should like to say this with the permission of certain people)
that this subduple proportion should be set forth in music only by appropriate numerical symbols or by canonic inscription. Since duple proportion
is contrary to subduple and is its opposite, if it should follow immediately
after the subduple, then the subduple itself disappears and is voided. This
is shown in the musical example here:

Subtriple Proportion

Subtriple proportion comes about when a smaller number of following notes is included in a larger number of preceding notes exactly three times, equalling it in power and in quantity, as, for example, 1:3, 2:6, and 3:9. This proportion makes each single note of the smaller number equal to three like itself so that the individual notes of the smaller number increase their normal quantity by three times. Moreover, it can be invoked in music by the canonic inscription: "It increases threefold." It is indicated in music by appropriate numbers as follows: $\frac{1}{3}$ $\frac{2}{6}$ $\frac{3}{9}$, and is destroyed by its opposite, triple proportion, following it immediately, as is clear in this example:

Subquadruple Proportion

Subquadruple proportion occurs when a smaller number of succeeding notes is included in a larger number of preceding notes exactly four times, and is equivalent to it in potency, as, for example, 1:4, 2:8, and 3:12. In this proportion each individual note of the smaller number is equal to four notes like itself so that it incurs a fourfold augmentation of its quantity. It is indicated in music in this way: $\frac{1}{4}$ $\frac{2}{8}$ $\frac{3}{12}$. It can be invoked by the canonic inscription: "It increases fourfold." Likewise, it is nullified by an opposite quadruple proportion, as is clear in the course of this harmonization:

Subquintuple Proportion

The subquintuple proportion occurs when a smaller number of subsequent notes is contained in a larger number of antecedent notes five times precisely and is equivalent to it in quantity and value, as 1:5, 2:10, 3:15, and 4:20. In this proportion the smaller number is equated with the larger so that each note of the smaller undergoes a fivefold increase of its quantity. Frequently it is invoked by the canonic inscription "It increases fivefold."

It is also indicated in composition in this way: $\frac{1}{5}$ $\frac{2}{10}$ $\frac{3}{15}$, and is voided by a quintuple opposite to it, which the accompanying harmonization proves:

We leave the other species of the submultiple genus, which are similar in technique, to be investigated by the ingenuity of musicians.

Chapter five   The Superparticular Genus and Its Species

The superparticular genus, which is the second of major inequality, is indicated when it is apparent that a larger number of following notes is being compared with a smaller number of preceding notes and the larger number comprehends the smaller number one time only plus one of its aliquot parts and is equivalent to it in potency and temporal value. An aliquot part is a fraction which, when multiplied by its own denominator, gives its whole exactly [that is, its whole as designated by the numerator], as a half multiplied by 2 completes its number wholly, and a third multiplied by 3, and a fourth multiplied by 4, and so on, a fact which is indeed clearly evident from the matters which are treated in Book III of the *Theorica.*

There are infinite species of this genus. The first is sesquialter, the second sesquitertia, the third sesquiquarta, the fourth sesquiquinta, and so on. You will perceive the order and sequence of these species when you have brought each single number into comparison with the smaller number contiguous and proximate to itself. Thus sesquialter will be 3:2, sesquitertia 4:3, sesquiquarta 5:4, sesquiquinta 6:5, and the others in the same way. In this genus it happens that a larger proportion is produced with smaller numbers but a smaller proportion is contained in larger numbers. For example, sesquialter 3:2 is larger than sesquitertia 4:3; the latter is also larger than sesquiquarta 5:4; and among the rest the same observation obtains. For one half is larger than one third, one third exceeds one fourth, and one fourth exceeds one fifth. By what degree a sesquialter exceeds a sesquitertia and a sesquitertia exceeds a sesquiquarta and the others exceed the rest we shall explain according to a general rule in a very detailed account in our *De harmonia* [I, 18 *passim.*]. But as for these *epimoria* species, let us examine them one at a time in natural order.

Sesquialter Proportion

The sesquialter proportion occurs when a larger number of succeeding notes contains a smaller number of preceding notes one and one-half times, and is equivalent in quantity and value, as 3:2, 6:4, 9:6, and 12:8. In this proportion three notes are equated with two like themselves in both name and quantity, so that each one of these three is diminished by one third of its normal quantity. It is represented in music in this way: $\frac{3}{2}$ $\frac{6}{4}$ $\frac{9}{6}$, which the composition at hand discloses:

It should be observed that in proportion, if that fraction by which a note is diminished is a figurable part of the note—for example, one third of a semibreve in perfect prolation (this is a minim) or one third of a breve in perfect tempus (this is, of course, a semibreve) or one fourth of a semibreve in minor prolation (this is a seminim) or in any other way you please —these diminished notes will be readily discerned and articulated, as is set forth in this example:[18]

18. Glarean, *Dodekachordon,* III.xii.234.

But if that quantity by which each note of the larger number is diminished is not a figurable, aliquot part of its whole—if, for example, it is a fifth of one semibreve, which is not included in the ordinary handling of notes—then the diminished quantities of these notes are joined in a certain kind of continuity so that the normal quantity of each note cannot be distinguished readily from another by a distinct separating mean. So, for example, one quantity and measure is continued out of another just the way a sounding string is distorted when it is struck on an instrument. For the initial striking of a string emits a lower sound, but when it is set in motion, it carries this sound to a higher pitch. We may also observe this phenomenon, to be sure, with our eyes when we inspect the colors of a rainbow. For they are in such proximity to each other that through a continuous mutation the color of one fuses into the next color with no mean separating any two colors.

Sesquialter proportion is often indicated in music without numerical characters, whenever, that is, it is written down with blackened notes or filled in with some other color to represent imperfect quantities of notes, like this:

As a matter of fact, my teacher, the musician Bonadies, used a single colored semibreve of minor prolation, a single breve of imperfect tempus, or only two colored notes, which are not susceptible to ternary division, for duple proportion, not for hemiola.

When you sesquialter single minims by blackening them, they will be called sesquialtered minims because then, if they all proceed according to a ternary division, there is no difference of notational representation between these sesquialtered minims and ordinary seminims. If, however, there are only six colored minims, which can either be sesquialtered minims or simple seminims, then if a single normal or white minim immediately precedes them, a minim with which the first two colored minims can be counted, then all six of these will be seminims. The same situation prevails if a single uncolored minim immediately follows this group of six. But if a single uncolored minim neither precedes nor follows them immediately, then all will be sesquialtered minims. If there are only five colored minims and a single uncolored minim precedes them immediately, then the first two colored notes will be seminims, but the last three notes will be called sesquialtered minims. If a single uncolored minim immediately follows these five, then the first three colored notes will be sesquialtered and the two final ones will be seminims, which are figured with the succeeding uncolored minim. If there are seven colored minims, then the first four are seminimed and the last three are sesquialtered. Concerning this matter the present example is subjoined:

Sometimes, however, a colored minim or another note can be transferred by means of syncopation. Such a note will also be subject to sesquialteration, and at one time or another it will depart from sesquialteration. We believe that this should be left to the discretion of the composer. However, it ought to be noticed generally that the sesquialter arranged in colored notes should not be written with its own special numerical characters lest by chance we should run unexpectedly into a conflict between two signs of sesquialteration which, taken together, result not in sesquialter but rather in duple-sesquiquarta proportion, as is clear in the numbers 9, 6, 4. Busnois inadvisedly put this in the contratenor acutus of the Sanctus in his mass *L'homme armé.*[19] Tinctoris sharply reproved him for this because he placed the number 3, by which he was accustomed to indi-

---

19. Antoine Busnois (d. 1492), a contemporary Burgundian of Ockeghem, composed a substantial repertory of chanson music which survives in a variety of MSS. His *Missa l'homme armé,* written c. 1475, is also cited by Tinctoris. It is printed in *Monumenta polyphoniae liturgicae,* Ser. I, No. 2 (Rome, 1948).

cate the sesquialter, ahead of the colored notes of the sesquialter, as follows:[20]

I am doubtful, however. I would not condemn this practice, because when
vocal compositions are performed in public, they should be understood and
sung by the performers without the hesitancy there which many have
shown. The character itself does not produce the proportion; the notes
themselves sesquialtered by coloration point up the difference from those
other notes which are ambiguous. Suppose six colored minims are arranged
either between, before, or after several normal, uncolored minims. The
latter of these can be sesquialtered and seminimed by the number 3 by
itself. When they are sesquialtered, the 3 will fittingly be placed in front,
for purposes of recognition, or below, as some people do, a fact which is
lucidly proved in the example at hand:

20. Tinctoris, *Proportionale,* III, in Couss., IV, 174.

Such minims sesquialtered by this coloration are generally not syncopated in practice, but colored semibreves and breves of this sort are customarily syncopated more often. Moreover, it should be observed that
when you see three colored minims, if a fourth such colored minim is before or after them and is to be figured in with these three in syncopation,
then these three will be seminims and the fourth colored seminim will be
grouped with them in distribution [even though separated from them by
larger notes], a fact which the accompanying example shows:

There are also those who express sesquialter proportion in music by the
sign of perfect prolation, that is, with a point placed within the sign of
tempus, as follows: ☉, ⊙. They perceive no difference between prolation
and proportion, a matter which rational reflection has not taken long to
confute. For sesquialter proportion makes three minims equal to two. Perfect prolation, however, imputes these three regular minims to each semibreve, and they are not to be equated with two. To be sure, this happens
in the same way for a breve of perfect tempus, which is resolved into three
semibreves but is nevertheless not to be equated with two semibreves
comprehended in a breve note of imperfect tempus. Guillaume Dufay, in
fact, noticing this, utilized sesquialter intelligently in the "Et in terra pax,"
in the "Patrem," and in the "Unam sanctam catholicam" of his *Saint An-
thony* mass, where he indicated perfect or major prolation and imperfect
tempus.[21] He assigned to each semibreve three normal minims that were

21. Also cited by Tinctoris in his *Proportionale,* III (Couss., IV, 171), this is prob-

in no wise to be equated with two. Philippe de Bourges also sensibly employed the same practice in a certain "Et in terra pax," arranging by means of the signature for perfect prolation three regular, normal minims for each semibreve—not equal to two minims of imperfect or minor prolation.[22] Likewise, Tinctoris and several others display this correctly in their compositions.

Nor do I approve of a common corruption among many people who, when they indicate sesquialter proportion in music by means of the number 3 only, set down imperfect tempus for perfect tempus and minor prolation for major prolation (which is absurd). They consider the number 3 a sign of alteration and perfection among the notes, whereas it is readily apparent that augmentation among the notes is produced from a diminution of the proportion, as is notated in this example:

ably the *Missa de Sancto Anthonii Viennensis,* a mass for three voices printed in Guillaume Dufay, *Opera omnia,* ed. H. Besseler (*Corpus mensurabilis musicae,* II; American Institute of Musicology, 1947).

22. Philippe, or Philippon, de Bourges was a French organist and a contemporary of Ockeghem. Biographical data is scanty. See *Biographie universelle des musiciens,* ed. F. J. Fétis, VII (Paris, 1870), 34; and also Robert Eitner, *Quellen-Lexikon der Musiker und Musikgelehrten* (Leipzig, 1900–1904), VII, 422, where it is suggested that he, Basiron, and Philippe des Bruges may be identical. Apparently, too, the Philippon who is represented in Petrucci's *Odhecaton* by the chanson *a 4,* "Rosa playsant," is Philippe de Bourges. Some of de Bourges' masses are preserved in manuscript in the archives of the pontifical chapel. It is quite likely that he spent some time in Italy.

A perfect breve and an altered semibreve are arranged only in perfect tempus, whose proper signature is the circle. Only major or perfect prolation, whose proper signature is a point affixed within the sign of tempus, joins together a perfect semibreve and an alterable minim. In imperfect tempus, which the semicircle signifies, however, the breve note always possesses only two semibreves, whether it is a regular breve note or one that is diminished in some proportion, except when it receives a point of augmentation; but the semibreve never receives the increase of alteration in imperfect tempus. By the same token a semibreve in minor prolation does not acquire perfection, nor can the minim be altered.

There are also those who do not diminish rests in sesquialter proportion as that proportion demands, believing that a kind of imperfection is brought about by that proportion. Concerning these people I would like to say, by their leave, that there must be a way to treat diminutions of proportions to which both notes and rests are subject and a different way to treat imperfections of notes which are recognized to have lost as much as one third of their value in computation. We have discussed this in detail in our tract *On Notes.*[23] Rests are not, in the latter case, generally subject to imperfection.

It seems right that this should also be noted in regard to sesquialter and other proportions: that when proportionate notes are presented in perfect quantity—proportionate breves and semibreves in perfect tempus, for example, and semibreves and minims in perfect prolation—these notes can be varied according to the accidents of their own perfect quantity, for an uncolored breve before a breve will be perfect, resolvable into three semibreves which are nevertheless equated with two according to the treatment of the proportion. Moreover, a second semibreve between two breves will be altered. An uncolored semibreve in perfect prolation before one like itself will contain three minims equated with two. The second of these two minims arranged between two semibreves will be altered. It is clear,

23. This may refer to the unpublished *Proportioni practicabili* which Gafurius completed sometime between 1481 and 1483.

according to this reasoning, that breve and semibreve rests are perfect, a fact which the accompanying harmonization affirms:

If, however, a sesquialter proportion is arranged among notes subject to imperfect quantity, then all the notes and rests will always be imperfect, so that if this sesquialter proportion is written in imperfect tempus, equating three breves to two, then each of these three breves always loses one third of its normal quantity. Similarly, three breve rests are computed proportionately (equal to two) so that each breve rest is diminished by one third of its normal quantity. The same thing must be observed concerning three semibreves of minor prolation and their rests. In sesquialter proportion it is clear that these must always sacrifice one third of themselves, as is set forth in this harmonization:

An arrangement of sesquialter proportion in music would be meaningless if the rests and notes were not treated exactly alike in diminution. Every proportion of major inequality written in music diminishes the individual notes and rests equally and uniformly according to the proportion's own natural power, and a proportion in minor inequality augments the notes and rests equally.

Many authorities also designate the sesquialter proportion arranged in colored notes, which they also call hemiola, by means of a sign of imperfect tempus and major prolation reversed, like this: ☉ . In my opinion this is erroneous. It is manifest from those matters which have been discussed that sesquialter proportion in music is indicated by coloration of the notes themselves. I prefer to call this a diminution equivalent to sesquialter proportion which is canceled when uncolored notes follow it immediately. I repeat, it is marked by appropriate numerical characters and is patently destroyed by its opposite, the subsesquialter proportion following it immediately, as is proved by this harmonization:

Sesquitertia Proportion

The sesquitertia proportion occurs when a larger number of following notes contains a smaller number of preceding notes one and one-third times and is equivalent to it in potency and temporal value, as 4:3, 8:6, and 12:9. This proportion equates four notes to three like themselves in name and quantity, so that each one of these four notes is diminished by a fourth of its normal value. It is notated in music as follows: $\frac{4}{3}$ $\frac{8}{6}$ $\frac{12}{9}$, and is cancelled by its opposite, a subsesquitertia, immediately following it, which is perceived in this harmonization:

Some musicians have desired that this sesquitertia be understood in music by the sign of imperfect tempus turned backward like this: ◔ . Prosdocimus of Padua, in the presentation of his brief work on Johannes de Muris' "Quilibet in arte practica," and Tinctoris, in his tract on proportion, sharply assail this practice.[24]

Sesquiquarta Proportion

The proportion is called sesquiquarta when a larger number of following notes comprehends a smaller number of preceding notes one and one-fourth times and is equivalent to it in quantity and temporal value, as 5:4, 10:8, and 15:12. In this proportion five notes are equated with four like themselves, so that each of the five is diminished by four fifths of its value. It is indicated in music in this way: $\frac{5}{4}$ $\frac{10}{8}$ $\frac{15}{12}$, and is nullified by a subsesquiquarta immediately succeeding it, as shown in this harmonization:

24. The brief work mentioned here is the *Expositiones tractatus practice cantus mensuralis* compiled by Prosdocimus in 1404, and like Gafurius' *Glossemata,* based on Johannes de Muris' *Practica musica.* The manuscript is conserved in the Biblioteca

Sesquiquinta Proportion

A sesquiquinta proportion occurs when a larger number of following notes contains a smaller number preceding one and one-fifth times and is equivalent to it in potency and value, as 6:5, 12:10, and 18:15. This proportion equates six notes with five like themselves, so that each single note of the six is diminished by one sixth of its quantitative value. It is indicated in music in this way: $\frac{6}{5}$ $\frac{12}{10}$ $\frac{18}{15}$, and it vanishes with a subsesquiquinta, its opposite, following immediately upon it, which the present example attests:

del Liceo Musicale in Bologna. "Quilibet in arte practica mensurabilis cantus . . ." is the opening line of text to the "Libellus practice cantus mensurabilis," the second part of de Muris' *Ars nova musicae* (Couss., III, 46–58). For Tinctoris' remarks, see his *Proportionale*, III, in Couss., IV, 172.

Sesquisexta Proportion

Sesquisexta proportion occurs when a larger number of succeeding notes comprehends a smaller number of antecedent notes one and one-sixth times and is equal to it in temporal value, as 7:6, 14:12, and 21:18. Seven notes are equivalent to six like themselves in this proportion, so that each of these seven notes is diminished by one seventh of its proper quantity. It is indicated in music in this way, of course: $\frac{7}{6}$ $\frac{14}{12}$ $\frac{21}{18}$, and is voided by its opposite, a subsesquisexta, as is evident here:

Sesquiseptima Proportion

Sesquiseptima proportion occurs when a larger number of following notes contains a smaller number of preceding notes one and one-seventh times, equalling it in potency, as 8:7, 16:14, and 24:21. In this proportion eight notes are equivalent to and computed with seven like themselves, so that each of these eight is diminished by an eighth of its value. It is indicated in music in this way: $\frac{8}{7}$ $\frac{16}{14}$ $\frac{24}{21}$. But if a subsesquiseptima proportion immediately follows it, it will vanish, since it is its opposite, as is written in this example:

Sesquioctave Proportion

A sesquioctave proportion takes place when a larger number of succeeding notes is equivalent to and comprehends a smaller number of preceding notes one and one-eighth times, as 9:8, 18:16, and 27:24. This proportion equates nine notes with eight notes like themselves, so that each one of the nine is diminished by a ninth of its proper quantity. It is indicated in music in this way: $\frac{9}{8}$ $\frac{18}{16}$ $\frac{27}{24}$, and it is voided by its opposite, a subsesquioctave, as is shown in this harmonization:

Sesquinona Proportion

A sesquinona proportion occurs when a larger number of succeeding notes is related to a smaller number of antecedent notes and made equal to it. The larger number contains the smaller number one and one-ninth times, as 10:9, 20:18, and 30:27. In this proportion ten notes are equal to nine like themselves, so that each of the ten is diminished by one tenth. It is represented in music as follows: $\frac{10}{9}$ $\frac{20}{18}$ $\frac{[30]}{[27]}$. Moreover, it is voided by its opposite, a subsesquinona, as the present example proves:

For the rest, the diligent musician can easily consider the remaining species of this superparticular genus by means of a similar approach.

Chapter six The Subsuperparticular Genus and Its Species

The subsuperparticular genus occurs when a smaller number of following notes related to a larger number of preceding notes is equivalent to the larger number in quantity and potency and is comprehended in it one time plus one of its aliquot parts, as 2:3, 3:4, 4:5, and so on. Its species are infinite. The first is subsesquialter, the second subsesquitertia, the third subsesquiquarta, the fourth subsesquiquinta, and so forth. These species must be discussed one by one.

Subsesquialter Proportion

Subsesquialter proportion is effected when a smaller number of following notes is included in a larger number of preceding notes only one and one-half times and is equal to it in potency and temporal value, as 2:3, 4:6, 6:9, and so on. In this proportion two notes are equivalent to and measured with three notes like themselves, so that each of these two is augmented by half of its normal quantity. It is indicated in music as follows: $\frac{2}{3}$ $\frac{4}{6}$ $\frac{6}{9}$, and is destroyed by its opposite, a sesquialter, following it immediately, as is perceived in this harmonization:

Subsesquitertia Proportion

Subsesquitertia proportion occurs when a smaller number of following notes is included in a larger number of preceding notes one and one-third times and is equivalent to the larger in temporal value, as 3:4, 6:8, 9:12, and so on. In this proportion three notes are equated and balanced with four like themselves both in name and quantity, so that each of these three undergoes augmentation of its normal quantity by a third. It is indicated in music in this way: $\frac{3}{4}$ $\frac{6}{8}$ $\frac{9}{12}$, and is destroyed by its opposite, sesquitertia, following it. The proportion is perceived in this example:

Subsesquiquarta Proportion

Subsesquiquarta proportion occurs when a smaller number of following notes is comprehended in a larger number of preceding notes one and one-fourth times and is equivalent to it in quantity and value, as 4:5, 8:10, and 12:15. This proportion equates four notes with five like themselves, so that each of these four is augmented by a fourth of its proper value. It is indicated in music like this: $\frac{4}{5}$ $\frac{8}{10}$ $\frac{12}{15}$. When a sesquiquarta follows it immediately, however, it will be destroyed and vanish, which the present example shows:

Subsesquiquinta Proportion

The subsesquiquinta proportion occurs when a smaller number of succeeding notes is contained in a larger number of preceding notes one and one-
fifth times and is equivalent to the larger, as 5:6, 10:12, 15:18, and so on.
This proportion equates five notes with six like themselves in name and
quantity, so that each of these five receives an increment of a fifth in value.
It is indicated in music in this way: $\frac{5}{6}$ $\frac{10}{12}$ $\frac{15}{18}$, and is destroyed by a sesquiquinta, its opposite. This is set forth in the accompanying harmonization:

We relinquish to the diligence of musicians the investigation of the remaining species of this subsuperparticular genus. Meanwhile, O most delightful singer, do not be disturbed if you should discover in the arrangement of some proportion an incomplete number of notes. As a matter of
practice, a passage which we do not set down in semibreves you will treat
as if it were in minims. Furthermore, among proportions which are designated only by the voiding of a preceding sign, you will occasionally find,
for the sake of brevity, an imperfect quantity among the notes and also in
the tenor parts a temporal computation of notes that is either excessive or
diminished for the same reason.

Chapter seven   The Superpartient Genus and Its Species

The superpartient, which is the third genus of major inequality,
occurs when a larger number of following notes in relation to a smaller
number of preceding notes contains the smaller number once and in addition one aliquant part derived from several aliquot parts. This larger number is equated with the smaller in potency and duration. Therefore, when
that aliquant part of the smaller number, which is also the difference and
excess of the two terms, shows two parts of the specified smaller number,
a superbipartient proportion will result.

The proportion also receives another, more specific name, so that if
these two aliquot parts of the smaller number are thirds, the proportion
will be called superbipartient thirds, as 5:3. If, however, they are fifths, the
proportion will be called superbipartient fifths, as 7:5, and if they are sevenths, it will be called superbipartient sevenths, as 9:7.

But when the aliquant part of the smaller term, the amount by which
the larger exceeds this smaller term, shows three aliquot parts of its smaller
number, the proportion will be supertripartient. It, too, is named more
specifically, so that if those three aliquot parts of the smaller term are
fourths of it, the proportion will be called supertripartient fourths, as 7:4.
If, however, the parts are fifths, it will be called supertripartient fifths, as

8:5. If they should be sevenths, it will be supertripartient sevenths, as 10:7.

But when the difference of the terms, which is called the aliquant part of the smaller, contains four aliquot parts of this smaller number, the proportion will be called superquatripartient. There is a more specific name for it, too, so that when, for example, each of these four aliquot parts are one fifth of this smaller number, the proportion will be called superquatripartient fifths, as 9:5. If these four parts should be sevenths of the smaller number, the proportion will be called superquatripartient sevenths, as 11:7 and 22:14.

For the remaining species the method of interpretation is exactly the same.

Furthermore, in this superpartient genus a proportion acquiring the name "partient" from an even number will join with the divided parts of the uneven number (the smaller one, of course). Take for example the superbipartient thirds, or 5:3. The partient number, which is the excess of the two terms, is the even number 2. Hence the proportion is superbipartient. But when the terms are divided, there is a remainder of two thirds of the odd number 3; then the proportion is called superbipartient thirds. If the partient number is uneven, it joins, logically, the divided parts of the even number, such as 7:4, supertripartient fourths. For in this case, the partient is the uneven number 3, the difference between the terms. Hence the proportion is called supertripartient. But the divided parts of the even number are four, and consequently the proportion is called supertripartient fourths.

Very often, too, in the same way, the partient, uneven number joins the divided parts of an uneven number, as in 10:7, supertripartient sevenths. But if both the partient number and the divided parts are manipulated under the classification of even numbers, they will not fit into the superpartient but into a superparticular relationship, as 6:4. This is not called superbipartient fourths but sesquialter, and 8:6 is not superbipartient sixths but sesquitertia. When, therefore, the excess or difference of the terms of any proportion is an aliquot part of the smaller term (and also if it contains several aliquot parts of this smaller term), that proportion should be considered, not in the superpartient, but in the superparticular genus, as 9:6. 9:6 is not called supertripartient sixths but sesquialter, because the larger term contains the smaller term one time and in addition one half of this smaller number (which is the same as three sixths of it).

There are infinite species of the superpartient genus; the first is superbipartient, the second is supertripartient, the third is superquatripartient, the fourth is superquintupartient, and the fifth is supersextupartient. The process goes on in this manner to infinity.

In natural numbers these first species may be considered as bases, in this order. The first species is produced out of terms between which a single term intervenes. In 5:3, for example, the number 4 is the mean, and in 7:5 the mean of the terms is 6. (In such a consideration we call the numbers terms.) The second species interposes two numbers, as in 7:4, in which the numbers 5 and 6 come in between. But if a proportion arises from 8:5, the numbers 6 and 7 intervene. The third species interposes three numbers between its terms, as in 9:5, whose means are 6, 7, and 8, and 11:7, whose means are 8, 9, and 10. The fourth species encloses four numbers between its extreme terms, as in 11:6, whose means are 7, 8, 9, and 10, and in 12:7, whose means are 8, 9, 10, and 11.

Similarly, whatever the number of the species is, there will logically be that many numbers interposed between the terms of the proportion; so that if it were the first species, one number would lie between its terms; if the second, two numbers would be enclosed between these terms; if the third, three; if the fourth, four; if the fifth, five; and so on. The first, the superbipartient, encloses one number between its terms. The second, supertripartient, shows two numbers to be contained between its terms. The third, superquatripartient, interposes three numbers between its terms. The fourth is superquintupartient, whose terms enclose four numbers. The others also proceed in this way in a simple and natural sequence of numbers.

These species, furthermore, are called subalternates, for they cross over into the status of genera. Hence they are also classified as genera by some authorities because one of the superbipartient proportions is superbipartient thirds, as 5:3, another is superbipartient fifths, as 7:5, another superbipartient sevenths, as 9:7, and so on. In fact, logicians call these specialized species.

Similarly, among the supertripartients, one is supertripartient fourths, as 7:4, another supertripartient fifths, as 8:5, another supertripartient sevenths, as 10:7. Likewise, of the superquatripartients, one is superquatripartient fifths, as 9:5, another superquatripartient sevenths, as 11:7, another superquatripartient ninths, as 13:9. Of the superquintupartients too, one is superquintupartient sixths, as 11:6, another superquintupartient sevenths, as 12:7, another superquintupartient eighths, as 13:8. And other such superpartient species are converted into genera, and in a way, into unlimited species by continuing in this same manner. For a genus is an aggregation of many species which in diverse ways share one and the same nature. And a species is a special quantity and quality of a genus. But let the series be described as follows:

The Superbipartient Thirds Proportion

The superbipartient thirds proportion occurs when a larger number of following notes contains a smaller number of preceding notes once plus one aliquant part made from two thirds of this smaller number. The larger number is equivalent to the smaller, as 5:3, 10:6, and 15:9. In this proportion five notes are equal to and measured with three like themselves, so that each of these five is diminished by two fifths of its normal quantity. It is represented in music as follows: $\frac{5}{3}$ $\frac{10}{6}$ $\frac{15}{9}$, and is destroyed by its opposite, subsuperbipartient thirds, a fact which is demonstrated in the accompanying example:

Superbipartient Fifths Proportion

The superbipartient fifths proportion occurs when a larger number of succeeding notes is equivalent to and contains a smaller number of preceding notes one and two-fifths times, as 7:5, 14:10, and 21:15. In this proportion seven notes are equated with five like themselves both in name and quantity, so that each of these seven is diminished by two sevenths of its normal value. It is indicated in music like this: $\frac{7}{5}$ $\frac{14}{10}$ $\frac{21}{15}$, and is destroyed by a subsuperbipartient fifths proportion, its opposite, as is readily observed in this composition:

Superbipartient Sevenths Proportion

The superbipartient sevenths proportion occurs when a larger number of succeeding notes is equivalent to a smaller antecedent number, containing it one and two-sevenths times, as 9:7, 18:14, and 27:21. This proportion equates nine notes with seven like themselves, so that each of these nine is diminished by two ninths of its normal value. It is indicated in music, of course, like this: $\frac{9}{7}$ $\frac{18}{14}$ $\frac{27}{21}$, and is destroyed by its opposite proportion, a subsuperbipartient sevenths, as is perceived in this composition:

Supertripartient Fourths Proportion

The supertripartient fourths proportion occurs when a larger number of following notes comprehends a smaller antecedent number one and three-fourths times and is equal to it in value, as 7:4, 14:8, and 21:12. In this proportion seven notes are equated and measured with four like themselves, so that each of these seven is diminished by three sevenths of its value. It is indicated in music in this way: $\frac{7}{4}$ $\frac{14}{8}$ $\frac{21}{12}$. It is destroyed, however, by its opposite, the subsupertripartient fourths, as shown here:

Supertripartient Fifths Proportion

The supertripartient fifths proportion occurs when a larger number of following notes contains a smaller number preceding one and three-fifths times and is equivalent to it in potency, as 8:5, 16:10, and 24:15. In this proportion eight notes are computed with five like themselves, so that each of these eight is diminished by three eighths of its normal quantity. It is indicated in music like this: $\frac{8}{5}$ $\frac{16}{10}$ $\frac{24}{15}$, and is voided by its opposite, the subsupertripartient fifths proportion, as evident here:

Supertripartient Sevenths Proportion

The supertripartient sevenths proportion occurs when a larger number of succeeding notes contains a smaller number preceding one and three-sevenths times and is equivalent to it, as 10:7, 20:14, and 30:21. This proportion equates ten notes with seven like themselves in duration, so that each of these ten is diminished by three tenths of its value. It is indicated in composition like this: $\frac{10}{7}$ $\frac{20}{14}$ $\frac{30}{21}$. Moreover, it is voided by its opposite, the subsupertripartient sevenths, as here:

Superquatripartient Fifths Proportion

The superquatripartient fifths proportion occurs when a larger number of following notes comprehends a preceding smaller number one and four-fifths times and is equivalent to it, as 9:5, 18:10, and 27:15. This proportion computes nine notes with five like themselves, so that each of these nine is diminished by four ninths of its proper quantity. It is indicated in music as follows: $\frac{9}{5}$ $\frac{18}{10}$ $\frac{27}{15}$, and voided by its opposite, a subsuperquatripartient fifths, as demonstrated in this harmonization:

Superquatripartient Sevenths Proportion

The superquatripartient sevenths proportion occurs when a larger number of following notes comprehends a preceding smaller number one and four-sevenths times, as 11:7, 22:14, and 33:21. In this proportion eleven notes are equivalent to seven like themselves, so that each of these eleven is diminished by four elevenths of its value. It is indicated in music as follows: $\frac{11}{7}$ $\frac{22}{14}$ $\frac{33}{21}$, and is also voided by its opposite, the subsuperquatripartient sevenths, as the subjoined example proves:

Superquatripartient Ninths Proportion

The superquatripartient ninths proportion occurs when a larger number of following notes contains a preceding smaller number one and four-ninths times and is equated with it, as 13:9, 26:18, and 39:27. This proportion computes thirteen notes with nine like themselves, so that each of these thirteen is diminished by four thirteenths of its quantitative value. It is indicated in music as follows: $\frac{13}{9}$ $\frac{26}{18}$ $\frac{39}{27}$, and voided by its opposite proportion, a subsuperquatripartient ninths, as here:

Superquintupartient Sixths Proportion

The superquintupartient sixths proportion occurs when a larger number of following notes contains a preceding smaller number once plus an aliquant part of it made up of five sixths of the smaller number, as 11:6, 22:12, and 33:18. In this proportion eleven notes are equivalent to and computed with six like themselves, both in name and quantity, so that each of these eleven is diminished by five elevenths of its proper quantity. It is indicated in music as follows: $\frac{11}{6}$　$\frac{22}{12}$　$\frac{33}{18}$. It is also voided by its opposite, a subsuperquintupartient sixths proportion, which the accompanying harmonization discloses:

Superquintupartient Sevenths Proportion

The superquintupartient sevenths proportion occurs when a larger number of following notes contains a preceding smaller number one and five-sevenths times, as 12:7, 24:14, and 36:21. This proportion makes twelve notes equal to seven like themselves, so that each of these twelve is diminished by five twelfths of its proper quantity. It is indicated in music as follows:

$\frac{12}{7}$ $\frac{24}{14}$ $\frac{36}{21}$. It is voided by a subsuperquintupartient sevenths, its opposite, as is evident here:

Supersextupartient Sevenths Proportion

The supersextupartient sevenths proportion occurs when a larger number of following notes comprehends a smaller preceding number one and six-sevenths times, as 13:7, 26:14, and 39:21. In this proportion thirteen notes are equivalent to and measured with seven like themselves, so that each of these thirteen is diminished by six thirteenths of its potency and quantity. It is indicated in music as follows: $\frac{13}{7}$ $\frac{26}{14}$ $\frac{39}{21}$, and voided by the subsupersextupartient sevenths proportion, as perceived in this harmonization:

We leave the investigation of the remaining subalternate and also of the specialized species of this superpartient genus to the diligence of musicians.

Chapter eight The Subsuperpartient Genus and Its Species

The subsuperpartient, which is the third genus of minor inequality, opposite, of course, to the superpartient, occurs when a smaller number of following notes related to a larger number of preceding notes is comprehended in the larger number once plus one aliquant part made up of several aliquot parts of the smaller number, this smaller number being equal to the larger in value. There are subalternate species of this genus: subsuperbipartient, subsupertripartient, subsuperquatripartient, subsuperquintupartient, and so on. Moreover, there are specialized species: subsuperbipartient thirds, subsuperbipartient fifths, subsuperbipartient sevenths, and similarly, subsupertripartient fourths, subsupertripartient fifths, subsupertripartient sevenths. The others proceed according to the same system. These are to be discussed one by one.

Subsuperbipartient Thirds Proportion

The subsuperbipartient thirds proportion occurs when a smaller number of following notes is contained in a larger number of preceding notes once plus one of its aliquant parts constructed from two thirds of this smaller number and is equivalent to the larger, as 3:5, 6:10, 9:15, and so forth. In this proportion three notes are equivalent to and measured with five like themselves both in name and quantity, so that each of these three undergoes augmentation by two thirds of its normal quantity. It is notated in music as follows: $\frac{3}{5}$ $\frac{6}{10}$ $\frac{9}{15}$. It is destroyed by its opposite, superbipartient thirds, immediately following it, as is clearly perceived in this harmonization:

Subsuperbipartient Fifths Proportion

The subsuperbipartient fifths proportion occurs when a smaller number of following notes is contained in a larger number preceding one and two-fifths times, as 5:7, 10:14, 15:21, and so on. In this proportion five notes are equivalent to and measured with seven like themselves, so that each of these five receives an increment of two fifths of its proper quantity. It is indicated in music in this way: $\frac{5}{7}$ $\frac{10}{14}$ $\frac{15}{21}$, and is voided by its opposite, superbipartient fifths, as this harmonization proves:

Subsupertripartient Fourths Proportion

The subsupertripartient fourths proportion occurs when a smaller number of following notes is comprehended in a larger number of preceding notes one and three-fourths times as 4:7, 8:14, and 12:21. This proportion equates four notes with seven like themselves, so that each one of these four is augmented by three fourths of its value. It is designated in music as follows: $\frac{4}{7}$ $\frac{8}{14}$ $\frac{12}{21}$, and is voided by a supertripartient fourths, its opposite, as shown in this harmonization:

Subsupertripartient Fifths Proportion

The subsupertripartient fifths proportion occurs when a smaller number of following notes is contained in a larger number of preceding notes one and three-fifths times, as 5:8, 10:16, and 15:24. In this proportion five notes are equivalent to and measured with eight like themselves, so that each one of these five receives an increment of three fifths of its proper quantity. It is designated in music in this way:$\frac{5}{8}$ $\frac{10}{16}$ $\frac{15}{24}$, and is voided by its opposite, supertripartient fifths, as is evident here:

Subsuperquatripartient Fifths Proportion

The subsuperquatripartient fifths proportion occurs when a smaller number of following notes resides in a larger number of preceding notes one and four-fifths times, as 5:9, 10:18, 15:27, and so on. This proportion equates five notes with nine like themselves, so that each of these five is increased by four fifths of its normal value. It is indicated in music like this:$\frac{5}{9}$ $\frac{10}{18}$ $\frac{15}{27}$, and voided by its opposite, superquatripartient fifths, as is clear in this example:

Subsuperquatripartient Sevenths Proportion

The subsuperquatripartient sevenths proportion occurs when a smaller number of following notes is contained in a larger number preceding one and four-sevenths times, as 7:11, 14:22, and 21:33. In this proportion seven notes are equivalent to and measured with eleven like themselves, so that each of these seven increases by four sevenths of its proper value. It is indicated in music as follows: $\frac{7}{11}$ $\frac{14}{22}$ $\frac{21}{33}$, and voided by its opposite, super-quatripartient sevenths, as is shown by this harmonization:

We leave the consideration of the remaining species of this genus, both the subalternates and the specialized species, to the diligence of musicians.

Chapter nine   The Multiple Superparticular Genus and Its Species

The multiple superparticular, which is the fourth genus of major inequality, made up of the first two genera, occurs when a larger number of following notes comprehends a smaller number of preceding notes several times and in addition one aliquot part of the smaller number. Its species, considered in various categories, are infinite.

The first category proceeds from the first multiple genus mixed with the superparticulars one by one in their natural order, as duple sesquialter 5:2, duple sesquitertia 7:3, duple sesquiquarta 9:4, duple sesquiquinta 11:5, and so on. The second group evolves from the second multiple genus in conjunction with all the superparticulars in natural order, as triple sesquialter 7:2, triple sesquitertia 10:3, triple sesquiquarta 13:4, triple sesquiquinta 16:5, and so forth. The third category joins together all the forms of the superparticular genus to the third multiple, as quadruple sesquialter 9:2, quadruple sesquitertia 13:3, quadruple sesquiquarta 17:4, quadruple sesquiquinta 21:5, and so forth. In the fourth category the individual superparticulars adhere to the fourth multiple genus, as quintuple sesquialter 11:2, quintuple sesquitertia 16:3, quintuple sesquiquarta 21:4, quintuple sesquiquinta 26:5, and so forth. Similarly the categories of this genus and the species of the categories are infinite.

Duple Sesquialter Proportion

The duple sesquialter proportion occurs when a larger number of following notes contains a smaller number of preceding notes two and one-half times and is equal to it in potency and temporal value, as 5:2, 10:4, 15:6, and so on. In this proportion five notes are equivalent to and measured with two like themselves in name and quantity, so that each note of these five is diminished by three fifths of its proper quantity. It is notated in music like this: $\frac{5}{2}$ $\frac{10}{4}$ $\frac{15}{6}$, and destroyed by its opposite, a subduple sesquialter, as is seen in this harmonization:

Duple Sesquitertia Proportion

The duple sesquitertia proportion occurs when a larger number of following notes contains a smaller number of preceding notes two and one-third times, equalling it in potency, as 7:3, 14:6, 21:9, and so on. This proportion equates seven notes with three like themselves, so that each one of the seven notes is diminished by four sevenths of its value. It is indicated in music in this way: $\frac{7}{3}$ $\frac{14}{6}$ $\frac{21}{9}$, and voided by its opposite, subduple sesquitertia, as is perceived in this harmonization:

Duple Sesquiquarta Proportion

The duple sesquiquarta proportion occurs when a larger number of following notes contains a smaller number of preceding notes two and one-fourth times, as 9:4, 18:8, 27:12, and so on. In this proportion nine notes are equivalent to and measured with four like themselves in quantity and temporal value, so that each of these nine is diminished by five ninths of its proper quantity. It is indicated in music in this way: $\frac{9}{4}$ $\frac{18}{8}$ $\frac{27}{12}$, and destroyed by its opposite, subduple sesquiquarta, as evident in this harmonization:

Duple Sesquiquinta Proportion

The duple sesquiquinta proportion occurs when a larger number of following notes comprehends a smaller number of preceding notes two and one-fifth times, as 11:5, 22:10, and 33:15. This proportion equates eleven notes with five like themselves both in power and temporal value, so that each of these eleven is decreased by six elevenths of its normal quantity. It is designated in composition in this way: $\frac{11}{5}$ $\frac{22}{10}$ $\frac{33}{15}$, and destroyed by its opposite, subduple sesquiquinta, as is evident here:

Triple Sesquialter Proportion

The triple sesquialter proportion occurs when a larger number of following notes contains a smaller number of preceding notes three and one-half times, as 7:2, 14:4, 21:6, and so on. In this proportion seven notes are equivalent to and measured with two like themselves, so that each of these seven is diminished by five sevenths of its quantity. It is indicated in music in this way: $\frac{7}{2}$ $\frac{14}{4}$ $\frac{21}{6}$. It is voided, moreover, by its opposite, subtriple sesquialter, as is evident here:

Triple Sesquitertia Proportion

The triple sesquitertia proportion occurs when a larger number of following notes contains a smaller number of preceding notes three and one-third times, as 10:3, 20:6, and 30:9. This proportion equates and measures ten notes with three like themselves, so that each one of these ten suffers a loss of seven tenths of its value. It is designated in music in this manner: $\frac{10}{3}$ $\frac{20}{6}$ $\frac{30}{9}$, and is destroyed by a subtriple sesquitertia, its opposite, immediately following it, as the harmonization at hand shows:

Triple Sesquiquarta Proportion

The triple sesquiquarta proportion occurs when a larger number of following notes comprehends a smaller number of preceding notes three and one-fourth times, as 13:4, 26:8, 39:12, and so forth. In this proportion thirteen notes are equivalent to and measured with four like themselves, so that each of the thirteen is diminished by nine thirteenths of its proper quantity. It is indicated in music as follows: $\frac{13}{4}$ $\frac{26}{8}$ $\frac{39}{12}$, and is voided by its opposite, subtriple sesquiquarta, as is evident in this harmonization:

Quadruple Sesquialter Proportion

The quadruple sesquialter proportion occurs when a larger number of following notes contains a smaller number of preceding notes four and one-half times, as 9:2, 18:4, and 27:6. This proportion equates nine notes with two like themselves, so that each of these nine is diminished by seven ninths of its value. It is designated in music as follows: $\frac{9}{2}$ $\frac{18}{4}$ $\frac{27}{6}$, and destroyed by its opposite, subquadruple [sesquialter], as here:

Quadruple Sesquitertia Proportion

The quadruple sesquitertia proportion occurs when a larger number of following notes contains a smaller number of preceding notes four and one-third times, as 13:3, 26:6, 39:9, and so on. In this proportion thirteen notes are equivalent to and measured with three like themselves, so that each of these thirteen is diminished by ten thirteenths of its value. It is designated in music in this way: $\frac{13}{3}$ $\frac{26}{6}$ $\frac{39}{9}$, and is voided by its opposite, a subquadruple sesquitertia, as shown in the accompanying harmonization:

Quadruple Sesquiquarta Proportion

The quadruple sesquiquarta proportion occurs when a larger number of succeeding notes comprehends a smaller number of preceding notes four

and one-fourth times, as 17:4, 34:8, 51:12, and so on. This proportion
makes seventeen notes equal to four like themselves, so that each one of
these seventeen is diminished by thirteen seventeenths of its proper quan-
tity. It is indicated in music in this way: $\frac{17}{4}$ $\frac{34}{8}$ $\frac{51}{12}$, and is likewise destroyed
by its opposite, subquadruple sesquiquarta, as is evident here:

Quintuple Sesquialter Proportion

The quintuple sesquialter proportion occurs when a larger number of following notes contains a smaller number of preceding notes five and one-
half times, as 11:2, 22:4, 33:6, and so on. In this proportion eleven notes
are equivalent to and measured with two like themselves, so that each of
these eleven is diminished by nine elevenths of its proper quantity. It is
indicated in music as follows: $\frac{11}{2}$ $\frac{22}{4}$ $\frac{33}{6}$, and voided by its opposite, subquintuple sesquialter, as is evident in this example:

Quintuple Sesquitertia Proportion

The quintuple sesquitertia proportion occurs when a larger number of following notes comprehends a smaller number of antecedent notes five and one-third times, as 16:3, 32:6, 48:9, and so on. This proportion equates sixteen notes with three like themselves, so that each of these sixteen is diminished by thirteen sixteenths of its value. It is indicated in music as follows: $\frac{16}{3}$ $\frac{32}{6}$ $\frac{48}{9}$, and is voided by a subquintuple sesquitertia, which the present harmonization proves:

Quintuple Sesquiquarta Proportion

The quintuple sesquiquarta proportion occurs when a larger number of following notes contains a smaller number of preceding notes five and one-fourth times, as 21:4, 42:8, 63:12, and so on. In this proportion twenty-one notes are equivalent to and measured with four like themselves, so that each of these twenty-one is diminished by seventeen twenty-firsts of its proper quantity. It is indicated in music this way: $\frac{21}{4}$ $\frac{42}{8}$ $\frac{63}{12}$, and is voided by its opposite, subquintuple sesquiquarta, as evident here:

We leave to the diligence of musicians the other categories of this genus, with its species to be considered by a similar technique.

Chapter ten   The Submultiple Superparticular Genus and Its Species

The submultiple superparticular, the fourth genus of minor inequality and the opposite of the multiple superparticular, occurs when a smaller number of following notes is comprehended in a larger number of antecedent notes several times plus one aliquot part of it, and the smaller number is equivalent to the larger. There are infinite species of this genus similarly made up of diverse categories. The first category is treated by means of the subduple joined to the individual superparticulars. Its first species is the subduple sesquialter, the second subduple sesquitertia, the third subduple sesquiquarta, the fourth subduple sesquiquinta, and so on. The second category combines the individual superparticulars with the subtriple in this succession: subtriple sesquialter, subtriple sesquitertia, subtriple sesquiquarta, subtriple sesquiquinta, and so on. The third category mixes together the individual superparticulars with the third submultiple, the subquadruple—that is, for example, subquadruple sesquialter, subquadruple sesquitertia, subquadruple sesquiquarta, subquadruple sesquiquinta, and so on. Anyone can readily consider the other categories in logical sequence.

Subduple Sesquialter Proportion

The subduple sesquialter proportion occurs when a smaller number of following notes is contained in a larger number of preceding notes two and one-half times, as 2:5, 4:10, and 6:15. In this proportion two notes are equivalent to and measured with five like themselves, so that each of these two undergoes augmentation by three halves of its proper quantity. It is indicated in music like this: $\frac{2}{5}$ $\frac{4}{10}$ $\frac{6}{15}$, and is voided by its opposite, duple sesquialter, immediately following it, as is perceived in this harmonization:

Subduple Sesquitertia Proportion

The subduple sesquitertia proportion occurs when a smaller number of following notes is comprehended in a larger number of preceding notes two and one-third times and is equivalent to it in potency and temporal measure, as 3:7, 6:14, 9:21, and so on. This proportion equates three notes to seven like themselves, so that each of these three is increased by four thirds of its proper quantity. It is indicated in music in the following way: $\frac{3}{7}$ $\frac{6}{14}$ $\frac{9}{21}$, and is destroyed by its opposite, duple sesquitertia, as is here evident:

Subduple Sesquiquarta Proportion

The subduple sesquiquarta proportion occurs when a smaller number of following notes is observed in a larger number of preceding notes two and one-fourth times, as 4:9, 8:18, and 12:27. In this proportion four notes are equivalent to and measured with nine like themselves, so that each one of these four increases by five fourths of its proper value. It is indicated in music in this way: $\frac{4}{9}$ $\frac{8}{18}$ $\frac{12}{27}$, and is destroyed by its opposite, duple sesquiquarta, as here:

Subtriple Sesquialter Proportion

The subtriple sesquialter proportion occurs when a smaller number of following notes is contained in a larger number of preceding notes three and one-half times, as 2:7, 4:14, 6:21, and so on. This proportion equates two notes similar in potency to seven like themselves, so that each of these two is augmented by five halves of its proper quantity. It is designated in music in this way: $\frac{2}{7}$ $\frac{4}{14}$ $\frac{6}{21}$, and it is voided by the triple sesquialter, its opposite, as the accompanying harmonization proves:

Subtriple Sesquitertia Proportion

The subtriple sesquitertia proportion occurs when a smaller number of subsequent notes is contained in a larger number of antecedent notes three and one-third times, as 3:10, 6:20, 9:30, and so on. In this proportion three notes are equivalent to and measured with ten like themselves, so that each of these three is augmented by seven thirds of its proper quantity. It is designated in music like this: $\frac{3}{10}$ $\frac{6}{20}$ $\frac{9}{30}$, and is voided by its opposite, triple sesquitertia, as is perceived in the subjoined harmonization:

Subtriple Sesquiquarta Proportion

The subtriple sesquiquarta proportion occurs when a smaller number of following notes is contained in a larger number of preceding notes three and one-fourth times, as 4:13, 8:26, 12:39, and so on. This proportion equates four notes to thirteen like themselves in potency and temporal value, so that each of these four receives an increment of nine fourths of its normal value. It is indicated in music as follows: $\frac{4}{13}$ $\frac{8}{26}$ $\frac{12}{39}$, and is voided by its opposite, the triple sesquiquarta, as the accompanying harmonization reveals:

Subquadruple Sesquialter Proportion

The subquadruple sesquialter proportion occurs when a smaller number of following notes is comprehended in a larger number of preceding notes four and one-half times, as 2:9, 4:18, 6:27, and so on. In this proportion two notes are equivalent to and measured with nine like themselves, so that each of these two is augmented by seven halves of its proper quantity. It is indicated in music as follows: $\frac{2}{9}$ $\frac{4}{18}$ $\frac{6}{27}$, and is destroyed by its opposite, the quadruple sesquialter, as is evident here:

Subquadruple Sesquitertia Proportion

The subquadruple sesquitertia proportion occurs when a smaller number
of following notes is comprehended in a larger number of preceding notes
four and one-third times, as 3:13, 6:26, 9:39, and so on. This proportion
makes three notes equal to thirteen like themselves in potency and temporal value, so that each of these three undergoes augmentation of its pro-
per quantity by ten thirds. It is indicated in music in this way: $\frac{3}{13}$ $\frac{6}{26}$ $\frac{9}{39}$,
and is voided by its opposite, quadruple sesquitertia, as the present har-
monization affirms:

Subquadruple Sesquiquarta Proportion

The subquadruple sesquiquarta proportion occurs when a smaller number of following notes is comprehended in a larger number of preceding notes four and one-fourth times, as 4:17, 8:34, 12:51, and so on. In this proportion four notes are equal to and measured with seventeen like themselves, so that each one of these four is increased by thirteen fourths of its proper quantity. It is indicated in music in this way: $\frac{4}{17}$ $\frac{8}{34}$ $\frac{12}{51}$, and voided by its opposite, quadruple sesquiquarta, as the present harmonization attests:

Chapter eleven   The Multiple Superpartient Genus and Its Species

The multiple superpartient genus, the fifth of major inequality, exists where a larger number of succeeding notes contains a smaller number of antecedent notes several times plus one of its aliquant parts, which is made up of several aliquot parts. There are infinite categories of this genus, which proceed with the individual multiples pairing with every one of the superpartients.

The first category is made up of the first species of the multiple genus united with the individual superpartients, such as duple superbipartient, duple supertripartient, duple superquatripartient, and so forth. These are called subalternate species because each is converted into the power of a genus, since one of the duple superbipartients is duple superbipartient thirds, as 8:3, another duple superbipartient fifths, as 12:5, another duple superbipartient sevenths, as 16:7, another duple superbipartient ninths, as 20:9, and so on. In fact, they call this type of species specialized. With the other categories a similar method of procedure is applicable.

The second category joins the individual superpartients to the second species of the multiple genus. The subalternate, specialized series of this category is as follows: triple superbipartient thirds, as 11:3, triple superbipartient fifths, as 17:5, triple superbipartient sevenths, as 23:7, and so on.

The third category unites the third species of the multiple genus to each of the superpartients. Its series is quadruple superbipartient thirds, as 14:3, quadruple superbipartient fifths, as 22:5, and quadruple superbipartient sevenths, as 30:7.

In the fourth category the individual superpartients are attached to the fourth species of the multiple genus in this order: quintuple superbipartient thirds, as 17:3, quintuple superbipartient fifths, as 27:5, quintuple superbipartient sevenths, as 37:7. For the most part such a process is treated through the application of subalternate superpartients to the individual multiples—a duple superbipartient, duple supertripartient, duple superquatripartient. For the rest, the technique fits in different ways. These are discussed one by one.

Duple Superbipartient Thirds Proportion

The duple superbipartient thirds proportion occurs when a larger number of succeeding notes comprehends a smaller number of antecedent notes twice plus one aliquant part made up of two thirds of the smaller number, as 8:3, 16:6, 24:9, and so on. In this proportion eight notes are equivalent to and measured with three like themselves, so that each of these eight is diminished by five eighths of its proper quantity. It is indicated in music like this: $\frac{8}{3}$ $\frac{16}{6}$ $\frac{24}{9}$, and is voided by its opposite, subduple superbipartient thirds, as this harmonization shows:

Duple Superbipartient Fifths Proportion

The duple superbipartient fifths proportion occurs when a larger number of succeeding notes contains a smaller number of preceding notes two and two-fifths times, as 12:5, 24:10, 36:15, and so on. This proportion makes twelve notes equal in potency and temporal value to five like themselves, so that each single one of these twelve suffers a loss of seven twelfths of its proper quantity. It is indicated in music in this way: $\frac{12}{5}$ $\frac{24}{10}$ $\frac{36}{15}$, and is destroyed by a subduple superbipartient fifths, its opposite, as is evident in this harmonization:

Duple Supertripartient Fourths Proportion

The duple supertripartient fourths proportion occurs when a larger number of succeeding notes comprehends a smaller number of preceding notes two and three-fourths times, as 11:4, 22:8, and 33:12. In this proportion eleven notes are equivalent to and measured with four like themselves, so that each of these eleven is diminished by seven elevenths of its proper value. It is designated in music in this way: $\frac{11}{4}$ $\frac{22}{8}$ $\frac{33}{12}$, and voided, moreover, by its opposite, subduple supertripartient fourths, as the present harmonization attests:

Duple Supertripartient Fifths Proportion

The duple supertripartient fifths proportion occurs when a larger number of following notes contains a smaller number of preceding notes two and three-fifths times, as 13:5, 26:10, 39:15, and so on. This proportion equates thirteen notes with five like themselves, so that each of these thirteen is diminished by eight thirteenths of its proper quantity. It is notated in music in this way: $\frac{13}{5}$ $\frac{26}{10}$ $\frac{39}{15}$, and voided by its opposite, the subduple supertripartient fifths, as is evident here:

Triple Superbipartient Thirds Proportion

The triple superbipartient thirds proportion occurs when a larger number of following notes comprehends a smaller number of preceding notes three and two-thirds times, as 11:3, 22:6, 33:9, and so on. In this proportion eleven notes are equivalent to and measured with three like themselves, so that each one of these eleven is diminished by eight elevenths of its proper quantity. It is designated in music as follows: $\frac{11}{3}$ $\frac{22}{6}$ $\frac{33}{9}$, and is destroyed by a subtriple superbipartient thirds, its opposite, as arranged in this harmonization:

Triple Superbipartient Fifths Proportion

The triple superbipartient fifths proportion occurs when a larger number of following notes contains a smaller number of preceding notes three and two-fifths times, as 17:5, 34:10, 51:15, and so on. In this proportion seventeen notes are equivalent to and measured with five like themselves, so that each one of the seventeen is diminished by twelve seventeenths of its value. It is designated in music as follows: $\frac{17}{5}$ $\frac{34}{10}$ $\frac{51}{15}$, and is voided by a subtriple superbipartient fifths, its opposite, as the present harmonization affirms:

Triple Supertripartient Fourths Proportion

The triple supertripartient fourths proportion occurs when a larger number of following notes comprehends a smaller number of preceding notes three and three-fourths times, as 15:4, 30:8, and 45:12. This proportion equates fifteen notes with four like themselves, so that each of these fifteen is diminished by eleven fifteenths of its proper quantity. It is indicated in music as follows: $\frac{15}{4}$ $\frac{30}{8}$ $\frac{45}{12}$, and is voided by its opposite, subtriple supertripartient fourths, as is evident here:

Triple Supertripartient Fifths Proportion

The triple supertripartient fifths proportion occurs when a larger number of following notes contains a smaller number of preceding notes three and three-fifths times, as 18:5, 36:10, 54:15, and so on. In this proportion eighteen notes are equivalent to and measured with five like themselves, so that each of these eighteen is diminished by thirteen eighteenths of its proper quantity. It is designated in music in this manner: $\frac{18}{5}$ $\frac{36}{10}$ $\frac{54}{15}$, and is destroyed by a subtriple supertripartient fifths, its opposite, as perceived in this harmonization:

Quadruple Superbipartient Thirds Proportion

The quadruple superbipartient thirds proportion occurs when a larger number of following notes comprehends a lesser number of preceding notes four and two-thirds times, as 14:3, 28:6, 42:9, and so on. This proportion equates fourteen notes with three like themselves in potency and temporal measure, so that every single one of these fourteen is diminished by eleven fourteenths of its value. It is indicated in music like this: $\frac{14}{3}$ $\frac{28}{6}$

$\frac{42}{9}$, and destroyed by a subquadruple superbipartient thirds, its opposite, as the present harmonization discloses:

Quadruple Superbipartient Fifths Proportion

The quadruple superbipartient fifths proportion occurs when a larger number of following notes contains a lesser number of preceding notes four and two-fifths times, as 22:5, 44:10, and 66:15. In this proportion twenty-two notes are equivalent to and measured with five like themselves in potency and temporal value, so that each of these twenty-two is diminished by seventeen twenty-seconds of its proper value. It is indicated in music like this: $\frac{22}{5}$ $\frac{44}{10}$ $\frac{66}{15}$, and voided by its opposite, the subquadruple superbipartient fifths, as proved in this harmonization:

Quadruple Supertripartient Fourths Proportion

The quadruple supertripartient fourths proportion occurs when a larger number of succeeding notes comprehends a smaller number of preceding notes four and three-fourths times, as 19:4, 38:8, 57:12, and so on. This proportion computes and measures nineteen notes together with four like themselves, so that each of these nineteen is diminished by fifteen nineteenths of its proper quantity. It is designated in music as follows: $\frac{19}{4}$ $\frac{38}{8}$ $\frac{57}{12}$, and voided by the subquadruple supertripartient fourths, its opposite, which the present harmonization proves:

By a similar procedure the diligent investigator will study the remaining subalternate, specialized species of this genus for himself.

Chapter twelve   The Submultiple Superpartient Genus and Its Species

The submultiple superpartient, which is the fifth genus of minor inequality and is opposite to the multiple superpartient, exists when a smaller number of following notes is contained in a larger number of preceding notes several times plus an aliquant part containing several aliquot parts. This smaller number is equivalent to the larger in potency and temporal value, so that each single note of the smaller undergoes an increase by as many particles of its proper number as there are notes composing the difference of these numbers. This also happens among the other genera of minor inequality.

Similarly, the individual submultiples give rise to infinite categories of this genus embracing superpartient forms. The first category is made from the subduple, as, for example, subduple superbipartient, subduple supertripartient, and subduple superquatripartient. Furthermore, such species are subalternates, since each one passes over into the power of a genus, as subduple superbipartient thirds, subduple superbipartient fifths, and subduple superbipartient sevenths. Moreover, these species are called specialized species.

The same method of treatment holds for the other categories. The second category is made out of the subtriple, such as subtriple superbipartient, subtriple supertripartient, subtriple superquatripartient, and so on. The third category is derived from the subquadruple, as subquadruple superbipartient, subquadruple supertripartient, and subquadruple superquatripartient. Specialized species of this type are placed under the subalternates. Let us line up their series as follows.

Subduple Superbipartient Thirds Proportion

The subduple superbipartient thirds proportion takes place when a smaller number of succeeding notes is comprehended in a larger number of antecedent notes two and two-thirds times, as 3:8, 6:16, 9:24, and so on. In this proportion three notes are equivalent to and measured with eight like themselves, so that each of these three is augmented by five thirds of its proper quantity. It is indicated in music as follows: $\frac{3}{8}$ $\frac{6}{16}$ $\frac{9}{24}$, and is destroyed by its opposite, duple superbipartient thirds, as this harmonization demonstrates:

Subduple Superbipartient Fifths Proportion

The subduple superbipartient fifths proportion occurs when a smaller number of succeeding notes is contained in a larger preceding number two and two-fifths times, as 5:12, 10:24, and 15:36. This proportion equates five notes with twelve like themselves in potency and temporal value, so that each one of these five acquires an increment of seven fifths of its proper quantity. It is indicated in music in this way: $\frac{5}{12}$ $\frac{10}{24}$ $\frac{15}{36}$, and is destroyed by its opposite, duple superbipartient fifths, as evident here:

Subduple Supertripartient Fourths Proportion

The subduple supertripartient fourths proportion occurs when a smaller number of following notes is contained in a larger number of preceding notes two and three-fourths times, as 4:11, 8:22, 12:33, and so on. In this proportion four notes are equivalent to and measured with eleven like themselves, so that each of these four is augmented by seven fourths of its proper quantity. It is designated in music as follows: $\frac{4}{11}$ $\frac{8}{22}$ $\frac{12}{33}$, and is destroyed by its opposite, duple supertripartient fourths, as is perceived in this harmonization:

Subtriple Superbipartient Thirds Proportion

The subtriple superbipartient thirds proportion occurs when a smaller number of following notes is comprehended in a larger number preceding three and two-thirds times, as 3:11, 6:22, 9:33, and so on. This proportion makes three notes equal to eleven like themselves, so that each one of these three undergoes an augmentation of its value by eight thirds. It is designated in music in this way: $\frac{3}{11}$ $\frac{6}{22}$ $\frac{9}{33}$, and it is destroyed by its opposite, triple superbipartient thirds, as is evident here:

Subquadruple Supertripartient Fourths Proportion

The subquadruple supertripartient fourths proportion occurs when a smaller number of following notes is contained in a larger number of preceding notes four and three-fourths times, as 4:19, 8:38, 12:57, and so on. In this proportion four notes are equivalent to and measured with nineteen like themselves, so that each of these four is augmented by fifteen fourths of its proper quantity. It is indicated in music in this way: $\frac{4}{19}$ $\frac{8}{38}$ $\frac{12}{57}$, and it is destroyed by quadruple supertripartient fourths, its opposite, as is perceived in this harmonization:

We entrust the investigation of the remaining forms of this genus to the diligence of musicians.

Chapter thirteen   The Conjunction of Several Dissimilar Proportions

Different proportions following one another logically yield various relationships of subsequent notes to preceding notes. If, for example, in music, a triple proportion follows immediately upon a duple proportion, at that point a sextuple proportion will result from the total quantitative value of the notes of that indicated triple proportion in relation to the prior number of notes, that is, to those which had been written ahead of the duple proportion. This fact is perceived, of course, in the numbers 1, 2, 6.

For 2:1 is duple, 6:2 is triple, and 6:1 makes the sextuple proportion which its opposite, a subsextuple, following immediately is known to destroy. The reason for this lies in the deduced equality of the extremes enclosed by the terms 1, 2, 6, 1. This is quite clearly perceived in the temporal distribution and articulation of the notes in the accompanying musical example:

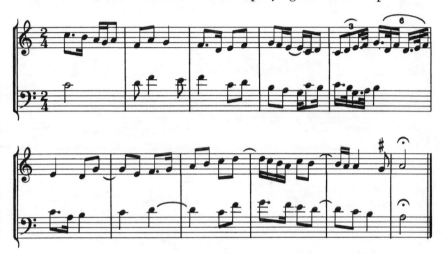

Thus each proportion, in relation to a preceding proportion, always matches its notes to the number of preceding notes, so that the notes are seen to correspond to the treatment of the first proportion as though it were the basis of the relationship. We have shown this by arithmetical calculation in the final chapter [8] of Book III of the *Theorica*.

Indeed, the first two species of the superparticular genus, the sesquialter and sesquitertia, following one another in a composition, match the ensuing notes in a duple relationship to the former notes. This is perceived in the arrangement of the numbers 2:3:4. When a sesquiquarta is added to these proportions, it measures the following notes to the anterior group of notes in duple sesquialter proportion, as is evident in the numbers 2:3:4:5. Furthermore, when a sesquiquinta proportion is added, it will perfect a triple proportion in relation to the first group of notes, as is shown by the series 2:3:4:5:6. For 6:2 fulfills a triple relationship.

With a subsequent subtriple proportion, however, all the proportions that have been set forth will be destroyed, for an equality of the extreme terms results, as this arrangement proves: 2:3:4:5:6:2. This procedure occurs also in music, by the same reasoning, as is patent in the following harmonization:

Further, it is clear that any two contiguous, successive species of the superparticular genus beyond the sesquialter and sesquitertia, which are the first and larger than the other *epimoria* relationships, cannot make up a duple proportion. Since they are set forth in numbers which are larger than those of the first two species, they will necessarily yield a smaller proportion, so that if I arranged a sesquitertia and a sesquiquarta with the numbers 3, 4, 5, the terms extreme to each other could not effect a duple proportion. When a sesquiquinta is added, however, the extremes will relate to each other in duple proportion, as follows: 3:4:5:6. For 6:5 yields a sesquiquinta, but 6:3 yields a duple correspondence, which a succeeding subduple proportion, its opposite, immediately destroys by the equality of the extremes that is brought about. This is evident in the numbers 3, 4, 5, 6, 3. For 3:6 makes a subduple proportion, but this 3 holds the previous 3 in equality by balancing the ensuing notes with the number of antecedent notes, as is perceived in this harmonization:

Moreover, in a treatment of this kind, no matter what the proportion is, when it is extinguished by its opposite following it immediately, then the rest of the preceding constituent proportions are also destroyed. This fact may be deduced from the preceding examples, for the subduple not only destroyed the duple proportion of the extremes but it also nullified the sesquitertia, sesquiquarta, and sesquiquinta constituents of the duple.

Successive forms of each and every genus follow one another in various manipulations which the careful musician can readily observe by himself.

Chapter fourteen   The Proportions Giving Rise to Musical Consonances

We are led to expound upon the nature and progression of those proportions which, with proper measurement, establish the consonances of music.

In the multiple genus the octave, twelfth, and the double octave are obtained from the duple, triple, and quadruple species. In the superparticular genus the sesquialter, sesquitertia, and sesquioctave define the fifth, fourth, and the whole tone. To be sure, even though I have spoken at length in the *Theorica* [III, 8] regarding these matters, yet it is useful to explain them more concisely here in their musical context.

When you add a sesquioctave to a given sesquitertia, the terms extreme to each other will emerge in a sesquialter relationship. This is evident in the numbers 6, 8, 9. For 8:6 makes a sesquitertia and 9:8 a sesquioctave. Further, 9:6 yields a sesquialter proportion, and a sesquitertia introduced above it will fix the extreme terms in duple correspondence, as is disclosed in the numbers 6, 8, 9, 12. 12:9 establishes the sesquitertia; 12:6, however, the duple. When a sesquialter proportion is introduced above, a triple relationship of the extremes will result at that point, a fact which is demonstrated in this series: 6, 8, 9, 12, 18. The numbers 18:12 effect a sesquialter, but 18:6, a triple. When you add a sesquitertia to such a triple, you effect a quadruple proportion of the extremes, as follows: 6, 8, 9, 12, 18, 24; for the number 24 to the number 18 shows a sesquitertia, but 24:6, a quadruple. When its opposite, a subquadruple, is subjoined to such a quadruple, however, the latter and its component parts soon vanish, because the subsequent notes are united with the earliest quantitative value. The equality of the extreme terms establishes this, as is evident in the numbers 6, 8, 9, 12, 18, 24, 6; for the number 6 makes a subquadruple to 24, but 6 to the previous 6 is restored to equality, a fact which the following harmonization illustrates in notes:

Chapter fifteen   The Production of Multiple Proportions from Multiples and Superparticulars

Finally we must notice that a sequence of multiple species is produced from multiples and superparticulars.

The first species of the multiple genus—that is, the duple—and the first superparticular—that is, the sesquialter—when joined together produce in their extremes the second multiple, that is, a triple. This is clear in the numbers 1, 2, 3. With a subtriple added above, however, the triple is destroyed on account of the equality of the extremes, as follows: 1, 2, 3, 1.

The same result is obtained in the quantities of the notes in accordance with their temporal value, a fact which the present harmonization discloses:

The second species of the multiple genus, namely the triple, and the second species of superparticular, that is, the sesquitertia, yield in logical sequence the third multiple species, that is, the quadruple, as is evident in the numbers 1, 3, 4. When they are set down in composition, they also bring together the ensuing notes in a quadruple relationship with the anterior notes. Its opposite, a subquadruple, immediately extinguishes this, as the present harmonization proves:

Again, the third species of the multiple genus, that is, the quadruple, and the third superparticular, that is, the sesquiquarta, when combined create the fourth multiple, the quintuple. The arrangement of the terms 1, 4, 5 proves this. The same thing is accomplished in musical composition. The ensuing notes are related in quintuple guise to the antecedent notes, but this arrangement is effaced when an opposite subquintuple follows, as is evident in this harmonization:

Further, the manner of deriving multiple proportions from multiples and superparticulars is quite uniform in procedure. The fourth multiple species and the fourth superparticular bring about the fifth multiple, as is proved in the numbers 1, 5, 6. The fifth species of the multiple genus plus the fifth superparticular bring about the sixth multiple, which is evident in the numbers 1, 6, 7. In addition, the sixth species of the multiple genus and the sixth superparticular establish the seventh multiple with the numbers 1, 7, 8. The others are treated in the same way according to the natural progression of numbers.

Now, most gracious reader, I have presented my thoughts on musical practice with perhaps no less talent and industry than you wished for, though your wish was unspoken. For of course, since you must have grown weary reading my books on theory, you needed this just as some sharp foods are needed to revive and refresh the taste. Nor did I think I could escape blame if, when I taught the art of music and unveiled its innermost secrets (if I may use the phrase), I held back in silence from this part as well, which is called *practica* and consists of and is perfected by the actual practice of music itself.

But if in a work such as this one, some error is detected, learned men should not take offense from this, because I shall leave it to the most skilled mathematicians and musicians to evaluate and criticize my writings. But when anyone does take offense at my use of a vocabulary which is not classical, or which is too modern, I should like him to attribute this fault to the subject matter in which we are involved. Neither should he fail to recognize the fact that many writers, if they wish to treat subjects accurately, have had to declare war on the ancient use of words and the rules of the grammarians. I decided not to raise the issue in my preface because I am writing these things for educated and sensible men who would pardon me, even without my asking. But I have observed the throng of uneducated people who are clothed in the shadow of knowledge; when they only nibble at my thoughts, they immediately curse them and tear them to shreds. When they have studied them over again thoughtfully and without passion, they will honor them with suitable and perhaps fruitful praise.

Here ends *The Practice of Music*
by Franchinus Gafurius of Lodi,
comprising four books.

Printed at
Milan through
the effort and expense
of Johannes Petrus of Lomazzo
by Guillermus Signerre of Rouen[25] on
the last day of September in the Year of Our Lord, 1496,
during the blessedly auspicious
reigns of the very great
Pope Alexander VI,
and the ever
revered
King of the
Romans, Maximilian,
and Ludovico Maria Sforza
Anglus, invincible
Duke of
Milan.

25. Johannes Petrus of Lomazzo was also the publisher of the second edition of the *Theorica* and of Caza's vernacular edition of *Practica,* II, the *Tractato vulgare del canto figurato,* both printed in Milan in 1492. Guillermus Le Signerre was one of two brothers active in Milan at the end of the fifteenth century; for a discussion of his role in the printing of the *Practica,* see "Texts and Editorial Policy," pp. xxvi–xxix above.

A concise identification of Gafurius' printed works, their titles, colophons, and some of their physical characteristics is given in Paul Hirsch, "Bibliographie der Musik-theoretischen Drucke des Franchino Gafori," in *Festschrift für Johannes Wolf* (Berlin, 1929), pp. 65–72. See also William Dana Orcutt, *The Book in Italy During the Fifteenth and Sixteenth Centuries* (New York, 1928); and F. J. Norton, *Italian Printers, 1501–1520* (London, 1958).

INDEX

INDEX

Agricola, Alexander, 154, 155*n*
Albertus de Saxonia, 165, 166, 166*n*
Alexander VI, Pope, 267
Ambrose, Saint, Bishop of Milan, 48, 48*n*, 158
Ambrosian Chant, 20*n*, 31, 43, 47, 48, 59, 62–63, 156, 158–60. *See also* Psalmody
Amphion, 11, 11*n*
Anselm of Parma, 26, 26*n*, 30, 33, 75, 75*n*, 81, 85, 92, 94, 125
Antiphon: defined, 61
Arion of Lesbos, 11*n*
Aristides Quintilianus, 23*n*, 29*n*, 68, 68*n*, 69, 75, 76, 76*n*
Aristotle, 11*n*, 13, 13*n*, 19, 19*n*, 21, 21*n*, 29, 29*n*, 73, 90, 112, 129, 137, 141, 141*n*, 162, 167. *See also* Musical Problems
Aristoxenus of Tarentum, 11, 11*n*, 29*n*, 70, 70*n*
Augustine, Saint, Bishop of Hippo, 12, 12*n*, 62, 68–69, 82
Ausonius, 85, 85*n*

Bacchius Senior, 23*n*, 28, 28*n*, 29*n*, 39, 70*n*; 123, 125
Bagpipe, 162
Baritone: defined, 150
Bede, Venerable, 69, 69*n*
Binchois, Gilles, 138, 138*n*
Boethius, 14, 14*n*, 19*n*, 23, 26*n*, 29, 70*n*; 73*n*, 124, 141
Bonadies, xvi, 78*n*, 108, 108*n*, 192
Bramante, 4*n*
Brassart, Jean, 138
Briennius, Manuelis, 23*n*, 28, 28*n*, 124, 171*n*
Britannicus, Angelicus: editions of *Practica musicae* printed by, xxx
Brumel, Antoine, 154, 155*n*, 156*n*
Burana, Francesco, 28*n*
Busnois, Antoine, 193, 193*n*

Campanus, Johannes, 165, 165*n*
Canon, 135
Capella, Martianus, 28, 28*n*
Caza, Francesco: Italian edition of *Practica musicae* by, xxxi, 267*n*

Charles VIII, King of France, 3*n*
Chordotone, 27, 27*n*, 40, 115, 127, 128, 130, 156, 166. *See also* Monochord
Chrysippus, 7, 8*n*
Cicero, 11, 11*n*, 70*n*
Coloration, xxiii, 106–8, 165–263 *passim*
Compère, Loyset, 154, 155*n*, 156*n*
Conagus, Lucinus, xviii, 7, 8*n*
Curtius, Lancinus, 14*n*

Demosthenes, 8*n*
De Zannis, Augustinus: edition of *Practica musicae* printed by, xxx
Diogenes, 118*n*
Diomedes, 67, 67*n*, 68
Dixerunt discipuli (antiphon), 86*n*
Dufay, Guillaume, 138, 195, 196*n*
Dunstable, John, 86, 86*n*, 138

Ecce quam bonum (psalm), 59
Eloy d'Amerval, 85, 86*n*
Erasmus, Desiderius, 95*n*
Euclid, 7, 8*n*, 29*n*, 165
Euouae, 50–62 *passim;* defined, 48

Faber Stapulensis, Jacobus, xv, 48*n*
Fauxbourdon, 140
Ficino, Marsilio, 4*n*
Francis I, King of France, 18*n*
Franco of Cologne, 75, 75*n*, 78, 78*n*, 79, 81, 124

Gafurius, Franchinus, life of, xv–xvii; influence of classical tradition on, xvii–xviii; as a composer, xxi–xxii; use of proportion, xxii–xxiv
—*Practica musicae:* musical examples in, xxii, xxiii; Latin editions of, xxvi–xxxi; Italian editions of, xxxi, xxxii
—other works: xviii–xx; *Theorica musicae*, xix, xvi, 5, 5*n*, 14*n*, 15, 27*n*, 67, 141, 166, 169, 189, 259, 262, 267*n; De harmonia*, xix, 18, 18*n*, 24, 27*n*, 37, 39, 40, 42, 43, 67, 123, 127, 128, 156, 161, 166, 189; *Glossemata*, 78*n*, 99*n*, 112*n*, 117*n*, 202*n; Flos musicae*, xx, 144; *Proportioni practicabili*, xx, 197*n*